THE PROCESS

IS THE

PUNISHMENT

THE PROCESS IS THE PUNISHMENT

Handling Cases in a Lower Criminal Court

MALCOLM M. FEELEY

Russell Sage Foundation

NEW YORK

First published 1979

First paperback edition 1992

Preface and Foreword to the paperback edition
© 1992 by Russell Sage Foundation

Library of Congress Catalog Number: 79-7349
ISBN: 0-87154-253-6
ISBN: 0-87154-255-2 (pbk.)

The paper used in this publication meets the minimum requirements of American National Standard for Information Sciences—Permanence of Paper for Printed Library Materials, ANSI Z39.48-1984.

RUSSELL SAGE FOUNDATION
112 East 64th Street, New York, NY 10021

10 9 8 7 6 5 4 3 2 1

IN MEMORY OF

John Aloysius Feeley

AND

Mildred McCollum Feeley

CONTENTS

CHAPTER 3

CHAPTER 4

CHAPTER 5

ACKNOWLEDGMENTS

I began this study during my stay as a Russell Sage Foundation Fellow in the Law and Behavioral Science Program at the Yale Law School and completed it while I was Research Fellow in the Daniel and Florence Guggenheim Foundation Program in Criminal Justice there. I am deeply appreciative to these two foundations and to the Yale Law School for their generous support during this period. My greatest personal debt is to Stan Wheeler, director of the Russell Sage Program at Yale, and Dan Freed, director of the Law School's Guggenheim Program, who offered advice, criticism, and unflagging encouragement for my venture, and they must certainly take a large measure of the credit for whatever merits this book possesses.

Abe Goldstein and Harry Wellington, deans of the Law School during my stay there, presided over an environment that was hospitable to sociolegal research. During the last phase of my work, Ed Lindblom, director of the Institution for Social and Policy Studies, and his then assistant director, Douglas Yates, secured for me a quiet and comfortable setting in which to write and a group of colleagues and students on whom to test my ideas. No scholar could ask for more.

A host of other people aided my work in various ways. Jack Katz will never quite know how influential he was in the development of my thinking at a crucial stage of my research. Bob Kagan, Austin Sarat, Wallace Loh, Joanne Epps, Andrew Rutherford, Dennis Curtis, Michael Kelly, Stuart Scheingold, and Paul Nejelski all either read and commented on portions of my manuscript or provided especially useful advice.

I was fortunate to have a number of outstanding students and research assistants whose work was invaluable. They are Kurt Hallock, Dean Goodman, Diane Pike, John McNaughton, Rich Edwards, and Setsuo Miyazawa.

It goes without saying that this book could not have been written without the cooperation and counsel of those whose behavior I was scrutinizing, the participants in the criminal justice system. There are far too many people for me to single out, and I must be content to mention just a few who were especially helpful. Foremost is my now close friend, Jon Silbert, who first as a colleague and then in private practice took considerable time and trouble to show me around the courthouse, introduce me to people, and remain to answer a constant stream of questions about criminal procedure and courthouse customs. Paul Foti and Morton Lewis, chief prosecutor and public defender, respectively, at the time of my study, were always accessible. Both they and their staffs were generous with their time and candid in their comments. Numerous judges gave of their time as well, and if I single out Barry Schaler, I do not mean to slight the many others. Tommy Corodinno of New Haven's Legal Assistance Association and Joseph Shortall, then assistant executive secretary of the State Judicial Department, supplied me with much useful information. I must also thank the entire staff of the court and the numerous defendants, victims, and witnesses whom I watched and to whom I talked in corridors.

Several people read what I thought was to be a final draft of the manuscript and in doing so made numerous and detailed comments, which led to significant revisions and improvements. They are Dan Freed, Stan Wheeler, Abe Goldstein, Herb Jacob, and Margaret Feeley, and I am deeply grateful for their thoughtful and detailed comments. Edna Scott and Diane Slider transcribed page after page of interview and observation notes and later typed major portions of successive drafts of the manuscript, all with characteristic good cheer and efficiency. I owe a note of appreciation to David Fellman for finding me a nest egg to cover the cost of typing the final draft of the manuscript. I must also acknowledge my indebtedness to Marlene Ellin at the Russell Sage Foundation, for her skillful editing.

Finally, I must express my deep appreciation to the two who matter most, my wife Margaret and my son Jacob. Margaret has remained a steady source of support and encouragement during this long project, and Jacob came along at just the right time to relieve the tedium and offer a friendly diversion.

FOREWORD

The paperback edition of *The Process Is the Punishment* is a welcome sign that legal realism is neither dead nor sick. Malcolm Feeley's 1979 study has already taken its place as one of the major studies of how laws are administered in the United States. The intensive scrutiny of legal doctrine that law school culture perpetuates has been recognized as a distorted map of how legal institutions operate or even should operate. In their daily lives, human beings act within contexts that are both immediate and remote. Doctrine is remote—written, interpreted, and misinterpreted far from the complex realities of organizations, the pressures of community challenges and supports, and the infinite capacities and infirmities of plaintiffs, defendants, prosecutors, attorneys, and judges.

In the study of law, the law and society movement has been an effort to view law as something wider and deeper than the legal doctrine enunciated in case and statute. In 1935, Thurman Arnold, that great demystifier of legal reasoning, pointed to the contradiction between legal doctrine and the realities of everyday life in legal institutions. "The principles of law," he wrote, "are supposed to control society, because such an assumption is necessary to the logic of the dream. Yet the observer should constantly keep in mind that the function of law is not to guide society but to comfort it." (*The Symbols of Government,* p. 34.) Much research since then has substantiated Arnold's insight into the symbolic functions of legal doctrine and the realities of the daily behavior of courts, lawyers, police, and citizens.

As Arnold also realized, it is not the higher reaches of the legal system—the appellate courts—through which most citizens come in contact with the legal institution. It is the lower courts that constitute the only site that almost all supplicants or defendants come to know. Nor is the trial the common event in the citizen's experience with legal disputes or enforcement. *The Process Is the Punishment* documents the paucity of trials in the routine flow of criminal cases. It is in the process of arraignment that most of the work of the court gets done. Here the case is dismissed, guilt is pleaded, fines are imposed. Here the citizen incurs the costs of loss of pay, of inconvenience, of auto impoundment charges, of attorney's fees. He or she suffers the indignities of dispute and defense and the other travails of organizational involvement. Whatever the outcome of the case, the experience is at best one worth avoiding.

Studies of the lower courts, before and since the original publication of Feeley's book, have given us a more realistic sense of what citizens experience in contact with legal institutions. In the same vein, the studies of police have made us aware of the negotiation and discretion that is involved in the origination or rejection of criminal cases. We come to recognize more clearly the limited role of legal doctrine in the processes of law enforcement and law usage. So too, studies of business practices and of insurance negotiation with claimants have underscored the vast extent to which civil cases reaching courts are a tiny tip of the iceberg of disputes. Even of those civil cases that do get court attention, few continue to the trial phase.

To twist an old adage, law is too important a subject to be left to lawyers. The United States is said to be a highly litigious society, yet most disputes are never settled by courts or even contemplate the legal institution as a place for resolution. Most crimes are not even reported to police. What Marc Galanter has called "indigenous law" is a large part of our daily lives. The study of legal institutions must also be concerned with who, how, and when police and courts are brought to bear in the lives of citizens.

The Process Is the Punishment is a convincing and striking description of how law operates in the context of what sociologists call "situated action." By this term they refer to the complex character of the immediate situation as distinct from the abstractions, which generalization and rules contemplate. The specific act of the defendant, his or her character and background, the organizational constraints and historical patterns of the court, and the nature of the lawyers all contribute to actions and outcomes deeply responsive to local contexts. Legal doctrine is general, abstract, and takes little recognition of the organizational and situational elements in which daily activity takes place.

Despite the locality and informality of the lower courts, the pattern of contextual understandings appears again and again in the numerous studies of the lower courts, which have emerged, many since Feeley's study. As the author asserts in his new Preface, his account of the New Haven court eleven years ago may differ from the same court now and certainly from other courts in other jurisdictions, but the general perspective toward our understanding of how law functions, which his study amplifies, remains a major paradigm for the student of legal behavior.

In these ways, the law and society movement has led us to examine more than legal doctrine and to provide us with a conception of the "legal system," which is much wider and less systematic than a law school version of it. Feeley's book is a significant contribution to that movement. But it is more. It raises the question of law but it also raises the important question of the relation between law and justice.

In *The Concept of Law,* H.L.A. Hart describes the "open texture" of legal rules as a general characteristic of natural languages. Where we seek to control behavior by universal standards, the rules cannot take account of the often unpredictable nature of facts and the multitude of relevant features, which the concrete situation and the specific person present (Hart, pp. 121–124). It is not only that language is a limited guide to individual cases. The situated case, in its particularity, presents features that the general rule cannot recognize or sometimes appreciate. The character of the person, the consequences of action at the time and in the place, the exigencies of organizational operation, the many aspects of individual cases may contradict the realization of a just, or fair, decision by the formal rule.

Feeley's recognition of this is a major contribution to the ongoing discussion of the courts and informal justice. Defenders of a strictly formal adherence to due process and the adjudicative ideal (what Arnold meant by the dream) find the limited occurrence of trials a matter of great dismay. Feeley's concept of "substantive justice" suggests that the matter is much more complex than that. The sense of justice is not abandoned but permeates the disposition of individual cases. Punishment is not alleviated by the process but is itself a costly matter. Formal justice and substantive justice are not the same.

The Process Is the Punishment does not solve all the problems it raises by any means. No single study can be expected to do that. For those who are critical of the courts and the police for their exercise of discretion, the cup is half empty. For those who want to temper the general by the specific, the cup is half full. The quotation from Herbert Packer (p. 288) states the problem quite well. The problem is the lawlessness of discretion and substantive justice. Justice is, after all, a condition that even Socrates had difficulty defining. One citizen's justice may be another citizen's travesty of justice. Justice is a political or judicial issue and thus a matter of general rules. Yet, as Feeley demonstrates, it is also one of specificity, of substance rather than form. How can a society, through legislation and judicial standards, give direction to a process that is inherently discretionary in its particularity? Feeley does not provide an answer, but he does do a great deal to formulate the question realistically.

The related problem is that of the relation between the adjudicative ideal of due process and the trial to the behavior of prosecutors and defendants. While trials may be few, they may nevertheless serve to give direction to the actors in the legal game. They may provide the imagined situation that directs settlements, police discretion, and the lower court personnel in reaching dispositions, which avoid trial. As in insurance cases, the imagined outcome of the trial plays a role in the negotiation between possible plaintiffs and defendants. Similarly, appellate law may not be a good map of what courts do, but it may nevertheless play an important role in the courts by the ways in which the participants take it into account.

Feeley's study suggests that the world of the adjudicative ideal, of due process and formal law, would be a sterile, organizational disaster, often unjust and unfair. As social scientists often do, he turns what may seem to be irrational into a process that is not as punishing to law and justice as it seems on first sight. In this fashion, Feeley has succeeded in humanizing the court organization.

While he would not go so far, there is much in common between *The Process Is the Punishment* and the remark of the Boston political boss of the early twentieth century. Asked by Lincoln Steffens if he could get a murderer off, Martin Lomasny agreed that he could. Could he do so a second time? Steffens asked. Lomasny agreed that he could. "Do you call that Justice?" said Steffens. Lomasny replied, "People don't want Justice. They want Mercy."

JOSEPH R. GUSFIELD
March 1992

PREFACE

For this edition, issued eleven years after first publication, my initial impulse was to revise and update *The Process Is the Punishment*. Upon reflection, however, I feel that the book stands on its own. Emphasizing recent changes in the court might unwittingly undermine concern with the generic, underlying processes and relationships, which constitute the central focus of the book. And so I resisted the temptation.

I realize that time has not stood still in New Haven. Indeed, the Court of Common Pleas no longer even exists. Just as I was completing my study, Connecticut merged its two-tiered trial court system into a single "unified" court. However, separate "parts" were created, and one "part" continues to deal with the sorts of cases examined in this study. Regardless of formal structure, such division of labor is found in many other courts across the country and as such reveals the dynamics of adjudication of less serious matters.

Despite these and still other changes in New Haven and the criminal justice system more generally, the underlying processes that were the focus of the book have not altered appreciably in the years since the book's initial publication. The book examines political sponsorship in the recruitment of judges, prosecutors, public defenders, and related court personnel. Although the personalities and no doubt the relative importance of various local and state political sponsors have shifted, the book itself shows that these are fluid factors, and focuses more on the roles and process of sponsorship and recruitment than on the correlation between any particular type of sponsors and positions. When it does focus on decision making, it examines pretrial detention and release, the appointment of public defenders, adjudication, sentencing, and pretrial process costs—decisions common to all courts. I have found no evidence that these institutions have altered appreciably in the intervening years.

The nature of crime as well as the composition of the city's population, also have changed since I completed my initial study. In particular the city's minority population, and the minority population as a proportion of defendants in the courts, have increased. And drug-related offenses are now more common. But here, too, such changes do not alter in any appreciable way the central issues examined in the book. No doubt radical changes in personnel, the defendant population, procedures, or the types of charges would affect in crucial ways how the court functions. But one sad fact of social life is that criminal courts everywhere are populated by the poor and the disadvantaged and the problems that bring them into contact with the criminal courts do not vary radically. Indeed, the courts are one of society's primary institutions for managing such people and their continuing problems. I do not mean to suggest that the defendant population and the nature of the charges handled in courts may not differ across jurisdictions, or that comparative analysis would not yield significant findings, but this study aims at explicating underlying dynamics and processes.

In asserting that the book continues to provide an accurate analysis of a lower criminal court, I do not claim that it portrays "every court" in the same way that Willy Loman in *Death of a Salesman* captures "everyman". Rather, I believe that its central concerns address ubiquitous practices and processes. This is most clearly evident in the book's effort to examine the aspirations of officials who, when charged with "applying" the law, confront the impulse to assess moral character and render substantive justice, and the confounding feature of process costs in a system whose best impulses are to provide more due process. As Max Weber, among others, has taught us, these tensions are not unique to lower courts. But they are writ large in a low-stakes, high-volume system, which grants decision makers vast discretion and operates with low visibility.

Although the book describes courthouse personnel at length, its aim is not exhaustive description of people, but presentation of roles and institutions, and examination of general processes. The analysis is firmly rooted in organizational theory and open systems theory, and emphasizes interdependencies, adaptation, institutional maintenance, adversarial relationships, and institutional morality—issues that are present in any organization, even an "open system" like the court. Since publication of *The Process,* this approach has been embraced by a number of other students of adjudication, and I like to think the book played some small part in promoting this perspective within the field.

My belief in the continuing relevance of the book is also reinforced by experiences since its initial publication: First, I have remained in touch with some lawyers and judges in the New Haven Court, and have returned to visit the court upon occasion. Despite elapsed time, the court remains familiar.

Second, my central concern with the organizational dynamics and the paradox of "the process is the punishment" has been strengthened by additional experience watching criminal proceedings in Minneapolis, New York, Wisconsin, California, Malmo, London, Kobe, Tel Aviv, and elsewhere. Despite sometimes significant differences in jurisdiction and procedure, as well as in political culture and demography, there are important similarities in all these courts. The similarities appear in organizational dynamics, adaptations, process costs, and the quest to reconcile formal rational reasoning with direct moral assessment.

Third, every summer I teach a short course to judges from

across the country, and assign parts of my book to them. And I have heard from still other judges and lawyers who have read the book. Many of them report that my characterization of the New Haven lower court resonates with their own experiences.

Finally, in recent years I have been involved in historical studies of criminal prosecution and adjudication in the United States and England, and have found that the dynamics explored in my field work in New Haven parallel impressions gained through exploration of court records, judges' diaries, and contemporary accounts of lower courts in several locations in England and the United States over the past two hundred and more years. I don't mean to imply that nothing has changed, but that the impulse to negotiate, the quest for substantive justice, the desire to avoid costly procedure, and the like are present across time. The abstractions of the law and procedure are always and everywhere refracted through similar sets of institutional realities and impulses.

One of the book's central themes is the limits of due process, and I hope that it has contributed to the increased concern with this issue in recent years. When I addressed issues relating to the problems associated with the logic of the quest for more justice through ever greater elaboration of procedure, few law and society scholars were concerned with them. The due process revolution was still in full bloom, and by and large the academic literature celebrated it as an unproblematic good, and equated increased process with increased justice. However, since first publication of the book, concern with the problematic features of individual-focused due process has become more pronounced, and a number of critical assessments of due process rights, especially as they apply to high-volume, low-stakes issues, have appeared.

Indeed, since initial publication, concern about the limits of due process has emerged as the central theme in a growing body of work by scholars as diverse as communitarian conservatives, critical legal studies scholars, and empirically oriented social scientists. Some of this work, like this study, is firmly rooted in organizational theory, and explores the tension caused by the aspiration of rights when confronted with the implications of institutional imperatives. It has developed these themes as they affect adjudication in such diverse issues as social security claims, welfare administration, educational entitlements, civil commitments, landlord–tenant conflicts, employment discrimination claims, and the like.

The Process and these other works are certainly not broadsides against due process. Nor do they purport to provide comprehensive frameworks for assessing rights-enhancing processes. Rather, they emphasize the costly dilemma of invoking due process rights in various settings and under various conditions.

Some of the more recent work is rooted in macrosociological theory, which seeks to illuminate the social functions of institutional practices. A number of scholars have used their studies as vehicles to launch sweeping explorations of modern legal developments and to mount broad attacks on individualism inherent in classical legal liberalism. Some have concluded that liberal legalism and the language of individual rights masks power differentials between the parties in legal conflicts, and fails to acknowledge structural factors that reinforce enduring inequalities. In so doing, they have challenged the basic premises of liberal legalism and concluded that a regime of rights, far from serving a liberating function, is in fact the enemy—an insidious form of social control.

This vigorous reexamination of liberal legal institutions is welcome. In the law and society field, it reflects a growing concern with the social functions of law and the legal process. The methods of these scholars vary widely, but their concerns are squarely in the traditions of Marx, Durkheim, Foucault, and others. Their sweep is usually both wider, in terms of social functions, and deeper, in terms of variation across time, than is the scope of more organizational-level analysis.

I am sympathetic with such macrosociological concerns and levels of analysis, but *The Process Is the Punishment* is clearly rooted in the concerns of organization and open systems theory, which takes the social structure—the environment—more or less as given. That is, it explores how the environment is reflected in the organization and how the organization adapts to the environment. But it does not explore in any systematic way the broad social functions of courts.

Some have suggested that the failure to address social functions is a weakness of organizational-level analysis, and of this volume. My response is that we should not confuse levels of analysis. Organizational theory, as I have used the term here, also focuses on issues of importance and enduring concern. They too are at root generic. Regardless of social structure, the dynamics of legal institutions are affected by the nature of recruitment, decision making, the impulse to move beyond the alienating formalism of legal rules, the tensions between standard routine and discretionary judgment, pressures to adapt in significant and problematic ways, and the like. Clearly there are important overlaps between macrosociological theory and organizational-level analysis, but, at least as I have used the terms here, they address somewhat different concerns. Those working at either level should remind themselves of this fact, and understand the different levels as complementary and not competitive.

MALCOLM M. FEELEY
Berkeley, California
February 1992

INTRODUCTION

Next to the police, the lower criminal courts play the most important role in forming citizen impressions of the American system of criminal justice. Even excluding traffic offenses, each year several millions of people are drawn into contact with these courts as defendants, complainants, or witnesses. Moreover, an appearance in court may have reverberations that affect a person's spouse, family, friends, and employer.

In systems operating with a two-tiered criminal court system, roughly divided by misdemeanor and felony jurisdiction, about 90 to 95 percent of all cases are handled in these lower courts. Armed robbery, rape, and homicide are rare exceptions in comparison with the overwhelming number of petty offenses which swamp the lower courts. The pressures of coping with this large number of petty cases shape court practices and in turn affect the ways in which more serious cases are handled.

Different levels of courts have distinct pathologies. The seriousness of the offense (and consequently the possible severity of outcome) affects the ways court officials approach their work. When a suspect is likely to be sent to jail for several years, his case is handled with far greater care than is a case likely to result in a small fine. Unless they are carefully bounded by reference to seriousness of charges, generalizations about how criminal courts operate can be grossly misleading. Even within the same court, what is routine for one type of case may not be for another.

In this study, my observations focus primarily on the lower court in New Haven, Connecticut, the Court of Common Pleas

as it is now called. It has sentencing jurisdiction over misdemeanors and lesser felonies. The generalizations I hazard
about the flow of criminal cases and the nature of court organization which stem from this examination of a single court are
usually restricted to lower courts or to the handling of "little"
cases. As I emphasize in this study, the pathologies of criminal
courts vary widely, largely in accordance with the magnitude of
the "stakes" involved. A recurring and continuous phenomenon
in lower courts may not occur at all in higher courts that handle
"bigger" cases.

Although this book focuses on a single court in a single city,
it is by no means an analysis of a unique institution or an
institution in a unique setting, nor does it focus on features of
the institution and its setting that are unique or even particularly
distinctive. Most students of the criminal process agree that the
operations of the criminal courts are shaped by little-understood
factors, and that decisions are made as a consequence of an
uncharted, complex, and interdependent set of relationships.
Both of these factors militate against a comparative approach
which by definition must *impose* at the outset a developed
framework on the research. While there have been a number of
studies comparing outcomes in several court settings, by and
large these have been superficial reports which did not convince
even their authors that they adequately controlled for major
relevant factors. In contrast, the best of the recent comparative
analyses of criminal courts have examined the more structured
felony courts and focused on only two and three jurisdictions.
But even their authors took pains to point out the limitations of
their comparisons. So far as I know, there are no published full-
length comparative studies of *lower* criminal courts.

Comparative analysis implies a deductive research strategy,
elaborating on a typology, testing hypotheses, or applying a
theory. At a minimum, it requires *advance* knowledge of relevant factors, for it must impose requirements on the data collection so that the data will be truly comparable and the variables

operationalized in equivalent fashion. I am not convinced that current knowledge of criminal court processes is well developed, and unless or until there is a substantial body of carefully drawn descriptive and inductive research on which typologies can be drawn and until classifications are made, the benefits of an analysis of a single setting may be as great as, if not greater than, those of comparative studies.[1]

This is not to suggest that this study and case studies generally do not have any devices to focus inquiry or to guard against preoccupation with the idiosyncratic. The best of them do; they rely on a test of substance and theoretical interest. Does the analysis focus on a substantial problem? Is the inquiry cast in general, theoretically intriguing terms? Are generic problems central to the analysis? If the answers to these questions are affirmative, then it is likely that the resulting analysis will provide a *general* explanation, one that maintains an interest in and focus on the generic rather than on the particular. To the extent that this takes place—and I have made an effort to see that it has in this book—the researcher undertaking a study of a single setting or a single institution has no need to apologize for not adopting the hallmark of social science, comparative analysis, and in fact may be able to make the claim that, unfettered by the constraints of predetermined data collection requirements, he is freer to pursue general theory.

A concern with the substantively important and the theoretically generic has guided this study at every stage. The central question is, How is the criminal sanction administered? As it is explored, this question assumes various forms: How is the criminal sanction administered in a lower court in light of its low visibility and vast powers of discretion? How are rules used in this process? How does a concern with substantive justice shape the process? How does a legal system cope with a high volume of "low stakes" cases? How do transaction costs affect the process? Answers to these questions should illuminate not only criminal, but civil court issues as well, and address issues that are of increasing concern to students of modern, complex societies.

The concerns that guide this study have not been plucked from thin air or "discovered" by random observation. They have their roots in the perennial theoretical issues of social science and other research on criminal justice administration.[2] The concern with the court organization and structure, and particularly the importance of environment and social context in shaping it, draws on a long tradition of research on criminal courts and other public institutions. Whereas the particular ways in which organization and social context shape the operations of the New Haven court will not be generalizable to all or even most American cities, the important lesson in this analysis is that the interdependencies of the separate components of the system and their collective relationship with the larger environment have important effects on how justice is perceived and administered. Indeed, substantial changes in the way courts operate may more likely be brought about by changes *outside* the courthouse than within it.[3]

Social scientists have long been interested in the development and application of rules and the tension between formal and substantive justice.[4] The law is only an approximation of some portion of a polity's values, and of necessity it must be stated in general and abstract form, for no set of rules can be detailed enough to anticipate or provide for all particular situations in which they are to be applied. Because of this, and because the law is overdetermined, allowing conduct to be defined variously by more than one rule, discretion is inevitable. Even under the best of circumstances, those who administer the law must mold abstractions, "fill in the gaps," and in the process work their own views of *substantive justice* into the administration of the law. Although the importance of values of individuals within the court is moderated by the collective nature of much decision making and by group pressures, the role of individual values in the evolution of a group consensus of substantive justice is important. Informed by the concerns of such writers as John Hogarth, Willard Gaylin, Martin Levin, William K. Muir, Philip Selznick, and Lon Fuller, this study focuses on the substantive nature of justice that court officials bring to their work.[5] Again, while it is impossible to know precisely how generalizable the particular constellation of values in New Haven is, this study shows how lower court processes are structured to invite and indeed necessitate the rise of substantive justice. Although these values will vary by individual and by community, this study shows they must be considered in any complete account of criminal case processing.

Finally, I examine decision-making and processing costs, which are important factors in accounting for the ways the court handles cases and defendants respond to the court. In a great many instances these processing costs turn the principles of criminal procedure on their head, reducing the presumed objects and end results of the process, adjudication and sentencing, to incidental actions. These costs of the pretrial process are not only important sanctions in their own rights, they in turn shape and are shaped by the nature of the court organization and the conceptions of substantive justice. Again, I do not claim that the particular ways in which these costs are felt in New Haven are characteristic of the ways pretrial costs affect criminal cases in all other cities. Clearly there are significant variations.[6] I do hope, however, that this discussion shows how important these processing costs are in shaping court procedures generally.

Even if one agrees with my argument for the benefits of an intensive analysis of a single setting, one final question remains: Why New Haven? The answer was obvious for me: location and access. I was at Yale during the period I conducted this research, and the courthouse was just a few blocks away from my office. This proximity allowed me to spend a great deal of time in the courthouse, maintain close connections over a long period, and as the reader of chapter five will find, to move back and forth between data collection and data analysis, a luxury few field researchers have. Most researchers can spend only a few weeks or months at their research site, and then must return home to analyze and write up the data; those conducting comparative studies are confronted with the additional need to fit data into a precoded format not designed for that particular setting.

The importance of access cannot be overemphasized. Courts are parochial institutions; each possesses its own peculiar information system and shorthand language for maintaining it, and it is precisely for this reason that I am skeptical of many comparative and quantitative studies of criminal courts. The court in New Haven, as are courts elsewhere, is like a closed community, and it took me some considerable time before I could penetrate it. I had to gain the confidence of its members, learn their language, and become a familiar face to them. A brief excursion into the courthouse simply would not have sufficed.

One last set of questions about the research site remains. Is New Haven typical? Can what we learn here be generalized to other cities as well? So far I have dealt with this question in general terms, but a specific answer is called for. My response is similar to the response of other students of New Haven's institutions: This is not really the right question. No single city can be regarded as "typical." The correct test is not to show that New Haven is typical of all American cities or typical of middle-sized cities, but rather to show that it is *not* so atypical as to be unique. I marshal evidence on this point with respect to rates of crime and arrests in chapter three, and for an extended treatment of this concern, I refer the skeptical reader to the introductory chapters of Robert Dahl's *Who Governs?* and Raymond Wolfinger's *The Politics of Progress*, both of which argue that New Haven is *not particularly* distinctive.[7] I emphasize "not particularly," because in the final analysis all cities and locations are distinctive. As Raymond Wolfinger observed:

Looking at other Connecticut cities, one notes that Bridgeport has a Socialist Party whose durable leader was mayor for 24 years;

Hartford has an economy in which the insurance industry plays an unusually important part; and so on. . . . A truly "typical American City" cannot be found and the best one can hope for is a research site that is typical of its type. New Haven meets this criterion; it is not a municipal freak.[8]

What Wolfinger argued for the city as a whole is true for the city's court as well. This was not an assumption I made at the outset, but rather a conclusion I drew after spending considerable time in court. Initially, I wondered whether or not the presence of one of the nation's leading law schools just a few blocks away might have a profound effect on the nature of justice administered in the courthouse. My conclusion was no; it does not have a profound effect, not even a major effect, and perhaps not even a measurable effect. Yale is noticeable in the courthouse, but less so than it is in many of the city's other public institutions, and there is no evidence to suggest that its effect is discernibly different from that of any other university in any other community. Occasionally a student is arrested and brought into court; at times classes make visits to the courthouse to observe the proceedings, or courthouse officials are invited to speak to student groups; from time to time a law school student interns in the court. On the whole, the educational credentials of the attorneys practicing in the New Haven criminal courts are fairly impressive, perhaps because of the presence of Yale. But as Anthony Platt and Randi Pollock conclude in their study of a public defender's office in a West Coast city, this phenomenon may be a general consequence of the times.[9] The activism of the 1960s coupled with the dramatic expansion of the rights of the criminally accused seemed to have attracted a distinctively well-credentialed group of young attorneys to courthouses everywhere, and a few years later many are still there.

Some readers of drafts of this book detected what they thought was an incongruity in style: I identified the city and court, but not the particular individuals whom I quoted or whose actions I described. But there are reasons for this: While writing this book, I carefully examined and at times took strong issue with the approach and findings of other research reports based on observations of courts in New Haven and elsewhere, and hope that my findings will be subjected to the same scrutiny. That is why I have identified the city. In the final analysis I will leave it to others to judge how broadly or narrowly the findings I report can be generalized. But there are also several reasons for not identifying the particular individuals whom I quote or whose behavior I describe in my study; most often I avoided it to honor confidentiality, at times to save people embarrassment, and at others simply not to clutter up the book with a host of once- or twice-mentioned names. I would hope that the evidence and observations I present here will be tested against additional information on this city as well as against information on other cities. Only if such collective work takes place can social science proceed successfully.

THE PROCESS

IS THE

PUNISHMENT

CHAPTER 1

The Lower Courts: Process

and Punishment

Introduction

Lower criminal courts are a world apart. They bear little resemblance either to the popular image of trial courts or to actual practices of higher trial courts which handle far fewer cases. In the lower courts trials are rare events, and even protracted plea bargaining is an exception. Jammed every morning with a new mass of arrestees who have been picked up the night before, lower courts rapidly process what the police consider "routine" problems—barroom brawls, neighborhood squabbles, domestic disputes, welfare cheating, shoplifting, drug possession, and prostitution—not "real" crimes. These courts are chaotic and confusing; officials communicate in a verbal shorthand wholly unintelligible to accused and accuser alike, and they seem to make arbitrary decisions, sending one person to jail and freeing the next. But for the most part they are lenient; they sentence few people to jail and impose few large fines. Their facilities are terrible. Courtrooms are crowded, chambers are dingy, and libraries are virtually nonexistent. Even the newer courtrooms age quickly, worn down by hard use and constant abuse.

The depressing air about the courtrooms carries over to the mood of the people who populate them. By conventional standards nearly all of the defendants are failures, both in life and in crime. They are poor, often unemployed, usually young, and frequently from broken homes. Most of them lack self-esteem, motivation, skill, and opportunity. A great many of them have come to rely on alcohol and drugs, and problems related to their use often bring these people into court. Breach of peace and disorderly conduct are the most common charges handled by the lower courts; they often stem from actions fueled by alcohol. For many of the defendants, petty theft is a way of life that they pay for with an occasional appearance in court.

Defendants in these courts, particularly those in urban areas, are disproportionately Black, while court officials are predominantly white. This contrast serves to reinforce both the defendants' and the officials' belief in two separate worlds divided by a chasm of wealth, status, and power. In this way, these courts serve as a catalyst for suspicion and contempt.

Court officials themselves are part of this depressing landscape. Judges, bored by their jobs, become callous toward defendants who are so different from themselves. Prosecutors, dulled by their repetitive work, may be noncommunicative and appear to be vindictive. Defense attorneys, depressed by feelings that their efforts are not appreciated, can easily begin to treat their clients carelessly. The solemnity that the words "crime" and "criminal court" imply aside, lower court officials—judges, prosecutors and public defenders alike—feel frustrated and belittled. Trained to practice law, they are confronted with the kinds of problems that social workers face, but if they respond as social workers would, then they are denied respect from their counterparts who do "practice law" in the higher courts. The very language used to describe the business of the lower courts reflects their low status. Cases in lower courts are universally labeled as "garbage," "junk," "trash," "crap," "penny ante," and the like. These words not only describe the way in which court officials come to think of their work, they also reveal how they think of the defendants before them, and, ultimately, themselves as well.

But despite their limited powers, these lower criminal courts are vitally important. While the criminal justice system is most often discussed in terms of the "big" cases, the large number of "petty" offenses in the lower courts occupies most of the time of criminal justice officials. In systems with a two-tiered trial court system, about 80 to 90 percent of all criminal prosecutions begin and end in the lower courts. Armed robbery, rape, and homicide are exceptional—indeed almost unique—events in comparison to the overwhelming numbers of petty offenses which swamp the lower courts. In the city which is the focus of this study—New Haven, Connecticut—for every armed robbery disposed of in the higher Superior Court, there are a hundred cases of larceny handled by the lower Court of Common Pleas; for every case of aggravated assault, there are dozens of cases of breaches of the peace.

Next to contact with the police, contact with these courts is the most important way in which citizens form impressions of the American system of criminal justice. Even excluding traffic offenses, each year several millions of people are drawn into direct contact with these courts as defendants, complainants, witnesses or jurors, or as friends or relations of someone else in one of these roles. For most of them this experience is one of their few encounters with the judicial process, and the impressions they form are likely to color their view of the entire system of justice. Whatever majesty there is in the law may depend heavily on these encounters.

Some Explanations for the Operations of Lower Courts

Half a century ago, Roscoe Pound diagnosed the ills besetting these lower criminal courts.[1] The rapid population growth in the nineteenth century spawned a host of local courts with

5

limited overlapping jurisdictions. Practicality dictated the need for part-time personnel, distrust of professionalism led to the appointment of nonlawyer judges, and passion for democratic ideals led to the election of criminal justice officials such as sheriffs, prosecutors, judges, and clerks. Courts were often catapulted into the center of the political process, and in urban centers they gradually came under the influence of the emerging political machines. Courthouse positions were coveted political prizes and important elements in maintaining political organization.[2]

Under such circumstances rules were applied arbitrarily. They fell with special harshness on the masses of poor people who were crowded together in the nation's mushrooming population centers, often newly arrived immigrants who were neither familiar with local customs nor able to comprehend the confusion of the courtroom. Careless officials and crowded facilities compounded the problems, and cases were often processed without careful consideration. The result, Pound argued, was popular dissatisfaction with justice and suspicions that conditions were even worse than they really were.

It is [the handling of petty prosecutions] that the administration of criminal justice touches immediately the greatest number of people. It is here that the great mass of an urban population, whose experience of law is too likely to have been only an experience of arbitrary discretion of police officers and offhand action of magistrates, tempered by political influence might be taught the spirit of our institutions and made to feel that the law was a living force for securing their interests. The bad physical surroundings, the confusion, the want of decorum, the undignified offhand disposition of cases at high speed, the frequent suggestion of something working behind the scenes, which characterize the petty criminal court in almost all of our cities, create in the minds of observers a general suspicion of the whole process of law enforcement which, no matter how unfounded, gravely prejudices the law.[3]

Since Pound first diagnosed these causes and consequences of the dissatisfaction with justice, there has been a revolution in criminal law, spawned in part by the movement for judicial modernization which Pound himself helped found, and spurred on by the rulings of the United States Supreme Court. The past fifty years have seen a continuous movement toward formalization of procedure, rationalization of jurisdiction, and upgrading of personnel. The rights of the accused have been expanded and strengthened by Supreme Court rulings, and nowhere are the implications of this change as dramatic as they are in the lower criminal courts. The substance of criminal law has become more precise, the process of adjudication has become more formal, and the rights of the accused have been substantially enlarged. Opportunities once reserved for well-to-do defendants are now within reach of almost everyone accused of a criminal offense. Alternatives once available only in the most serious cases are now in theory open to anyone accused of any type of criminal offense. An indigent charged with drunk and disorderly conduct may now avail himself of roughly the same set of rights and opportunities as a wealthy businessman charged with stock fraud.

Perhaps the single most important Supreme Court ruling for the lower criminal courts was *Argersinger* v. *Hamlin*,[4] which held that those unable to afford counsel who are charged with any type of criminal offense that might result in a jail term have a right to appointed counsel. As a result of this ruling, an institution which just a few years ago was organized haphazardly, staffed with nonlawyer judges, and rarely graced with the presence of an attorney for the accused, now has most of the formal characteristics associated with upper level trial courts that handle major crimes.

The constitutional revolution has had profound implications. It has changed the nature of courtroom organization. It has led to the creation of a drastically expanded office—that of Public Defender (PD). It has provided new options and opportunities that a decade ago were wholly unavailable without advice of counsel. Perhaps above all, it has altered expectations about

7

what a case in lower criminal court can be. Charges once considered "nuisances" can now command the full attention previously reserved for major felonies. Defendants once routinely shepherded through the process by the prosecution now have an attorney to advise them.

But the revolution is by no means complete. Despite the constitutional and institutional changes, the lower courts continue to operate in a manner reminiscent of an earlier era. The conditions and practices described by Pound and others around the turn of the century still strike a familiar chord. Instead of proceeding by careful argument and quiet deliberations, courts continue to make decisions by noisy exchanges and rushed judgments. Instead of adopting full-fledged adversarial proceedings, they continue to rely on quick negotiations. In contrast to the lengthy fact-finding and truth-testing usually conducted during a cross examination, there are superficial reviews of police reports. Constitutional changes notwithstanding, the lower courts are reluctant to treat formally that which has traditionally been treated informally, and they refuse to consider solemnly that which has usually been taken lightly. They will not regard as a *crime* that which has typically been treated as a *nuisance*.

In a letter to friends expressing concern over the conditions in New Haven's lower court, novelist John Hersey described a typical scene, and then concluded with a question which could have been penned by Roscoe Pound fifty years ago, or, as he suggests, by Charles Dickens fifty years earlier:

The Sixth Circuit courtroom, which some New Haven lawyers call the Pit, is a great dingy box of passions. Two stories high, its flaking ceiling supported by metal stanchions, with tall dusty windows and creaking floors, it is a hell that would have appealed to Charles Dickens. What faces one sees there! —ravaged, jaunty, dazed, disenchanted, raging, resigned. A man in his forties (found intoxicated) clutching in his arms a stuffed tiger nearly as tall as he, his constant companion and only comfort; a natty type accused of gambling, in a whipcord bush jacket and knickers and smartly polished leather puttees; three weedlike red-eyed minors in blue jeans, accused of armed robbery; a woman booked as a whore, with a pokey-soiled wig and a hacking cough, badly in need of night's more merciful light; an empty-faced teenager, held for possession, with his mother, who is played out to the very end of her kitchen string, on hand to stand up with him. . . . This place is society's open sore. A hundred cases a morning. Breaking and entering, assault, gambling, pimping, prostitution, found drunk, armed robbery, non-support, welfare fraud, disturbing the peace.

Now this may well be asked: What credentials does the author of this letter have to take issue on questions of criminal justice with a state Supreme Court Justice? It goes without saying that I am not an expert on jurisprudence, and I have presumed to write such a letter as this only because of my novelist's sense of what happens to *all* the human beings, judges included, in the ambiance of court-oriented criminal justice with its atmosphere of pragmatism, of getting the job done in the crudest but quickest way; with, in the end, its cynicism, its assumption that riffraff are probably guilty, its lesson to the accused poor that justice is a matter of wheeling and dealing, of influence ("I can get you a suspended sentence if you'll cop the plea"), and so of copping out, playing the game, fitting in with the system's requirement that the job of the courts be done, above all, with dispatch. The noble ideal, "innocent until proved guilty," gives way to a corrupt and crime-feeding one, "let off easy if copped as guilty."

When will we turn our eyes to what goes on in the Pit?[5]

Hersey's impressions are reinforced by the findings of more systematic investigations. In my survey of over 1,600* criminal cases and observation over a period of several months, I found that:

- Although all defendants have a right to a trial by jury, not one defendant in a sample of 1,640 cases insisted upon one.
- Even though arrestees with limited funds have a right to a court-appointed counsel, only one-half of all defendants journeyed through the criminal process with an attorney at their side.
- Those who went without attorneys were not confined to those charged with the most minor offenses. Roughly 20 percent of those

* The total number of cases varies in specific instances throughout the book.

9

charged with felonies, and one-third of those receiving jail sentences, were not represented by counsel.

● Even in those cases in which counsel was present, his contribution was questionable. "Interviews" with clients were often little more than quick, whispered exchanges in the corridor, and proceedings before the bench consisted of little more than a defense attorney's recapitulation of what his client told him. There was little independent investigation of facts.

● Despite the fact that the state of Connecticut is recognized for its liberal pretrial release statute which provides for release conditions to be set according to the accused's ties to the community, most arrestees were at the mercy of the police who set bail according to a "schedule" based on the seriousness of the charges.

● Although most arrestees were eventually released prior to trial, 10 percent of them were detained until disposition. While this figure may seem insignificant, it is twice the number who were sentenced *after* conviction. In other words, twice as many people were sent to jail prior to trial than after trial.

● Even though the Supreme Court has gone to great lengths to insure that its rulings are not empty vessels, the Court of Common Pleas continued to dispense justice "Church Street style." Arrestees were arraigned in groups and informed of their rights *en masse*. At times the arrestees were not even aware that they are being addressed. Judges did not always look at them, and even if a judge made an effort to be heard, he could not always be understood over the constant din of the courtroom.

● Although the Sixth Amendment to the Constitution guarantees the right to a speedy trial, seemingly simple cases dragged out endlessly. Cases in which there was no trial, no witnesses, no formal motions, no pretrial involvement from the bench, and no presentence investigation still required as many as eight or ten different appearances spread over six months.

● Conversely, many complex cases were cut short because the accused had agreed to plead guilty at arraignment after the prosecutor advised him to "be smart and get it over with today."

● Other cases were cut short because the defendant failed to appear in court. Unless the charges were particularly serious or the accused was notorious, the court made no serious effort to locate defendants who did not appear but hoped that their attorneys, the bail bondsmen, or the police on another arrest would return them eventually to court. But even when they were returned, the court did little to sanction them for their failure, preferring to overlook the matter rather than separate the "reasonable" from the "unreasonable" excuses.

• Despite the deliberateness envisioned for due process, the court organized its work to move at a rapid pace. Court convened in midmorning and usually adjourned by midafternoon. Defendants came and went in rapid succession. While a few cases took up as much as a minute or two of the court's time—and a small handful involved the court in protracted proceedings—the overwhelming majority of cases took just a few seconds. In these situations the court was not a deliberative body, nor was the judge an assessor of facts or law. Instead, the courtroom encounter was a ritual in which the judge *ratified* a decision made earlier.

• Although Connecticut statutes carefully classify criminal offenses into a sevenfold scheme of seriousness and provide for a sliding scale of maximum penalties in proportion to the seriousness of the offense, there was no measurable relationship between seriousness of charge and severity of sentence. Those charged with the more serious offenses, including most of those found guilty of felony charges, by and large received the same types of sentences as those convicted for lesser misdemeanors.

• Those with prior records did not fare significantly worse than first offenders. Sentences could not be accounted for by standard "legal" factors, seriousness of charge, or prior record.

There is no dearth of explanations to account for this continuing "crisis" in the courts. Some argue that the *press of heavy caseloads* prohibits slow deliberation. Others argue that we are witnessing the twilight of the adversary system and the *ascendency of a criminal justice bureaucracy* which operates in assembly-line fashion. Some point to the *pervasiveness of plea bargaining*, claiming that uncaring defense attorneys, ruthless prosecutors, and indifferent judges encourage pleas of guilty in order to avoid the difficult and time-consuming tasks of mounting a defense, proving guilt, and umpiring a contest. Still others suggest that the *lack of qualified personnel* accounts for the problems of the courts. It is difficult to reject such explanations. Each appeals both to intuition and to common sense. Each contains a substantial measure of truth. But neither separately nor together do these explanations add up to a complete account of what shapes the decision process in the lower criminal courts.

Courts have always been burdened with heavy caseloads, and there is some evidence that they may be better off today than they were in the past.[6] It is not at all clear that the criminal courts are overburdened, nor that they would perform their tasks appreciably differently if their caseloads were reduced. It is indisputable, however, that courts tend to *organize their work* so that they must operate at a frantic pace. A reduction in workload may simply mean making an adaptation in the organization and instituting shorter working hours.[7]

The practices of lower criminal courts cannot be explained as the product of a decline in the adversary system. If we are witnessing the twilight of the adversary system, then when was the dawn? The high noon? Experience teaches that the ideal always outstrips reality, and history reveals that the past is filled with ample faults of its own. Despite the intensity with which many value it, the adversary system has rarely been put into full operation. Throughout the history of criminal law, guilty pleas and negotiated settlements appear to be the norm rather than the exception.[8] Indeed, throughout most of our history, guilty pleas have usually been negotiated between the state and an *unrepresented* defendant. Only recently have accused indigents had the opportunity to rely on counsel in this process. Nor do the terms "bureaucracy" and "assembly line" satisfactorily describe the practices observed in the lower courts. In fact, such terms are more rhetorical than real.[9] A court is not an assembly line, and court officials are not automatons mindlessly stamping out endless copies of the same product. It is neither a bureaucracy organized to pursue clearly articulated goals, nor is it an institution which possesses the means to discipline its members to accept such goals. Rather, the criminal court is more like a marketplace, a complex bargaining and exchange system, in which various values, goals, and interests are competing with one another.

To describe the court as a bureaucracy is to ignore the excessive hypertrophy of the criminal process, its decentralization of authority, its deference to professionalism, and the virtual absence of any real hierarchical structure. The bureaucratic label implies a degree of coherence and a commonality of purpose that simply do not exist. Similarly, the assembly-line metaphor ignores the complexity of the criminal process, and the casualness and confusion characteristic of decision making in the lower criminal courts.

The fact that trials are infrequent is often presented as evidence of the demise of the adversary system and the abandonment of concern with justice. But this assertion is a gross exaggeration, a generalization based more on the occasional horror story than on the vast majority of cases. There are a great many reasons why defendants plead guilty. Some feel compelled to confess for wrongs that they have done. Others recognize the inevitability of conviction and prefer to minimize the embarrassment of protracted court proceedings. They may not like the uncertainty and the tensions brought on by a trial. In petty cases in particular, there may be little incentive to go to trial. Defendants often know that their sentence is likely to be a suspended jail term, a small fine, or a conditional discharge, and prefer to plead guilty at arraignment in order to "get the case over with" as quickly as possible. For them it is quite simply a rational decision, an alternative which they have the full right to exercise.

Furthermore, to consider the trial as the only indicator of the adversary system is to ignore the many other types of combative devices available to participants in the criminal process. Vigorous negotiations between defense and prosecution often appeal to "the law" and take place "as if" they were being umpired by a judge—which indeed both parties know they could be if they wanted to go to the trouble. Informal discovery, fostered by many courts, often provides valuable information which in other settings might emerge only as a result of more formal proceedings. There are a host of motions available to the defense—bills of particulars, probable cause hearings, motions to suppress, and so forth—which for all practical purposes can turn the pretrial process into a mini-trial. A defendant's plea of guilty or a prosecutor's decision to drop charges after a ruling on a motion can be equivalent to a verdict of guilty or a directive to acquit after trial.

Lack of qualified personnel and adequate resources constitutes still another explanation for the situation in the lower courts. "If only we had more . . . If only we had better . . ." is a refrain heard again and again from critics of the criminal justice system. But lack of resources and qualified personnel is a complaint leveled against most public agencies, if not all large-scale organizations. Before we consider this argument as a cause we must ask: How much is enough? What does "qualified" mean? Unless these questions can be clearly specified and unless we can show that certain characteristics yield certain differences in outcomes, this complaint must be taken with a grain of salt.

Additional Factors Affecting the Administration of Justice

Although all of the factors enumerated above help account for the practices of the courts, they do not provide a complete answer. We must look beyond them and consider other important factors as well.

This book explores three additional themes which I believe provide a deeper appreciation for the problems of the courts— particularly the *lower* courts—and yield a more complete understanding of their operations. First, courts are complex institutions, and what they do is in part a function of how they are organized. The backgrounds of court officials, the ways in which they are recruited, and how their offices and tasks are structured, all affect what they do. In order to understand the operation of the courts, we must understand both their relationship to the environment and their internal organization.

Second, law is above all, a normative ordering. It gives expression to deeply felt sentiments within a society. Courts are staffed by representatives of this society, and what they do is in part a function of their own sense of justice. Many observers of the courts have become preoccupied with procedural justice, and have consequently failed to appreciate the intensity of the normative concern which informs the decisions of so many officials in the criminal process. Any complete examination of the criminal process must take these values into account.

Third, legal processes are costly. While Supreme Court decisions expanding the right to free counsel, transcript, appeal, and so forth, have gone a long way toward reducing costs to the accused and making these rights more accessible, they are still not free. Pretrial detention, bail, repeated court appearances, and forfeited wages all exact their toll on the criminally accused; in the lower courts these costs can quickly outweigh sanctions imposed at later stages of the process, at adjudication and sentencing. To the extent that these and other "by-product" costs of the pretrial process loom large in the minds of the accused, courts are not and cannot be what they claim they are, for these costs shift the locus of sanctioning away from the formal stages of adjudication and sentencing onto the process itself. We will examine this situation by juxtaposing the sanctions of sentence against the sanctions imposed in the pretrial process.

The Court as an Open System

Within recent years it has become more or less conventional to characterize criminal courts as bureaucratic organizations and to account for observed practices in terms of the emerging dominance of bureaucratic structures and goals.[10] This position can be summarized as follows: The traditional concerns of the adversarial system have all but given way to preoccupation with bureaucratic self-interest and organizational maintenance. The reasons for this trend are the reasons for the rise of all bureaucratic institutions—the press for efficiency. Swamped with mushrooming caseloads and the demands of ever-increasing procedural requirements, courts have been forced to abandon their traditional concern with the administration of justice by trial and turn to bureaucratic devices to "process" cases by plea negotiation.

But to conclude that courts are bureaucracies because they handle large numbers of cases and depend heavily on the guilty plea is to draw a premature, and I think improper, conclusion. Bureaucratization implies much more than the rapid performance of repetitive tasks. It implies hierarchy, relatively clear agreement on organizational goals, the existence of efficacious means for securing compliance to these goals, and a substantial degree of organizational autonomy from the larger environment.

Few of these conditions apply to the criminal courts, and when they do they are usually weak. Indeed, the evidence mounted by those who characterize the courts as bureaucracies can easily be turned full circle and used to support an opposite conclusion. The essence of bureaucracy, as Max Weber noted, is that decision making is dictated according to a "calculable set of rules," that is, that bureaucracy is characterized by routine application of clearly enunciated rules. The antithesis of bureaucracy is discretion, the ability to base decisions on individual judgments rather than on rules. And it is the *discretionary* capabilities of the prosecutor and judge and the many options of the defense which facilitate rapid processing of vast numbers of cases. While there are certainly elements of bureaucratic organization in the courts, this exercise of discretion has more in common with decentralized, nonhierarchical forms of bargained decision making than it does with bureaucracy. The closest analogs to the court as an organization are hospitals and universities, institutions which organization theorists have great difficulty characterizing as bureaucracies and indeed even as organizations.[11] As for the other distinctive characteristics of bureaucracies, courts possess few of them. There is no single authority supervising the activities of judges, prosecutors, defense attorneys, defendants, support personnel, and other occasional participants, nor is there even any central coordinating mechanism.

Courts may be considered bureaucracies only by a loose and casual definition of the term. If by bureaucratic one means impersonal, confusing, prone to error, impenetrable to outsiders, arbitrary, unable to provide rationales for action, and self-absorbed, then many courts may accurately be characterized as bureaucratic. But these characteristics are actually quite unbureaucratic. They also apply to behavior on the floor of the stock exchange or among the spectators at a football game, settings few would characterize as bureaucratic. To define bureaucracy as a Kafkaesque nightmare of disorganization and place the courts under it may capture the confusion of the defendant's perspective, but it also robs the term of its analytic power.

To argue that it is not particularly useful to characterize courts as bureaucracies is not to argue that they operate according to the ideals of a full-fledged adversary process. But, in fact, they more closely approximate the model of organization implicit in the traditional theory of the adversary process than they do bureaucratic organizations. At least in the common law countries, the adversary system provides for decentralization of authority, a minimum of hierarchy, and considerable discretion to negotiate settlements. Even appellate courts have severely circumscribed supervisory capacities. They must wait for cases to be brought to them, and by tradition when they do review a lower court decision, they rule on the narrowest possible grounds. This is quite unlike a bureaucratic business enterprise, in which supervisors take an aggressive and expansive stance in selecting decisions for review. And this restraint is true for judges, prosecutors, and defense attorneys alike. While some chief prosecutors organize their offices into hierarchical structures, their authority is limited to their office, which is only one component in the criminal justice system. And even within their office there is considerable deference to the professional judgment of assistant prosecutors. Close supervision is likely to be confined to a handful of visible cases and the training of new personnel.

While the theory of social control in the adversary process bears a superficial resemblance to bureaucratic control in practice, the criminal justice system has more in common with the functioning of a market than with the operations of a bureaucracy. Like bureaucratic organizations, the legal system envisions that much decision making is governed by the impartial application of rules, but unlike bureaucracy, the adversary system is designed to be self-regulating. As with the division of labor and interest in the market, it is expected that the self-interest of the individual parties will be sufficient to assure that appropriate decisions are made. Efficient solutions are arrived at, not because there are shared goals to which all adhere, but because there are *conflicting* interests, and the pursuit of those interests is expected to produce fair and efficient decisions. If this view is correct, the organization of courts may owe more to Adam Smith's theory of the market than to Max Weber's theory of bureaucracy.

The administration of criminal justice clearly does not operate in precise accord with the ideal theory of the adversary process, but the distinctive features of the criminal court system are decentralization and fragmentation. Instead of being organized to pursue a common set of goals, the criminal court system is comprised of a collection of often antagonistic agencies whose own behavior is determined as much by their conflicting interests and views of justice as it is by their shared interests.

Courts however can be understood as organizations.[12] While theorists of large-scale organizations have traditionally focused on business and government bureaucracy, contemporary organization theorists have adjusted to the multiplication of institutional structures in modern complex societies. These theorists have adopted a looser conception of organization than the one usually defined for business bureaucracies. Drawing from general systems theory, they have characterized many organizations as open systems. While bureaucratic organization focuses on shared goals, system-wide oversight, compliance-inducing sanctions, and hierarchy, systems theory is more expansive. It defines a system as any set of elements in which there are regular and recurring patterns of interaction.

To characterize the criminal process as a system[13] is to sidestep the debate about bureaucratic structure and shared goals and focus instead on the nature and pattern of interrelations within the system. It is to concentrate on the individual interests of the components of the system, and to seek to determine how each is pursued in light of the others' interests.

An important concept in systems theory is equilibrium, the steady state or resultant position of the various elements in the system. Equilibrium need not be a point at which there is common agreement on goals. It is the result of exchange, reciprocity, adaptation, and adjustment, not necessarily of agreement. The task of systems theory is to explore the way in which elements—actors who may be pursuing diverse interests and goals—continue to function in the face of this conflict. From a systems perspective, no single factor can be expected to explain the equilibrium. There is no particular reason to expect formal rules to be effective, or manifest goals to be accepted, although these may be among the factors that affect the system. From this perspective, the task of the social scientist is to identify and understand the multiplicity of incentives and interests.

The criminal court must be seen as an *open* system, exposed to continuing and not always predictable influences from its environment. Only when the court is viewed from this broad perspective does much of the behavior of court officials become understandable. For instance, the major figures in the courtroom are employees of separate and distinct organizations: the judicial department; the prosecutor's office; the public defender's office. Some belong to civil service employees unions, and others are self-employed. These continuing ties shape people's perspectives and circumscribe their alternatives. Additionally, courts are part of the community; what they do is in part a function of what the community expects of them and who it supplies to staff them.[14] Since courts do not even control their caseload, they must continually adjust to operations outside their control, such as citizen complaints and police practices. In order to understand the operations of courts and the functions they perform for the community, it is necessary to locate them in a larger context, to see them not only as systems which have created their own internal dynamic, but also as institutions responding to their environment.

What does this mean in more concrete terms? The criminal court system consists of a set of primary actors: prosecutors; defense attorneys; judges; defendants; and frequently the bail bondsmen and police; and a set of auxiliary personnel: bailiffs; sheriffs; clerks; complainants and witnesses; representatives of pretrial programs. Adapting Eisenstein and Jacob's concepts to a smaller court system, we can regard some of these people as the "courthouse workgroup."[15] Their informal work routines, how they value a case, how they perceive their jobs, how they pursue their separate and common interests, how they adapt to and counterbalance each other's interests, and what means of influence they possess, all affect the decisions which they jointly make. They maintain a delicate balance, stable yet always shifting slightly.

This workgroup does not operate in isolation. Each of its members also belongs to another institution as well, a "sponsoring organization" in Eisenstein and Jacob's terms, and how they handle cases is in part determined by the interests, goals, and resources of these institutions.[16] Even the most vindictive prosecutor is not likely to press for a maximum sentence in a routine prostitution case, knowing his chief will overrule him because the sentence would go against office policy. Nor would a public defender file several lengthy motions in a minor case, a course of action occasionally followed by a few private attorneys. Such actions would run counter to the unwritten policy in an office where secretarial services are in short supply, and might be wholly unnecessary because of the generally trusting relationship between the PD's and prosecutor's offices.

Finally, courthouse officials come from the same environment, and they reflect and remain responsive to it. In the court under investigation here, most official positions have been filled as a result of political patronage. This is important for several reasons. Whatever differences may be generated by the division of labor within the courthouse are moderated by common backgrounds and shared loyalties. Whatever their differences in levels of professionalism and income, a great many officials are "ethnics" from a lower-middle-class milieu who have used politics and the court to "pull themselves up." Perhaps even more important is the generalized influence of political culture. The city which provided the location for this study has a traditional political culture, evidenced by the continued existence of a political "machine." As a consequence, politics is thought of in terms of practicalities and personalities, not abstractions and issues. It is not surprising, then, that the courthouse workgroup carries this way of thinking into its official duties.

In short, the criminal court is an open system. What appear to be rapid and routine decisions are really the expression of a complex process: the balancing of the individual and collective interests in the courthouse workgroup, with the constraints and goals of their sponsoring organizations, and the influences of the environment.

Substantive Justice and the Adjudicative Ideal

Although the manifest purpose of the criminal law is to deter crime—to keep people from ever coming within the grasp of the law—the purpose of the criminal courts is to identify and sanction the law's failures, to cope with those who do come within its grasp. In the Anglo-American legal tradition, the institutional means for accomplishing this is adjudication, a special and highly developed form of problem solving, rooted firmly in a belief in the value of the rule of law, and a belief which places a premium on due process.

The rule of law relies upon abstract rules for governing relationships among individuals. It presumes a process which bases decisions on general, *universalistic* principles, not *particularistic* or situational criteria. The impulse toward universalism is the desire to "transcend the special interests of persons or groups,"[17] to grasp for and objectively apply broad, universally applicable "principles." In contrast, the impulse toward particularism is the claim of distinctiveness, uniqueness, or the claim of status or common association, often on the basis of religion, family, or friendship.

But the distinguishing characteristic of adjudication, some have suggested, "lies not in the substance of the conclusion reached, but in the *procedures* by which that substance is guaranteed," a process which "assures to the affected party a particular form of participation, that of presenting proofs and arguments for a decision in his favor."[18]

Nowhere has this conception of justice been so well established and given such full expression as in the criminal law. The meaning of due process has reached its height in the criminal law, and a concern with *justice* is inextricably linked to the notion of due process.

Most of us take the concept of due process for granted. Yet a moment's reflection will supply a substantial list of other perfectly reasonable and acceptable means for solving problems arising from the violation of social norms, ways which are familiar to most people but which we may not regard as alternative conceptions of "justice."

For instance, criminal law adjudication rests squarely on a belief in moral choice, and requires the assignment of individual responsibility, the clear establishment of right and wrong. Another familiar way of dealing with trouble arising from rule violation is to try to *settle* the dispute by mediation in order to repair the damage it has done to the ongoing social order. With this approach, the assignment of responsibility may be of secondary concern. If adjudication focuses on the past in order to define the *precise* nature of the violation, assign responsibility, and prescribe punishment, then *dispute settlement* looks to the future in order to fashion a settlement designed to preserve future relationships.[19]

Another way to cope with violations of the law is firmly entrenched in modern philosophy of juvenile justice, a view which places primary emphasis on the *actor* rather than the act. In its classic form, this position views the allegation of wrongdoing as only the initial means of identifying the "true problem," the moral development of the person, and concern for this problem should inform the proceedings. If this position is pushed to a logical extreme, then the alleged wrongdoing or violation is of secondary concern, little more than a convenient means to identify people "in need of help." Just as a doctor is willing to treat the heart of a patient who comes to him with stomach pains, so too will the juvenile court *treat* a child who may have been "sent" to it for a minor offense, but is actually seriously in need of help.[20]

Still another impulse away from rigid adherence to norms of adjudication is the desire to temper the unforeseen harshness of "*abstract* principles" with compassion—or harshness—toward *real* persons. This impulse is itself not rooted in articulated, predetermined principles, and can be seen as *particularistic* and idiosyncratic, or lawless. In the administration of the criminal law, there is a strong drive for discretion. Decisions made under a strict application of rules often lead to outcomes that few find palatable. The lifetime consequences of a record of conviction for a college student out on a Saturday night lark are difficult to accept; the courts frequently wink at such cases (and wish the police had not made the arrest in the first place). Suspending the driving license of a father of four who requires a car to get to work may be more difficult than suspending the license of an eighteen-year-old high school student. Sending a frail, effeminate man to a prison known for its brutal homosexuality may be unpalatable to some judges. Inevitably those who "apply" rules, however laudable and well-intentioned the rules are in principle, are at times confronted with the consequences flowing from their application. Even the most perfect system of rules must be applied in an imperfect world, and at times this gives rise to the impulse to ignore or circumvent it. But many are disgusted as well at decisions which free a "known criminal" on a technicality—because the evidence was weak or a crucial witness failed to appear—and these people take the opportunity, if it is available to them, to express their moral outrage. This can take the form of an insult by the auxiliary personnel or stern lectures by the judge and prosecutor.

"Little" cases present their own particular problems for the court. Arrest is typically viewed as the first stage in the criminal process, as the *beginning* of an effort to resolve a dispute and render a verdict. But for police, arrest is often a convenient way of avoiding or *ending* trouble. They see it as a means to separate people who are quarreling before any "real trouble" begins. In such instances, adjudication is little more than a bookkeeping ritual, a formality necessary to terminate a problem which for all practical purposes has already been resolved.

While these various views of justice are often contrasted as alternative models of the criminal process, alien to the adversary process, in fact they all coexist within the criminal justice system. The courts are forums not only for competing interpretations of facts and rules, but also for competing conceptions of justice. Different types of cases, different types of defendants, and different officials may bring one or another of these conceptions of justice into play. A prosecutor may be reluctant to prosecute a man who has assaulted his wife, feeling that it would only irritate healing wounds and jeopardize chances for future tranquillity. Behavior which is clearly illegal may be overlooked if the accused agrees to see a social worker or psychiatrist. Officials are often willing to drop minor charges, feeling that the arrestees have learned their lesson by spending a sleepless night in jail. A judge may dismiss charges against a person with a "promising" future, not wishing to jeopardize that future. But someone else may be vigorously prosecuted for a minor charge because he is known to be a serious troublemaker.

Such decisions are efforts to render *substantive* justice; they spring from an impulse to move beyond the rigid, formal legal process and to consider the "whole" person. To the casual observer, the dizzying array of rationales for decisions may appear arbitrary and chaotic, but to one familiar with the court there is a logic—even if it is unwritten and unarticulated—to the process. The importance and intensity of these various visions of justice have often been ignored by observers of the criminal courts. After looking at the courts and failing to find full-fledged adversarial proceedings, they too quickly conclude that all concern for justice has given way to the pressures of heavy case-loads, organizational security, and bureaucratic self-interest. The abandonment of a concern with one particular form of justice is too often incorrectly seen as an abandonment of *all* concern for justice. While the self-interest of agencies is, of course, an important factor in explaining the disparity between the ideal and the real, the variety of senses of justice which criminal justice officials bring to their tasks is also of vital importance. A full explanation of what goes on in the criminal courts must consider the normative orientations of the officials who comprise the court.

Decision-making Costs: Two Models and an Alternative

Discussions of American criminal courts are dominated by two models, both of which are so ingrained in the thinking of observers of the criminal courts that they may be termed the "orthodox" views of the criminal process. The first is the *Due Process Model*, and the other the *Plea Bargain Model*. Both

contain a mixture of "is" and "ought," although the former—
the due process model—is most often thought of as the ideal-
ists' vision of the criminal justice system and the latter the
realists'. Both models contain a set of expectations about the
way cases are to be handled, and both seek to specify factors
which concern the participants. And both provide a set of responsibilities for the sanctioning agents in the system. But both
ignore, in important ways, the costs to the accused of participat-
ing in the criminal process, and as a consequence, both present
a distorted picture of the actual process of decision making in
criminal courts. Before we examine a third "corrective" model,
we will outline the basic elements of these two models.

The Due Process Model In pure theory, the adversary process presumes complete combat between the state and the accused. It is a zero-sum game; the accused and the state either
win or lose, and what one gains the other loses. In this context,
sanctions are penalties attached to outcomes based on a careful
determination of facts, which have then been applied to relevant
rules. The battle is vigorously waged according to clear and
precise rules, and if the defendant loses (is convicted), penalties are attached in the form of whatever stigma follows from
conviction and the deprivation imposed by the sentence. If the
defendant wins (is acquitted), there are no penalties. Although
the prosecutor is central in determining the outcome of the case,
the due process model places the primary sanctioning powers in
the hands of the jury and judge, for one or another of them
must establish innocence or guilt and set sentence.

Although some seem to think it does,[21] the due process
model does not require that all criminal cases go to trial; it requires only that the option be available to all who desire it. It
does, however, assume that combat is vigorous, that the state is
able to *prove* its case, and that the accused has the opportunity
to present challenges and make defenses. While the trial is the
formal and full-dress forum for doing this, motions and quiet
but firm negotiations between the prosecution and defense can
often accomplish the same ends.

The drive for due process is motivated by a zeal for fairness, and has been developed largely without regard to cost. But the process is not altogether impervious to the costs that the criminal justice system imposes at its early stages. Indeed, as Herbert Packer has argued, the system is explicitly designed to minimize them. Comparing due process to an obstacle course, Packer sees it as a number of successive stages, each designed "to prevent formidable impediments to carrying the accused any further along in the process."[22] Despite this protection, the sanctions this model is primarily concerned with are the penalties attached to wrongdoing, the stigma of conviction, and the subsequent sentence of the court. The process is directed toward these forms of punishment, and it assumes that they are the main concern of the criminally accused.

The Plea Bargain Model   The plea bargain model is the realist's revision of the system of due process outlined above, and in recent years it has come to be recognized as the model of how the system *actually* operates. It conceives of the system as a mixed-strategy game. Plea bargaining allows the prosecution and the defense to share in both gains and losses. By pleading guilty, the defense gains certainty of outcome, and a reduction of the sentence he otherwise would have received had he been convicted after trial. The prosecutor gains by securing a conviction without the effort of putting on a trial. The state is also a beneficiary because it secures an admission of guilt, punishes the guilty, and yet saves the expense of a trial.

Although not always explicitly acknowledged, there is another type of concern which supports the guilty plea process. By pleading guilty the defendant is not only likely to gain a reduction of the sentence, he also reduces the decision-making costs associated with mounting a defense. For those with private attorneys this may mean a smaller fee. For all defendants—with publicly appointed or private attorneys—it eliminates the embarrassment of a public trial, a spectacle that can be humiliating, time-consuming, and anxiety-provoking to the defendant and his family. In addition, the guilty plea process also saves time, a rare commodity, and one that is likely to loom large in petty cases, where the formal sentence is usually lenient.

The generally accepted reason for plea bargaining is a need for the rapid processing of large numbers of cases which clog the courts. Despite their differences of position, prosecutors, defense attorneys, and judges are said to have a common administrative interest in the rapid processing of cases which plea bargaining facilitates. For this reason, plea bargaining is often criticized by those who view the criminal process from the defendant's perspective. They complain that it is a process which sacrifices concern for truth and accuracy for expediency. Even if plea bargaining does induce an occasional innocent person to plead guilty, most observers agree that the practice survives because it offers discounted sentences to the great majority of defendants who could have been proven guilty. In the plea bargain model, the explanation for the truncated process is the discounted sentence, an offer necessitated by the administrative concerns of an overworked system.

In the plea bargain model, the central sanctioning agent is not the judge, but rather the prosecutor. Not only does he exercise his traditional discretion to establish charges, he also in effect determines guilt and sets the sentence. Although the prosecutor does not officially usurp the judge's authority to convict and sentence, the institution of plea bargaining depends upon the credibility of the prosecutor and the predictability that the judge will accept the prosecutor's recommendations.

An Alternative Model of the Lower Courts: The Pretrial Process Model The plea bargain model has come in recent years to represent the new scholarly orthodoxy of the understanding of criminal courts. As with much conventional wisdom, it contains a great deal of truth, but truth which contains untested assumptions that substitute for careful factual analysis. There are a number of problems with casual discussions of plea bargaining. For example, there is no consensus over the very meaning of the term "plea bargaining." Although many discussions point to the high rate of guilty pleas and the paucity of trials as evidence of the pervasiveness of plea bargaining, there are few careful studies which distinguish between pleas of guilty with *explicit* consideration and those without consideration. Nor are there many careful discussions of plea bargaining which focus on negotiations over facts. Most discussions suggest that the primary object of plea bargaining is administrative convenience; yet some of the more thoughtful examinations of "negotiations" suggest that bargaining sessions are often probing examinations into the *facts* of the case, facts which in turn can affect the appropriateness of the charges.[23]

And while trial rates remain low and may even have decreased in recent years, it is not at all clear to what extent other adversarial techniques remain intact, or have been strengthened, and can serve as substitutes for trials. Preliminary hearings, probable cause hearings, and informal discovery may serve many of the functions of a trial—to obtain and test crucial evidence and challenge assertions of fact and law—which in turn may lead to nolles, dismissals, or pleas of guilty in the face of an overwhelming case. To infer the lack of an adversarial stance and the existence of bargained settlement—for the pure purpose of administrative convenience—from the absence of trials is to ignore altogether the importance of these other "truth-testing" and highly combative processes. Reliance on a single term such as plea bargaining imposes a blanket of uniformity on a process in which great diversity and intensity in combativeness—short of trial—does in fact exist.

Plea bargaining poses special problems for the lower courts. These are characterized not only by the masses of cases which they process rapidly and perfunctorily; they are also distinguished from the higher trial courts by the pettiness of the offenses they handle and the leniency of the sentences they pass. If we looked only at jails, with their ubiquitous overcrowding, the criminal justice system might appear to be unduly harsh and severe. But if we sat in the gallery in a lower criminal court, the process might appear chaotic and arbitrary, but essentially tolerant and lenient. Defendants come and go rapidly in the midst of the confusion, but only occasionally is one sent to jail. Suspended sentences or small fines are much more typical, and defendants who never show up in court at all are not atypical either. In most of these situations it is difficult to imagine a defendant wanting to prolong his contact with the court long enough to go through a trial, or for that matter, any type of extended deliberation of his case.

In the lower courts, it is the cost of being caught up in the criminal justice system itself that is often most bothersome to defendants accused of petty offenses, and it is this cost which shapes their subsequent course of action once they are entrapped by the system. For every defendant sentenced to a jail term of any length, there are likely to be several others who were released from jail only *after* and *because* they pleaded guilty. For each dollar paid out in fines, a defendant is likely to have spent four or five dollars for a bondsman and an attorney. For every dollar they lose through fines, defendants who work are likely to have lost several more from docked wages. For every defendant who has lost his job because of a conviction, there are probably five who have lost their jobs as a result of simply having missed work in order to appear in court. And for every defendant who would like a trial, there are dozens who do not even bother to appear in court. Under such circumstances, even a decision to engage in protracted negotiations could *increase* rather than decrease costs to the defendant intent on getting his case over with the least possible effort.

When we view criminal sanctioning from this broader, functional perspective, the locus of court-imposed sanctioning shifts dramatically away from adjudication, plea bargaining, and sentencing to the earlier pretrial stages. In essence, the process itself is the punishment. The time, effort, money, and opportunities lost as a direct result of being caught up in the system can quickly come to outweigh the penalty that issues from adjudication and sentence. Furthermore, pretrial costs do not distinguish between innocent and guilty; they are borne by all, by those whose cases are nolled or dismissed as well as by those who are pronounced guilty. It is understandable why so many defendants in lower courts waive rights, ignore options, and plead guilty at first appearance. The costs of exercising the rights available under due process—or even of engaging in plea bargaining—are often greater than the gains they might produce. The desire to minimize pretrial process costs also helps to explain why so many fail to appear in court; they, too, are trying to avoid the costs of the process.

The pretrial process model identifies a different set of officials as the key sanctioners. In the due process model it is the judge who imposes sanctions. In the plea bargain model it is the prosecutor. In the pretrial process model, sanctioning powers are distributed among several different people. Sentence is still formally set by the judge, but usually prescribed by the prosecutor. The pretrial sanctions are administered by any of several different people. The arresting officer or the policeman at a station house may set the first conditions of release. He typically uses this opportunity to impose his own notion of rough justice on the accused, setting the conditions of pretrial release according to his sense of the "worth of the case." But the length of pretrial detention does not always depend only on what he does. It is often a function of the responsiveness of a bail bondsman, a businessman whose criteria for accepting clients are not dictated by the state. For a great many people, the conditions the bail bondsman imposes ultimately determine whether they will or will not be released on bond, and how costly that will be.

Defense attorneys also extract costs. Their fees may depend on their assessment of their clients' ability to pay. But fees are not the only costs they impose. Even a defendant who receives the services of a public defender without any direct expense to himself must still take the time and effort to discuss the case. At a minimum, this necessitates a second meeting and repeated

31

court appearances. Furthermore, attorneys are busy people. New business comes up suddenly, cases last longer than they were expected to, and a host of other uncertainties crop up to make a daily schedule problematic. As a consequence, appointments are frequently canceled and rescheduled with little or no prior notice; long waits are required in order to receive or transmit a bit of information; and meetings frequently take place on the run without full opportunity for explanation.

Continuances necessitate additional court visits by defendants. While these frequently work to their benefit, defendants often view them as a problem, as something to be avoided. Witnesses fail to appear, the defense attorney may be involved in a trial in another court, and his client may be made aware of it only after waiting through the morning for his case to be called. The prosecutor and defense attorney may not have taken time to talk over the case, and might casually agree to continue it for still one more day without thinking of the inconvenience this may cause the defendant and his family. Defendants without attorneys are typically told to appear early in the day but are invariably called last, after the court obliges private counsel and public defenders. Each continuance means the loss not only of a few minutes spent before the bench, but also of a major portion of the work day, something that few defendants and their employers are likely to view favorably. Although delay can and often does work to the benefit of defendants, it is not without its own considerable costs; frequently these are enough to dissuade a defendant from doing anything to prolong his case.

Trials are expensive and time-consuming, and are usually not either a real alternative to a plea of guilty or a real threat in a negotiation session. Given the pervasive leniency of the courts as a whole, it is not at all clear that there is much to be gained by prolonging contact with them through active negotiations. There is clearly much to be lost by extending the process and increasing the cost of participation to the defendant. To the extent that defendants want to keep down the costs of the pretrial process, the pretrial process model challenges the plea bargain model.

In theory, the due process model preserves the rights of all defendants. It insists on a standard of *legal guilt* as a basis of conviction, both to protect individual rights and as a means of controlling officials' behavior. For a great many cases in lower court, the pretrial process model challenges these assumptions, since the exercise of these rights only increases net costs to the defendant. There is little incentive to invoke *formally* the rights loosely referred to as due process, and there is virtually no incentive or opportunity to test them by appeal. For all practical purposes, the lower courts of first instance are also courts of last resort. It is unclear how effective these rules are in restraining official behavior and shaping case outcomes. Since it is often more expensive to invoke rights and remedies than to suffer injustices in silence, it is problematic if the rights and remedies actually would either protect individual rights or control official behavior. In fact, expanding them may produce the opposite effect. Not only might it produce more rules which may in turn be ignored with increasing impunity, it also might give the public an *appearance* of increasingly principled decision making while in fact doing little more than providing the props and lines for a ritualistic drama devoid of meaningful content.

Conclusion

This study seeks to determine how a lower criminal court conducts its business. It asks how this court adapts itself to the formal norms of due process and the adversarial system as it processes large numbers of "petty" cases. The investigation is concerned with three themes which elucidate the nature and functioning of lower criminal courts. Courts are complex institutions, and what they do is in part a function of how they are organized and how they relate to the larger environment. The backgrounds of officials, their relation to the community, how they are recruited, how their offices are structured, their own interests, and the interests of their agencies, all help account for the way criminal justice is administered. So too does the sense of justice officials bring to their tasks. The law is a normative ordering that touches people in an important way. Criminal justice officials are not exempt from this; most of them respond intensely to their tasks, and how they perform their duties is determined in part by their sense of justice. But they are concerned with *substantive* justice as distinct from procedural justice, a concern which is paramount in the theory of the adversary process but not necessarily in practice.

Finally, this book is concerned with the decision-making costs that loom particularly large in lower criminal courts, where the formal sanctions are frequently less awesome than the "by-product" costs of going through the system. Because of these primary sanctions in the pretrial process, courts are not and cannot be what they claim to be, for these sanctions shift the locus of punishment and central concern away from adjudication and sentencing to the "preliminary" stages of the process. Efforts to increase fairness by making the system more deliberate may in fact produce precisely the opposite results. They may make the process more costly, a punishment which would be meted out to the innocent as well as the guilty.

While each of these three themes appears and reappears throughout the book, each of them is considered at great length in particular sections. Chapters two through four focus on the organization and environment of the court. Chapter six considers the sense of substantive justice which has been fashioned into a consensus by the courthouse culture. Chapter seven examines the costs imposed in the pretrial process and compares them to the formal sanctions at sentencing.

CHAPTER 2

Setting and Context

Introduction

This chapter examines the Court of Common Pleas in the context of the community. It describes the city, the nature of the court's business, the court's relationship with the police department, and its formal structure. The chapter continues with an examination of the informal organization of the court, describing the recruitment process for court officials and the importance of the courts for local political organizations. This discussion is only introduced in broad terms here. The next two chapters treat in detail each of the offices and roles of the court's principal decision makers.

The City

New Haven is the third largest city in Connecticut. With a population of slightly under 138,000, it ranks behind Bridgeport and Hartford, both of which have populations approaching 160,000. Like these two neighboring cities—and like many other New England cities—it is old, originally founded as a colony in the mid-seventeenth century and incorporated as a city in 1784. Yale University is the community's single largest employer, but New Haven is also a manufacturing center. Like many other New England industrial cities, it has watched its businesses pick up and move elsewhere, and its residents either trail along behind them or relocate in the suburbs. During the decade 1940–1950, when the American urban population grew by almost 20 percent, New Haven grew by only 2.5 percent, and since 1950 the city has declined in population. In 1970 it had 25,000 fewer residents than it did two decades earlier, a decline of over 15 percent, and a decline much sharper than those of its sister cities, Bridgeport and Hartford.[1]

Mere numbers, however, do not provide an adequate picture of the changes in the city's population. Not only did the population shrink, but its composition also shifted dramatically. The postwar years saw the exodus of middle-class families to the mushrooming suburbs surrounding New Haven, and as they exited, they left older and cheaper housing which was filled by newer and poorer immigrant groups, first Italians and then increasing numbers of Blacks and Puerto Ricans. The nonwhite population grew from 6 percent in 1950 to 30 percent in 1970 (with Blacks constituting 26 percent of the nonwhite population and Hispanics the other 4 percent). The changes have been more than alterations in ethnic composition. Rising middle-class families also left their parents behind, and the proportion of older and poorer whites has grown along with the proportion of younger and poorer nonwhites.

However, New Haven is far from a dying New England manufacturing town. As Robert Dahl documents in his classic study, *Who Governs?* New Haven—more than many cities— has benefited from farsighted leadership and has attempted to grapple with the problems of urban deterioration.[2] Beginning in the 1950s, its political leadership actively set about to preserve the city center as a viable business location and to preserve and stabilize the city's declining economic and housing base. In comparison with many other cities in similar situations, it has been successful. It can boast of a prosperous downtown shopping area, a large and relatively attractive public housing program, and a relatively high and stable rate of employment.

Its citizens are also more civic-minded than those in many other cities, and its employees for city-sponsored public service programs are probably more talented than their counterparts in many other cities.[3] Although there is no doubt that the presence of Yale University must account for some of this, much of this civic activity has a broader base. After he was elected in 1953, Mayor Richard C. Lee embarked on an ambitious program of development for the city, and in doing so provided an important impetus for attracting talent to the new federally funded local programs that emerged in the 1950s and blossomed forth in the 1960s, after his departure. During the 1950s, for example, New Haven obtained more federal funds per capita for planning urban redevelopment than any other city in the United States except for the nation's capital.[4]

Success breeds success, and this same pattern continued into the 1960s and 1970s. New Haven attracted more than its share of federal funds in the War on Poverty, in part because of its strong political leadership and its ability to attract bright, intelligent people to its agencies. Long before the War on Poverty was declared, New Haven had created its own citywide version of community action and renewal, so that when the federal funds were made available, it could put them to immediate use.

New Haven also has a cadre of politically active "alternative" public programs. It boasts several small but lively and politically knowledgeable alternative newspapers, a number of food cooperatives, and active "third party" political organizations which regularly put up candidates for public office.[5]

Although it is difficult to make sweeping comparisons, it is safe to conclude that New Haven probably is better off than many other cities of similar size and composition. Beset with the standard ills of many old urban areas—shrinking population, declining tax base, deteriorating housing, smog, poor schools, encroaching superhighways, and an increasing under-employed minority population—it is fortunate to have a vigorous group of residents involved in actively trying to cope with and ameliorate its problems. To this extent, it represents neither the worst nor the best of American urban centers. It does not convey the sense of hopelessness and decay that observers report in such urban centers as Newark or Gary, nor does it convey the same sense of optimism as do new and more culturally homogeneous and prosperous cities as Des Moines or Minneapolis.

The Business of the Court

If we look only at crime, however, New Haven does not fare so well. It has a higher rate of crime than other American cities of comparable size. The average annual number of all *reported* serious crimes for the nation's ninety-six cities with populations between 100,000 and 249,000 is 5,449, while in New Haven it is 6,140.[6] The average annual number of aggravated assaults for these ninety-six cities is 246, as compared to 248 for New Haven; the number of burglaries for the group is 1,708, but for New Haven it is 2,208.[7] While it is above the national average, New Haven holds its own with its neighbors, falling midway between Bridgeport with 6,320 and Hartford with 5,889 annually reported serious crimes per 100,000 population. But in comparison with the state as a whole, which averages only 70.4 robberies per 100,000 population per year, New Haven averages 164; while the state averages only 87 aggravated assaults per 100,000, New Haven averages twice as many, or 163. And while the state has 1,084 burglaries per 100,000, New Haven has 3,783. In short, the city has more than its share of crime, but the rates are similar to those of comparable neighboring cities.[8]

These figures are subject to considerable qualification. They are based on crime data submitted to the FBI by local law enforcement offices and represent offenses reported to the police, not all actual crimes, unreported and reported alike. In addition, such crime data are subject to variations in meaning, distortion, and manipulation, so that despite the seemingly standardized reporting system, the FBI is at the mercy of those who produce the reports—local police departments which follow their own traditions for reporting offenses and are subject to a variety of local pressures in compiling them.[9]

New Haven also has a high *arrest* rate, substantially higher than that of neighboring Bridgeport and Hartford. Juvenile arrest data for 1970 show 1,540 arrests per 100,000 population in Bridgeport, 1,350 in Hartford, and 1,970 in New Haven. Adult arrests show a similar pattern.[10] Although these rates vary from year to year, the relative position of the three cities for both juvenile and adult arrests remains stable, with New Haven usually in the lead. Although it is impossible to determine whether this higher rate of arrests really indicates that there is more crime or simply more aggressive police practices, it nevertheless does lend support to the common local belief that New Haven has more than its share of crime, and certainly generates more business for its courts.

The business of the court runs the gamut of offenses. Table 2.1 shows the breakdown of the most serious charges against defendants during the three-month period I collected data on case dispositions, and reflects fairly accurately the distribution of cases handled by the court throughout the year. The table organizes the separate offenses into five categories—offenses against persons, property, public morality, public order, and justice—presenting figures for each individual charge and subtotals for each of these categories as well. While the total number of charges is spread rather thinly across the entire spectrum of offenses and categories, two offenses do stand out: breach of peace and disorderly conduct, which constitute 26.37

TABLE 2.1

Distribution of Individual Charges (most serious charge per case)
for Cases Handled by the Sixth Circuit Court (June-August 1974)*

1. Crimes against persons	N	%
Assault 1	19	1.16
Assault 2	34	2.08
Assault 3	46	2.31
Threatening	60	3.66
Reckless endangerment 1	7	.43
Statutory rape	1	.06
Rape 1	2	.12
Conspiracy to commit rape	1	.06
Deviate sexual intercourse 3	2	.12
Robbery 1	7	.43
Robbery 2	6	.37
Robbery 3	3	.18
Risk of injury	2	.12
Other	10	.61
Subtotal	200	12

2. Crimes against property	N	%
Larceny 1	1	.06
Larceny 2	29	1.72
Larceny 3	50	3.05
Larceny 4	85	5.19
Criminal mischief 2	3	.18
Criminal mischief 3	42	1.65
Trespass 1	6	.37
Trespass 2	15	.92
Trespass 3	27	1.65
Burglary 1	8	.49
Burglary 2	15	.92
Burglary 3	21	1.28
Illegal use of credit card	1	.06
Fraud obtaining state aid	3	.18
Forgery 1	7	.43
Forgery 2	2	.12
Forgery 3	1	.06
Tampering with motor vehicle	1	.06
Arson 3	1	.06
Other	11	.67
Subtotal	329	20

*This constitutes 100 percent of the sample—all types of criminal cases but one—which were handled during this three-month period. The exception is those cases in which the only charge was "found intoxicated." There were large numbers of such cases and they were handled separately and in a highly perfunctory manner. This offense was abolished by statute shortly after the data were collected.

3. Crimes against public morality

Prostitution	18	1.10
Soliciting sexual intercourse	3	.18
Patronizing a prostitute	6	.37
Gaming	70	4.27
Policy playing	10	.61
Pool selling	2	.12
Possession of marijuana	81	4.95
Possession of marijuana with intent to sell	7	.43
Possession of cocaine	2	.12
Possession of cocaine with intent to sell	4	.24
Possession of controlled drugs	12	.73
Possession of controlled drugs with intent to sell	5	.31
Possession of heroin	6	.37
Possession of heroin with intent to sell	5	.31
Illegal dispensing of other controlled drugs	1	.06
Selling liquor without permit	2	.12
Keeping liquor with intent to sell	3	.18
Other	11	.67
Subtotal	248	15

4. Crimes against public order

Breach of peace	432	26.37
Disorderly conduct	153	9.34
Loitering on school grounds	3	.18
Vagrancy	2	.12
Found intoxicated	31	1.89
Keeping/carrying pistol	3	.18
Carrying dangerous weapon (in/out auto)	35	2.14
Possession, sale, or discharge of fireworks	29	1.77
Other	21	1.28
Subtotal	709	43

5. Crimes against justice

FTA, F-D, or M-A	36	2.20

TABLE 2.1 *(continued)*

Violation of probation, parole, or conditional discharge	17	1.04
Nonsupport of wife/child (1 yr.)	12	.73
Resisting arrest (or interfering)	73	4.46
False information to police	2	.12
False report of an accident	3	.18
Other	6	.37
Subtotal	149	9
6. Miscellaneous Offenses		
All other offenses	4	.24
Total	1,639	99†

†Rounding error.

percent and 9.34 percent, respectively, of all cases. Following in descending order of frequency are: larceny (5.19 percent); possession of marijuana (4.95 percent); and resisting arrest (4.46 percent). Turning to the subtotals, the two largest categories are offenses against public order, which consist largely of breach-of-peace and disorderly conduct charges, and offenses against property, which consist largely of petty theft (various larceny and burglary charges) and attempted or suspected theft (criminal mischief and trespass charges).

Connecticut statutes classify criminal offenses according to the maximum penalty which can be imposed for their violation. Penalties range from a minimum of three months in jail or a $100 fine for a class C misdemeanor, through life imprisonment for a class A felony. Table 2.2 shows that the magnitude of the court's business is inversely proportional to the seriousness of its business. Over half of the cases came from the two least serious classes (C and B misdemeanors), and only 2 percent of the cases were class B felonies, the most serious offenses which the court handled during this period.

The profile of criminal defendants in New Haven's court is similar to that found in most other urban courts. As shown in Table 2.3, the defendants are disproportionately young, Black, and male; most have prior records; and if reliance on a public defender is a measure of wealth, most are poor. Forty-seven

TABLE 2.2

Distribution of Total Number of Most Serious Charges, by Class of Offense

Class	N	%
Misdemeanor C	400	24%
Misdemeanor B	546	23
Misdemeanor A	325	20
Felony D	184	11
Felony C	44	03
Felony B	38	02
Other/DK	101	06
Total	1638	99%*

*Rounding error.

percent are under 21 years of age, and all but 30 percent are under 30. Blacks constitute 58 percent of all defendants and Hispanics 8 percent. The respective proportions in the New Haven population for these groups are 25 percent and 4 percent. Given the ethnic composition of New Haven, there is a pronounced "overrepresentation" of Blacks and Puerto Ricans and an equally pronounced "underrepresentation" of whites in the lower court. The imbalance is even more pronounced for sex. Males constitute only 47.5 percent of the population in New Haven, but they account for fully 80 percent of all defendants in the court. Just over half—51 percent—of the defendants have prior New Haven arrest records, a figure that understates the real number of defendants who have had prior encounters with criminal courts because it does not include juvenile arrest records or all records from other jurisdictions.

The Police

The agency that produces most of this work for the courts is the New Haven Police Department,[11] a force which in 1972

TABLE 2.3

*A Comparison of Selected Characteristics of
Defendants in Circuit Court and
New Haven Residents*

	Defendants in Circuit Court	
Age	Court Sample (%)	**Residents of** New Haven (%)
15-17	07	
18-21	22	
22-25	19	
26-29	13	
30-33	09	
34-37	07	
38-41	06	
42-45	04	
46-49	05	
50-53	03	
54-60	03	
over 60	02	
Sex [12]		
Male	80	47.5
Female	20	52.5
Ethnicity [12]		
White	38	70
Black	53	26
Hispanic	08	04
Other	01	–
Prior Arrest Record in New Haven		
Yes	51	–
No	49	
Representation by Counsel		
None	51	
Free, appointed counsel	31	–
Private attorney	18	

was staffed by 420 sworn officers and 138 civilians. While it has experienced periods of reform-minded leadership, it remains a "traditional" police force, closely linked to the local political organizations.[13] The chief of police is appointed by the mayor and is responsible to him, as well as to a City Board of Police Commissioners. In theory the Commission is nonpartisan, which in New Haven means that its membership is equally divided between Republicans and Democrats. The primary function of the Board is to establish and implement procedures for hiring new personnel and granting promotions. Like most other city agencies, the Board is composed of the mayor's close allies, and the powerful Democratic party organization uses its powers of appointment to help perpetuate the dominance of the party.

Applicants to the force and for promotion are likely to be dependent upon a political "sponsor" to approach the Board on their behalf. Often this sponsor is someone on the Board itself, or an alderman who is friendly with a commissioner. In return for sponsorship, aldermen expect and receive support in the form of contributions, canvassing, and mobilization of votes for the party at election time. And as a unit the police themselves are active in local politics. The police union is highly organized, and public officials are not unmindful of the combined number of votes the union claims it can deliver. Nor are they unaware of the manpower for voter mobilization that over 500 people, familiar with all sections of the city, can provide. Like the court, the police department is intimately linked to the local party organization, with both appointment and advancement dependent upon the goodwill of a political "sponsor" to pave the way.

Despite this common linkage to the Democratic party organization, there is little regular contact between the police department and the prosecutor's office. By tradition police officers are not required to be present at the arraignments of those whom they have arrested, and they are rarely called as witnesses. Most of the prosecutor-police communication is by telephone, when a prosecutor calls to obtain amplification or clarification of the report the arresting officer has written. A police-court liaison officer is always present in court, but his main job is to supervise those still in police custody and to maintain a record of court dispositions which are passed on to the Department. At times he intercedes in a case to press the prosecutor to take a hard line. These cases usually involve incidents in which there was an injury or insult to the arresting officer, and in such instances the prosecutors will usually oblige with a recommendation for higher bond or a reluctance to drop the charges. Occasionally the police officer may approach the prosecutor to ask for a lower bond and lenient treatment because the accused is an informant whom the police are "looking after." Or an officer may occasionally request the prosecutor to "go easy" on a defendant because he is an acquaintance.

One might think that the police would be antagonistic to the prosecutors since almost half of their arrests result in nolles. One might also expect that prosecutors would be irritated with a police force whose success rate is only about one in two cases. In fact there is little antipathy between them. The police consider one of their functions to be "dispute avoidance," and view arrests as one means of carrying it out. For many minor incidents they see arrest as an end in itself, as a way of *terminating* a problem, not as the first stage toward adjudication, disposition, and sanction. The shock of arrest and a night in the lockup allows people to cool down and sober up, and may teach them "a lesson," so that police are not overly concerned to find that all their arrests do not result in convictions. They certainly do not view these nonconvictions as reflections on their professional abilities. Nor do the prosecutors consider their decision to drop charges to be an indication of poor police work. Like the police, they too view many arrests as ends in themselves, regarding subsequent court appearance as a symbolic ritual required for the administrative purpose of "disposing" of the case. Although occasionally prosecutors will complain about poor police practices—their carelessness in making an arrest, collecting and preserving evidence, or writing up a report—the prosecutor's office has not made any concerted effort to reduce these problems, and in fact does not view them as very serious.

In contrast, the chief prosecutor for the Superior Court is extremely concerned about police behavior. He has authored a textbook on arrest and police investigation practices; frequently lectures police audiences on developments in the Supreme Court's rulings on search and seizure, questioning of suspects, and other aspects of police work; works closely with police in their periodic campaigns against the narcotics trade and other vices; and regularly appears at the scenes of big arrests. While these differences are perhaps a function of personality, they may be caused by a difference in how seriously these people view their cases. Like the police themselves, the prosecutors in the lower court often take a "dispute processing" view of the criminal process and have no interest in gauging police effectiveness in terms of the rate of nolles or convictions their arrests produce.

The Two-Tiered System of Courts

The Court of Common Pleas is the lower of a two-tiered statewide court system. It has arraignment jurisdiction in all criminal offenses, concurrent jurisdiction over "five-year" (Class D) felonies, and full jurisdiction over all misdemeanors.[14] Effectively, its authority is limited to cases in which the maximum sentence does not exceed one year, although in cases involving multiple charges consecutive sentences above one year are permitted. Even though this court is often referred to as a "misdemeanor" court, fully 20 percent of the cases in my sample were felonies.

If a person is charged with a more serious felony, then he is arraigned in the Court of Common Pleas and bound over to the

47

Superior Court, the higher court in the two-tiered system. The Superior Court has its own separate facilities, judges, and a separate prosecutor's office and public defender system. At the outset of my investigation, I planned to focus on both the Court of Common Pleas and the Superior Court, believing that I would find frequent close connections between them. In particular, I was concerned with the tensions that might result from jockeying for the most advantageous forum. Some such tension exists, but not as much as one might expect. The primary reason is that in New Haven many arrests for felonies are made by warrants issued by the Superior Court, which require arrestees to be taken directly to that court, bypassing the arraignment in Common Pleas Court.[15] And although over 15 percent of my sample cases involved charges over which the Superior Court could exercise jurisdiction, defense attorneys in Common Pleas are anxious to keep them in the lower court with its limited sentencing power, and Superior Court prosecutors, always anxious to reduce their workload, do not complain that these cases are not sent to them.

The Emergence of the Court of Common Pleas

It is not surprising to find that most of the younger attorneys —prosecutors and defense attorneys alike—who regularly work in the Court of Common Pleas are extremely critical of it, while older attorneys view it with more tolerance. This division of opinion reflects differences in perspective and experience. The older attorneys recall what the court system "used to be like," and although some are wistful for earlier days, most are thankful for the progress they have seen the court make. The younger attorneys, closer to their law school idealism and less familiar with the practices of the past, compare the casual processes and crowded facilities of Common Pleas to the more deliberate processes and ample facilities of Superior Court. This difference in perspective is understandable, since the lower court system has undergone tremendous changes since 1961.

Prior to 1961, the court system of Connecticut was a patchwork of local-municipal, town, city, and justice-of-the-peace courts, each with slightly different jurisdictions. Smaller towns often had local magistrates, courts staffed by part-time judges and prosecutors, many of whom were not even attorneys. Decisions "appealed" from these courts could result in a trial *de novo* in a more formal court. Although the larger cities, including New Haven, have had a more formalized court system for years, they too were often staffed with part-time personnel and by people closely connected with local party organizations. If a new party took over the mayor's office after an election, it would also take over the courthouse. A new mayor or party leader would make new judicial and prosecutorial appointments from among the faithful. This affected the type of justice meted out in the court. According to one older attorney, "Cases were nolled, dismissed, or buried for strange reasons and no one would question them. Politically active court personnel were willing to do favors for their brother Democrats or Republicans who in turn would help the party or would otherwise become faithful constituents." Other older attorneys expressed similar views; all agreed that now political influence is limited to the appointment process and means very little, if anything, in terms of obtaining preferred treatment in handling cases.

Throughout the 1950s, court reform was of growing concern to citizen groups and an expanding state bar association. It was elevated to a major issue in Abraham Ribicoff's successful gubernatorial campaign in 1958, which resulted in the Court Reform Act of 1959. The Act rationalized the state's crazy-quilt system of lower courts with overlapping jurisdiction and replaced it with a single statewide system divided into eighteen circuits whose jurisdiction was limited to "five-year felonies" and the imposition of sentences no greater than one year. It eliminated the trial *de novo*, provided for a full-time judiciary and at least one full-time prosecutor in each of the eighteen circuits, and established the rudiments of a public defender system, an innovation which lagged behind the other components of the court and had to be pushed along by the landmark Supreme Court rulings of the 1960s.

Despite these reforms, the courts remain an integral part of the political patronage system in Connecticut. Prior to the Court Reform Act, judicial appointments were often used by local officials to reward faithful supporters and sidetrack ambitious competitors. This was true for judgeships as well as other courthouse positions. Prosecutors, public defenders, clerks, aides, secretaries, and investigators, all exempt from civil service requirements, were appointed on the basis of reward and favoritism, and were used effectively as devices for welding together local political organizations. The Reform Act removed formal powers of judicial appointment from the hands of local officials and placed it in those of the legislature upon the nomination of the governor. Power to appoint prosecutors, public defenders, and clerks was vested in the statewide judicial conference (comprised entirely of judges).

This change has not removed "politics" from the selection process; in fact it has not even shifted the locus of power of appointment very far. By all accounts, the Act which created the Circuit Court system was passed only because Democratic and Republican party leaders came to an understanding about a method for selecting judges and other court personnel that preserved (if not enhanced) their powers.[16] By gentlemen's agreement they decided to divide the new judgeships evenly between Republicans and Democrats, with the additional understanding that the governor was to defer to local political leaders on all appointments. The authority to appoint other officials attached to the court—ranging from prosecutors down to clerk-typists— was also lodged in the state conference of judges, but in fact has remained entrenched in the hands of powerful resident judges within each of the localities. These judges, because of their own close and continuing contacts with local party organizations, tend to reflect the preferences of local party officials. The judges' ability to hold this power was facilitated by the Act, which exempted almost all of the court staff, professional and clerical, from civil service status and limited the tenure of prosecutors, public defenders, and chief clerks to one year, thereby requiring annual reappointment and presumably continuing indebtedness.

It was largely for these reasons that a faction-ridden legislature could pass a seemingly sweeping Court Reform Act establishing a Circuit Court system which allowed a Democratic governor, Abraham Ribicoff, a windfall of several dozen judicial nominations. The rule for appointing judges has been honored since it first went into effect in 1961; a Democrat is usually appointed to replace a retiring or deceased Democrat, and a Republican replaces a Republican. It has also been followed upon those occasions when the Circuit Court judiciary has been enlarged. Despite the formal state organization, *de facto* appointment powers have remained the property of the presiding judges of each court, most of whom remain close to their local party organizations. Writing several years after the court reform legislation was enacted, one of its sponsors, now a federal judge, observed that ". . . the influence of politics has in no sense been eliminated, only camouflaged. Names of prospective appointees are regularly furnished by political sources, and normally just satisfied by judicial appointment."[17]

In 1973 the Connecticut legislature, stimulated in part by a recent Connecticut Supreme Court decision affecting the Circuit Court's jurisdiction, combined Circuit Court (criminal) with the Court of Common Pleas (civil), and created new judicial districts to replace the old eighteen circuits. The new court system is called Common Pleas, and what was once known as the Sixth Circuit Court (New Haven, Bethany, and Woodbridge) was designated the Court of Common Pleas for the Sixth Geographical Area, or the "Sixth G.A.," as it quickly came to be known. The most important feature of this Act was to combine the civil Common Pleas Court with the criminal Circuit Court. In the opinion of many, this has helped to upgrade the status of Circuit Court judges and personnel, and was a crucial step in the successful drive toward the unification of Common Pleas and Superior Courts, a reform which was finally enacted by the state legislature in 1976.

The debate over court unification highlighted many of the currents that shape the court personnel recruitment process. Proponents of unification argued that elevating the status of lower court personnel would assure a higher standard of justice. They argued that raising the salaries of Common Pleas judges, public defenders, and prosecutors to the level of those in the Superior Court not only would attract more legal talent to the court but also would remove its badge of inferiority and second-class status. Furthermore, proponents continued, the more stringent standards that were formerly used only to assess nominees for Superior Court would extend to *all* judgeships in the state.

Opponents of this plan—and they predominated among the ranks of local party organizations who wanted to preserve their prerogatives and Superior Court personnel who wanted to preserve their status—argued that the plan would lower the quality of justice. Their argument was that, given the inevitability of limited resources, it made sense to keep the two-tiered court system, separating the few really "serious" cases from the masses of "petty" offenses which necessarily must be handled routinely.

Although the "management" aspects of these arguments about division of labor were important, there was also a strong political undercurrent to the debate. The two sets of standards for scrutiny used by the State Bar Association's Committee on Judicial Appointments—it has upon occasion certified a person as "qualified" for Circuit Court but "unqualified" for Superior Court—has allowed the governor and party leaders greater freedom in selecting appointments to the lower court bench.

Some fear that if the status differential among judges is erased and a uniform standard of acceptability is created, the prerogatives of local party officials will be sacrificed to the governor and particularly to the Bar Association.

Power, Patronage, and Position

The power of political party organizations is not limited exclusively to the selection of judges. It permeates the entire court system, and reflects the tradition of machine politics in both city and state government. Political organizations in Connecticut, as elsewhere in America, depend heavily on the use of jobs to reward subleadership, and the courts provide a particularly rich array of positions. These include a number of relatively well-paid and prestigious positions for those with legal training, as well as a number of lesser positions for others, thereby helping to attract and hold supporters with a variety of backgrounds, levels of competence, and income aspirations. Judgeships in particular are highly coveted positions for many lawyers, and in some areas they are used not only as rewards for faithful service, but also to replenish the organization's war chests.[18]

While judgeships are usually reserved for those who have given long and faithful service, the reward structure for other positions is more varied. Prosecutors and public defenders are usually younger than judges because there is considerably less prestige attached to these jobs and the salaries are lower. Appointments are made less because of personal services to a party organization than because of the services of one's father, mother, or other close relative or friend. Many of the prosecutors and public defenders in the Court of Common Pleas have family members or other close relatives who were active in local political organizations, and who served as their "sponsors"; those who do not have such direct relationships are likely to have close family friends or business associates who do.

The other lower-paying nonprofessional positions in the court are also used by party organizations, primarily to reward lower-level activists. Rather than being filled by the organization's leaders and major subleaders or their sons and daughters, these positions tend to be filled from among the ranks of the more numerous lower-level spear carriers of the party, ward leaders and vote mobilizers. Although the particular reasons for an appointment vary widely, the process of selection is inextricably bound up with the goals and interests of the party organization, and appointments are made with an eye toward furthering the interests of the party by binding additional loyalties to it and adding to its sources of revenue. For example, court personnel are solicited at election time by one of the prosecutors and are expected to make contributions to the Democratic party. According to several court officials, many if not most do so on a regular basis. And even those few who have not received their positions as a reward to friends or family are made to feel indebted to the political organization.

The structure of party rewards outlined above must be modified in two important ways. Although since the early 1950s New Haven has increasingly become a one-party city dominated by an energetic Democratic party organization, there remains a remnant of a Republican party organization whose survival is in large part dependent upon cooperation with the Democrats in exchange for a share of patronage to reward its faithful few.[19] In addition, Republicans have at times occupied the governorship, thereby controlling judicial appointments. Both of these factors have led to interparty appointments, with Democrats occasionally appointing Republicans and Republicans appointing Democrats. Shrewd local Democratic leaders have effectively co-opted many Republicans by securing appointment of them or their friends to positions of public prominence, thereby eliminating them as competition or rewarding them for cooperation. Under Richard Lee's unprecedented sixteen-year tenure as mayor during the 1950s and 1960s this tactic was elevated to a high art, and at times with the cooperation of a Democratic governor resulted in a number of Republicans receiving appointments as judges and prosecutors.[20] Governors have also used interparty appointments to their best advantage; Democratic governors have extracted concessions from key Republican legislators in exchange for appointments, and the Republican governor has done likewise. Such arrangements produced what are known locally as "Meskill (the Republican governor from 1970 to 1974) Democrats," and "Dempsey (the Democratic governor from 1962 to 1970) Republicans."

Incumbent judges exercise powers of their own, especially in filling auxiliary court positions. Although the formal powers for filling these positions reside in a statewide judicial council, by tradition appointments remain firmly under the control of a committee of resident judges for each geographical area in the state, and particularly of the powerful chief resident judges in each area who have gained their positions through seniority. Most judges remain closely linked to their political party organization and are likely to have coinciding interests. However, some judges may not remain wholeheartedly loyal to the party, and once on the bench may curb their active interest in partisan politics. All this can, in turn, blunt the direct impact of patronage. A Republican can, for instance, ascend to the position of chief resident judge in a predominantly Democratic city and not be wholly bound to the dominant party's interests. Changes and feuds within the Democratic party itself may produce new leadership in the party, leadership to which the judges, sponsored by others years earlier, have little or no loyalty. Others aspiring to higher judicial positions may try to rise above party politics by withdrawing from contact with their old associates. Even this, however, does not result in a "merit" selection process. Rather than accommodating the party faithful, as designated by an incumbent party leadership, judges simply exercise their own brand of particularism. Some have created their own independent system of patronage, filling positions to fit their own personal interests. For instance, a judge in a neighboring community secured a bail commissioner's appointment for the woman he was living with at the time, and a number of auxiliary positions in New Haven are filled with the relatives, friends, and neighbors of sponsoring judges.

Although the appointment process for virtually all positions in the Court of Common Pleas in New Haven is organized principally as a way of rewarding or strengthening the Democratic party organization's power, and the judges' own concerns are usually secondary, it is difficult if not impossible to separate the relative influence of politics, family, and friendship. The intense ethnic loyalties, the interlocking structure of family relationships, and the overlapping nature of group associations in New Haven make such an effort all but impossible. It is only clear that all appointments are based on claims of loyalty and association which exist apart from the claims of the position itself. Merit, skill, expertise, and experience are all subordinated to the claims of loyalty to primary groups. One person with long experience in the Connecticut court system articulated the feelings of many other court officials with whom I talked when he observed:

It's not at all obvious to me that professional competence has anything to do with appointments in the court. It is purely by accident if the person selected turns out to be a good lawyer and interested in his job since this consideration is the farthest thing from the minds of those who do the sponsoring of the appointees. This is not to say that there are not good people in the offices, but only that it is a happy coincidence.

This process of selection appears to run counter to the expectations of students of rational-legal organization. Max Weber, for instance, argued that the administration of justice in the West was the prime example of rational organization. He asserted that it was a system based upon "the realization of the principle of division of labor in administration according to purely technical considerations, allocating individual tasks to functionaries who are trained as specialists and who continuously add to their experience by constant practice."[21] According to this view of rational organization, officials are selected for their technical competence and their proficiency in mastering the technology and rules with which they must work; their advancement is based upon proven competence in the exercise of these tasks. Yet despite the form of a rational organization, we find a heavy overlay of traditional values, and a minimalist view of personnel selection. Although judges, prosecutors, and defense attorneys must be attorneys, they need not have tried criminal cases, or indeed practiced law at all. Indeed many people who are selected as judges have not seen the inside of a courtroom in years, and those who have usually focused on civil rather than criminal work. The system appears to be an anomaly; it is a formal, rational system that obtains its staff in a traditional, nonrational manner, recruiting on the basis of political reward, friendship, and family ties rather than technical competence.

Conclusion: The Court and Its Environment

This is a paradox only if the system of administering criminal justice is conceived of as a closed system, a single-minded organization with a clearly articulated set of goals. Indeed, a great many scholars following Weber have viewed it as such, and have treated "deviations" from such goals as pathological shortcomings of the criminal courts. There is, however, another way of viewing the criminal justice system, one which employs a substantially different conception of organization. This view approaches the criminal process as an open system, one based primarily upon cooperation, exchange, and adaptation. Rather than being the primary focus of attention, formal "rules" and "disinterested professionalism"—the distinguishing characteristics of rational organization—can be viewed as only *one of a number of factors* shaping the actions of officials in the system and affecting considerations for appointment. The efficacious "rules" followed by court officials and participants are not necessarily ideal, professional rules; the goals they pursue are not necessarily formal "organizational" goals posited by the researcher or even formal goals espoused by leaders of the organization; and the interests of those who fill the positions do not necessarily coincide with the formal goals of the system.

Rather, the "rules" that the organization members are likely to follow are the "folkways" or informal "rules of the game" within the organization; the goals they pursue are likely to be personal or subgroup goals; and the roles they assume are likely to be defined by the functional adaptation of these two factors. The idealized perspective of the rational organization staffing itself in order to pursue effectively a single specified goal— justice according to due process, for example—is replaced by a perspective which sees the criminal justice system as a collection of rational individuals pursuing their own goals, and agencies that are often antagonistic to one another.

Above all, the criminal court system must be understood as an *open system*, as a part of other more inclusive social systems which constantly shape it in a host of different ways. This concept begins to explain the personnel selection process in lower criminal court. Although the criminal justice system is formally organized as a model of rational organization, the larger system of which it is a part is not. Political party association in New Haven as elsewhere is intensely practical, and leadership is highly personal, almost patriarchal, not easily transferred from one person to another. Loyalty rests with persons rather than with ideas or offices, and is rooted in their effectiveness in providing the tangible rewards of employment. From the perspective of the traditional political association, then, the criminal justice system is neither an end in itself nor a closed and separate organization pledged to fidelity to law, an organization whose sole function is to ferret out truth. Above all, it is a source of employment for the faithful. The courtroom competence of appointees is of marginal concern to those in the political process. They are only concerned that minimal legal requirements be met and that the party organization will not be embarrassed by the appointments. Apart from that there is little organizational interest, and there is strong incentive to oppose moves toward professionalism because they tend to diminish the role of the political association in the selection process.[22] This fact alone goes a long way to account for lackluster performances by some judges, carelessness by some prosecutors, and the inactivity and nonappearance of some lesser officials.

But the criminal court is not an entirely open system. It has a life of its own, and officials, even when they are recruited for prior political service, and even when they continue to maintain a deep loyalty to their party organization, can also develop strong commitments to their new office and their new roles. The results can cause conflicts. These values collide with the values of those outside the courts who control the appointment process. Old friends not given preferential treatment in court may complain, and "new" standards of conduct articulated by former politicos may cause resentment and at times bitterness.

This impulse for professionalism and increased respect for office fosters a continuing drive for competency and "merit selection," a process which if adapted would strengthen the voice of the legal community and more particularly the voices of officials in the criminal justice system itself.

Despite complaints about "political" domination of the appointment process, the Connecticut criminal justice system has moved steadily in the direction of professionalism and continues to do so. The Court Reform Act significantly altered the structure of the courts, replacing a haphazard local court system with a single statewide system, which is staffed by full-time judges with formal legal training. The state bar association has begun to take an active role in screening judicial candidates. The now-completed drive toward court unification has further tended to upgrade the status of the lower court, and will no doubt have an effect on the way business there is conducted. Within the past decade, a public defender system has not only been created; it has also been removed from the direct control of the judiciary which, many claimed, curbed the defenders' abilities to be vigorous champions of their clients. In addition, the United States Supreme Court has made itself felt in New Haven. Many of the changes noted above have been effected at least partially because of the Court's decisions, particularly those which have expanded the rights of defendants and extended their coverage to those accused of lesser offenses. A movement capped by *Argersinger* v. *Hamlin* in 1972[23] has required the state to provide counsel for defendants of limited means, and this in turn has spawned a host of other activities unheard of in lower courts only a decade or two ago and altogether impossible without representation. However overworked or underqualified public defenders may be, or however perfunctory the attention they give their clients' cases, their very presence in the court has altered the relationship between the accused and the prosecution in a way that makes them more nearly equal. If instituting public defenders has not created a court which operates according to the ideal norms of the legal profession, it has definitely contributed to the elimination of the more gross displays of arbitrariness and favoritism that once were commonplace in the court.

One can learn much about an institution by examining the way it obtains its staff. The organizations supply these new people, and the traditions, modes of thinking, and bases for decision that have guided them in the past will carry over into their new positions. In short, the culture which produces them and of which they remain a part will continue to shape their outlooks. Martin Levin describes the differences in the political cultures and the mode of judicial selection in Minneapolis and Pittsburgh, and convincingly argues that these differences account for much of the variations in sentencing.[24] What is important for judges is important for other positions as well. Prosecutors and defense attorneys are probably more important decision makers than judges, whose functions may have been reduced with the expansion of the right to counsel. What emerges in the next two chapters is a picture of a criminal court system staffed almost entirely by those recruited from traditional institutions, people whose life experiences and social advancement have been shaped by the particularistic values of ethnic, religious, political, and family associations, and whose behavior, once they are ensconced in the court, is a curious adaptation of these traditional values to the norms of professionalism.

This mixture of traditional and formal rational goals has its parallel in the process of decision making in the court, a process which combines some of the elements of rational legality, but is molded by the inclination to render swift, substantive justice, a form of decision which emphasizes dispute resolution rather than formal adjudication and the impulse to consider the "whole person" rather than the narrow "facts" of the case. This correspondence of recruitment, organization, and decision making is hardly surprising, for it is difficult to imagine that any system so thoroughly immersed in the values of particularism, cooperation, and exchange could operate in any other way.

The factors responsible for the rapid and perfunctory treatment of criminal defendants and the virtual absence of trials are not such structural ones as inadequate facilities or the press of heavy caseloads. They are the traditional values maintained by both the court and its immediate environment, values which may emphasize rapid and substantive rather than deliberative justice.

The perspective outlined above helps to provide an understanding of the behavior of courts which is so often considered pathological. The following chapter will make this increasingly clear.

CHAPTER 3

Judges, Prosecutors, and Defense Attorneys

Introduction

Although they are not always the central figures in the eyes of the criminally accused, the judge, the prosecutor, and the defense attorney are by far the most visible and potentially most important actors in the criminal process. The judge makes the formal determination of guilt or innocence, rules on motions, and sets sentence; the prosecutor adds, drops, or reduces charges, presses vigorously for conviction, or makes the decision to nolle; and the defense attorney can invoke rights, pursue options, and raise defenses his client has never thought about. How these officials perform their functions is determined in large part by the way their offices are organized; this organization, in turn, is shaped by the ways in which people are recruited to the offices, and how they perceive their roles. This chapter examines recruitment and organization in the offices of judge, prosecutor, and defense attorney.

Judges

There are fifty-nine judges in the Court of Common Pleas in Connecticut. They are appointed for terms of four years by the legislature, from nominations submitted by the governor. Initial nomination by the governor is tantamount to appointment for life; no gubernatorial nomination has ever been rejected by the legislature, and no appointee has ever failed to be renominated.[1] Each judge is appointed to a position in a resident court, and then rotates among any of several different courts within commuting distance. At the time of this study, all but two of the judges in Connecticut were males, and only three were Blacks. The same division was roughly true for the other professional positions in the court. Thirty-three judges were Democrats and twenty-three were Republicans; three did not reveal any party affiliation. There were more Democrats than Republicans because of the 1973 amalgamation of the lower civil Court of Common Pleas and the lower criminal Circuit Court. Prior to that the Circuit Court consisted of twenty-two Democrats, eighteen Republicans, and the three judges of unknown party affiliation (who were probably Republicans). Ordinarily, there is a gentleman's agreement between party leaders to maintain an even balance.

The Court of Common Pleas in New Haven had seven resident judges assigned to its criminal division, four Democrats and three Republicans. All were active in local politics and received their appointments as carefully considered *quid pro quos* for past political service. Those who "moved up the ladder" from prosecutor to judge continued to remain politically active, and their "promotions" were based on far more than their legal abilities. Even for Republicans, a promotion was part of a carefully considered Democratic machine strategy either to reward cooperative opponents or to sidetrack ambitious competition.

Most of the judges were fifty or older, and reached the bench after a lengthy minor political career and a vigorous behind-the-scenes campaign. One judge described his appointment as follows:

I was staff counsel to a very prominent legislator and got to know a number of leading legislators and the Governor. Toward the end of his term, I decided to try to get a judicial appointment. There were ten judgeships opened up and I began to try to campaign for one by talking to the various party leaders. By and large the Governor did not bother with the appointment process. He would appoint a few of his friends, but left most of it to the party's State Chairman. I knew him, so went to him directly—if they do not know him, others would approach him through someone who did. He said it would be tough—there were dozens of applications— but he did send my name over to the State Bar Association and I did get his approval and the appointment.

Other judges have similar backgrounds, differentiated only by the details of their political service. The former Chief Resident Judge of the New Haven court was a long-time Republican party activist, and served for many years as the Republican Town Chairman, but his appointment to the bench was a reward for cooperation with the Democrats. Another of the judges was active in Republican politics, earned his party's gratitude by waging a losing mayoralty campaign against a popular Democratic incumbent, and then later gained Democratic support by cooperating on several important local issues and by virtue of the fact that the Democrats wanted to weaken the opposition. A third judge, a Republican and a prominent leader in New Haven's active Italian-American community, was appointed by the governor just prior to his reelection campaign in an effort to make Democratic inroads into New Haven's large Italian-Republican voting bloc. The other judges had also been active in party affairs, and earned their offices by serving in such invisible but nevertheless important and time-consuming positions as party committeeman and treasurer for election campaigns.

People want to become judges in a lower criminal court for a variety of reasons. It is rarely because of an interest in criminal law, since few judges have had previous experience with criminal cases, and most have probably not even seen the inside of a courtroom for years. One obvious reason is the public prestige attached to the position. Most judges have led a long and active public life, and like the attention and respect attendant upon it. A judicial appointment guarantees that this will continue, but without the wear and tear of electoral politics. One judge observed that many of his colleagues had sought judicial appointments for "negative" reasons. Some were exhausted with the long hours that political life requires; others had had heart attacks or illnesses which caused them to seek a more leisurely pace. The judge quoted above was interested in a judgeship in part because he did not like the economics of a small law firm, with constant worries about billing and obtaining new clients. However, many other attorneys cannot even dream about a judgeship for economic reasons. A judge's salary is less than $30,000 a year, much less than what a successful lawyer in private practice can make. Perhaps this is why so many judges are so old when they are appointed to the bench. They probably have already put their children through college, amassed some savings, or begun collecting a pension, and can "afford" the drop in income that comes with the appointment.

Because of rotation, these seven resident New Haven judges are not the only ones who handle cases in the city's lower court. In my sample of 1,648 cases, almost all were handled by judges whose home base was a city other than New Haven. Some judges commuted from as far away as Hartford and Bridgeport, but most of them came from the closer towns of Meriden, Waterbury, and West Haven. The rotating judiciary seems to have originated in a much earlier era when a single judge was responsible for presiding over courtrooms in more than one city, and literally rode circuit to cover them. This tradition was reasserted in the Court Reform Act of 1959, and justified on the grounds it would prevent judges from becoming complacent or overly cooperative working with the same small group of prosecutors and defense attorneys day in and day out.

Rotation is an efficient system; judges can be shifted around to fit the varying needs of each court. For instance, if a judge in a smaller court is tied up on a lengthy trial or is ill or on vacation, a second or third judge can be assigned to his court on a temporary basis. It is also used to protect the judiciary from its detractors. Older judges, who are nearly senile, deaf, or blind, are at times assigned to the smaller courts where there is little business and where they are out of the view of probing newspaper reporters and activist attorneys, and can be guided by an understanding prosecutor. Other judges who are inclined to be slow and deliberate are also likely to be assigned to lighter duty, so that those who work harder or those who are more willing to conduct court at a faster pace can be assigned to the busiest courtrooms in the larger cities. Rotation is also used to keep unruly judges in line.[2] If the Chief Judge is miffed at one of his judges, he might assign him to a particularly unattractive area a long drive from his home, or to a courthouse with inadequate facilities or an overwhelming amount of business.

Rotation minimizes the appearance of collusion and overfamiliarity that continuous presence in a single courtroom would foster, but it also reduces the judge's already low interest in overseeing the administration of the court. When confronted with a noisy courtroom,[3] distasteful scheduling practices, unreasonable plea bargaining and sentence recommendations, incompetent personnel, or any of a host of other problems, a judge usually finds it easier to accommodate to the problem rather than overcome it. However demeaning they are to the judge, such practices may be functional for the court's permanent staff of prosecutors, clerks, and public defenders, and if he tries to alter them he might find himself in a clash with other judges, a politically powerful prosecutor, or the "sponsor" of one of the persons whose actions he is questioning. Ultimately it is easier to avoid such conflicts by avoiding certain courts alto-gether. More typically, a judge will silently endure the problems for the period that he is sitting in that courtroom. One judge I talked to about decorum in the courtroom quoted Sam Ray-burn's famous dictum: "To get along, you've got to go along."

Whereas most judges are older men who have little interest in assuming administrative duties in their courts, a few of the younger or more energetic judges take a different view of their job. But they are often frustrated:

> There is little incentive for a judge to innovate. They sit in any cir-cuit for only two or three months and then rotate, so they don't really care. Perhaps a concerned judge will make recommendations that he won't and can't see through. Generally, however, they don't even have enough interest to make recommendations.

An important by-product of rotation is that judicial responsi-bilities tend to gravitate into the hands of prosecutors and other officials who are permanently assigned to only one court. Cal-endaring practices, access to files, bail forfeiture decisions, and other practices properly controlled by a clerk under the direc-tion of a judge are in effect dominated by the local prosecutor, who in turn uses them for strategic purposes to punish or re-ward defendants, defense attorneys, and bail bondsmen. Even such responsibilities as sentences, bail decisions, warrant is-suances—all decisions formally under the control of judges—pass into the hands of the prosecutors. Judges rotating into a new court find it more convenient to take their cues from the prosecutors than to exercise independent authority. One judge I talked to always calls in the Chief Prosecutor on his first day in a new court to ask him what the "going rates" are for sentences and bail so that he will not disrupt local expectations.

Because most of the judges are so passive, their names evoke few intense responses from prosecutors and defense attorneys. There is a general consensus among prosecutors and defense attorneys in the state that Common Pleas judges are on the whole less competent than Superior Court judges,[4] and in New

Haven there is a consensus as to which judges are lazy or hard-working, biased or fair. But most attorneys—prosecutors and defense attorneys alike—feel that they can work comfortably with almost any judge. Defense attorneys do have preferences, and when they are able to act on them they try to avoid or obtain particular judges. Some judges are rumored to be especially hard on certain types of crimes (child molestation, for example), and an attorney handling such a charge may try to avoid the judge. Or a defense attorney may once have had a client receive an unexpectedly long sentence in a drug case from one judge and try to avoid him in similar future cases. If a defense attorney is planning to file a motion, he may try to maneuver his case away from a judge who is known to be particularly impatient with "nitpicking." But such special efforts are the rare exception, not the rule. Typically, attorneys complain privately about the judges and then take whoever is there, hoping for the best. By and large this approach proves satisfactory to them since the primary function of the judge is to *ratify* decisions made outside the courtroom, not to make them himself.

Even when there are strains between a defense attorney and a judge, the formal language of the law helps to minimize open personality clashes. Like the rhetoric of debate in Congress, language in the courtroom is extremely arcane and formal, and it can easily accommodate the most bitter denunciations and sarcasm in a way that does not unduly strain the rituals of court procedures or the rapid rhythm of case processing.[5] Moreover, since most crucial decisions are made through negotiations and agreements between the defense and prosecution, the most important person for a concerned defense attorney to worry about is not the judge but the prosecutor.

The judge's role is a study in contrasts. To the community, the judge is a symbol of authority and respect, a role which no doubt attracts many people to the bench. Within the courthouse, however, the powers of the judge are severely circumscribed. Like a rock in the middle of a whirlpool, the judge is placed in a swirl of activity which neither moves him nor is significantly shaped by him. In a process of adjudication characterized by prosecutors' nolles and defendants' guilty pleas, there are few rulings to make. And in a guilty plea process which depends upon the prosecutors' promising sentences, there is little for the judge to do after conviction. By and large, the judge's function is to ratify the decisions of the prosecutors and defense attorneys.

But even in those cases in which judges have "freedom" to sentence, they are left feeling frustrated. "What do you do," one judge asked, "in these petty cases? They're not serious enough to put a person in jail; yet you want to do something to show society's disapproval. Normally a fine would be appropriate, but so many of these people don't have any money. So we end up giving meaningless conditional discharges or probation, and it becomes something of a joke. It's frustrating; there's little we can do."

In the main courtroom the judge is not even manager of his own domain; the activity is too diffuse and the pace too quick. It is perhaps more accurate to say that the judge endures rather than presides over his courtroom. This phenomenon is illustrated in the following account by one judge:

I hate the noise in the New Haven arraignment court. It's intolerable, but there is little I can do about it. I once ordered the door to the back room locked up because people were constantly coming and going and the door was open and people were standing in the doorway talking. It was simply too noisy. But my order to keep the door locked lasted all of two days. Everybody bitterly complained, and the end result was that people would stand in the courtroom and talk rather than going to their offices. The public defenders complained that every time they had to talk to the client they had to run all the way down to their own offices or to the prosecutor's offices and as a result there was confusion when another of their cases was called in court. I finally relented after two days and unlocked the door.

Like schoolteachers who find it convenient to "allow" pupils to "act up" on the last day of class, judges find it convenient to overlook intrusions into the dignity of the courtroom. If the judge were to insist upon order, he would only call attention to his weakness and inefficacy. In the long run, his sense of dignity is best served by acting as if the problem did not exist.

Prosecutors

Paralleling the two-tiered court system are two separate prosecutor systems, one for Superior Court and one for Common Pleas. Like the Common Pleas judiciary, on paper the system appears to be centralized; prosecutors are formally appointed and reappointed by a council consisting of the state's entire Common Pleas Court judiciary. But as in the judiciary, initial appointment depends almost entirely on the influence of a local political "sponsor." For all practical purposes, appointment is made by the Chief Resident Judge of each court. When a vacancy occurs in a prosecutor's office, the Chief Resident Judge defers to the recommendations of his own party's officials and the other resident judges in the area. He is likely to "recommend" a candidate and have him routinely approved by the Office of the Chief State's Attorney and the statewide conference of judges. The Chief Prosecutor in the court in which the new appointee will be working may not have met or even be aware of the new appointee before he appears for work.[6]

As with judicial appointments, the reasons and incentives for selection may vary, but whatever the precise reasons, prosecutors attain and maintain their positions by mobilizing political support. One former prosecutor in lower court—himself the godson of a Democratic governor—described the process leading to his appointment as follows:

> I'm not from New Haven. I moved here [after graduation from law school] because my wife had a job here. So I called my god-

father, who, as you know, was Governor Dempsey. I told him that there were two openings in the prosecutor's office, and that I would be interested in one of them. I was told to go see Catherine Quinn who handled John Bailey's [Democratic Party State Chairman] patronage positions. I talked to her briefly about the fact that the positions were open, left a copy of my resume, and indicated that I was anxious to have one of the jobs. She didn't talk to me at all about my political connections, although I'm sure that she was aware of who my godfather was. She thanked me and that was the last I heard for some time. There was no further communication between us.

All of a sudden one day I got a call from [the chief resident judge of New Haven's circuit court], who called me and told me to be in court at 10 A.M. the next day. I went up there expecting to talk to him and waited until court adjourned, at which time he called me into his office, had me put my hand on the Bible and swore me in as a prosecutor—this is how I began to work. Before I knew it I was a prosecutor. It's not the way I would have liked it, because my wife and family were not present, but it was the way to get started. It was purely political. Judge ——— was extremely active in politics and it seems that whatever he wanted he got. At the time there were six other resident judges, but he took the lead in organizing the appointments for the prosecutors, public defenders, and as far as I know, the staffs of the court in his jurisdiction.

At the time of this study, the Court of Common Pleas had four full-time prosecutors, and all of them had secured their appointments in a similar manner, mobilizing the support of political "godfathers."

The career of the former Chief Prosecutor is a case in point. He was for many years a leading figure in the Italian wing of the city's Republican party organization, and was once his party's candidate for mayor. But he emerged as a party leader just as the city's Democratic party organization was beginning to dominate local politics, and owes his first judicial appointment largely to the Democratic leadership. His subsequent appointments to the prosecutor's office and later to the bench received strong bipartisan support. The Democratic party support was part of a strategy to weaken the Republican party, co-opting its most able leaders by appointing them to prestigious but politically neutral positions; he received support precisely because he was such a popular and potentially challenging Republican.[7]

The Chief Prosecutor at the time of this study—Paul Foti—was not as active in local politics, but still owed his appointment to political sponsors who were. Born and raised in the city's old Italian section, Foti was delivered by a midwife who subsequently became his godmother and close family friend. Her son later became a leading figure in the Italian community and was for many years the Republican Town Chairman before he was appointed to the bench. Throughout his career he acted as a sponsor for his younger neighbor and mother's godson.

After graduating from law school and completing military service, Foti returned to New Haven and eventually landed a part-time clerking position with a one-man law office, a job which offered him no real future. The position did, however, introduce him to the Democratic Town Chairman, who advised the young man that his future would be brighter if he became active in Democratic affairs. Foti heeded the advice, changed his party registration, and began to contribute time to local Democratic causes. He was soon rewarded with a part-time position as a court clerk, and as the court expanded so did his job. Later, with the support of both his Democratic and Republican connections, he obtained an appointment as an assistant prosecutor, and came under the tutelage of the Chief Prosecutor described above. When the latter received a judicial appointment, Foti was designated to fill the vacancy.

The other three full-time prosecutors had similar backgrounds. They all came from families long active in New Haven politics and obtained their positions shortly after graduating from law school. One, the son of a prominent Democratic politician who once sat on the Board of Police Commissioners, was also related to the Democratic Town Chairman. Another was the son of a maverick Democratic politician who was the city's corporation counsel in the mid-1950s, and later as a ward leader challenged his party's leadership by making a bid for mayor and fielding a slate of aldermanic candidates in the party's primary, normally a showcase for party consensus.[8] The third was the nephew of the publisher of the city's newspapers and a long-time family friend of two of the resident judges who together pressed for his appointment and, according to him, assured him of a position "before I graduated from law school or had passed the bar exam."

The four part-time prosecutors had similar backgrounds, but were older and once active in politics. One was a former Republican state senator who at one time had been regarded as a "shining light" in the party, but had long since dropped out of active politics. Another came from a family active in Democratic circles and was married to the daughter of a former Democratic Town Chairman. He remained active in party affairs and regularly solicited contributions for the party from his coprosecutors and court personnel.

Like so many other public jobs, a prosecutor's position is initially attractive, it offers a good starting salary and a fair amount of responsibility; but it offers little opportunity for professional growth, career advancement, or scheduled salary increases, so that it becomes less appealing as time goes by. After four or five years a young prosecutor has learned most of what there is to know, has reached the peak of his salary schedule, and can look forward to little other than perhaps becoming the Chief Prosecutor, transferring to the Superior Court, or hoping to be appointed to the bench. But it is impossible to count on such advancement, and it is often slow in coming. During the course of my study two assistant prosecutors resigned to enter private practice. Both were relatively content with their jobs, but cited limited opportunities and salary constraints as their primary reasons for leaving.

Although he was quite critical of a number of practices in the Common Pleas court, the Chief Prosecutor made little effort to change them, "because they are beyond my control." He wanted part-time prosecutors, whom he believed rush through their work in order to leave early, replaced with full-time people, but he did not take any active steps toward this. He would have liked a lower caseload or a larger staff. He would have liked more and better facilities and investigative resources. He was critical of many of the judges, some of whom he thought were approaching senility. He had a high regard for most defense attorneys, although he was disdainful of a handful of them, mostly private attorneys whom he thought were either incompetent or were more interested in obtaining easy fees than in helping their clients. But he argued that these matters too were either beyond his control or would require increased funding. They were matters for the legislature, not for him, to pursue.

This passivity was in part a matter of individual preference. He admitted to a dislike of "administration," and said he preferred to rub shoulders with his assistants in the midst of the action of the courtroom. He was also realistic about the amount of freedom and flexibility his office had. In effect, he did not control it. One defense attorney who was normally extremely critical of the prosecutor's and public defender's offices reserved his judgment about the Chief Prosecutor:

I hate to say anything about ————. He's in a pathetic position. He's a hard-working and bright guy. He's in every day at 8 A.M. He knows the criminal law and evidence. He's a competent state worker, but he has no control over his staff. He's saddled with whomever he gets, so I'm reluctant to criticize him because his problems are really beyond his control. There's absolutely no quality control in the prosecutor's office or anybody's office. The heads of these offices can't even fire their personnel—even a secretary—or get rid of them in any way.

Although the Chief Prosecutor and this attorney were correct in claiming that the most important changes are out of the Chief's control, the Chief's passivity was also firmly reinforced by his belief that his office—and the court as a whole—was doing an adequate job in dispensing rough justice. He thought that his staff was fair and equitable, that it bent over backward to protect defendants, that it was willing to overlook minor violations, and that it had a good working relationship with the local criminal bar and the Public Defender's Office. He saw little merit in many of the recurring proposals to "reform" the system, since they encourage antagonism between prosecution and defense, something in which he saw little value. This view was echoed by most of the other prosecutors on his staff. There was a shared sense that within the limits placed on them they did an adequate job, and that whatever shortcomings they had should be overlooked since they almost invariably favored defendants. The purpose of reform, as they saw it, was to relieve them of the need to work so long and so hard for so little, not to do anything substantially different.[9]

Although there was a broad consensus among the prosecutors, there were still important differences among them. Most obvious was the distinction between part- and full-timers. The part-time prosecutors, almost always assigned duties in the arraignment part of the court, had a strong incentive to rush through the calendar in order to return to their full-time jobs.[10] Most of them were reluctant to engage in protracted negotiations with defense attorneys or to pursue any type of "legal" argument likely to require sustained deliberation, research, or investigation. If a defense attorney suggested a case settlement which a part-time prosecutor believed was unreasonable or raised anything approaching a novel argument which could develop into a motion to suppress or dismiss, rather than offering a counterposition or considering the argument, the part-timer was likely to tell the defense attorney to see one of the full-timers or suggest a continuance. This transferred the burden of decision to someone else, necessitated another appearance, and contributed to delay in the court. Although part-timers were frequently criticized by their full-time counterparts and by defense attorneys for such actions, they were invariably placed in prime positions for procrastination. Assigned to the arraignment courtroom, it was their duty to screen all incoming cases, and when in doubt they felt it was appropriate either to delay the case or pass it upward. This is typical of "intake" positions in many types of organizations, so that it is difficult to determine if the fact that the "screeners" were part-timers was as important as some of their critics claimed. When a full-time prosecutor was assigned to work in this same environment, he quickly became adept at similar practices, preferring to decide the great mass of easy cases quickly and to transfer and defer judgment on the handful of problem cases.

There were few other differences among the prosecutors. A survey of those defense attorneys who appeared most frequently in Common Pleas produced nearly unanimous agreement as to which ones were "knowledgeable of the law," "willing to negotiate," and "stubborn" and which were not.[11] Not surprisingly, with but one notable exception, part-time prosecutors did not fare as well as their full-time colleagues. But defense attorneys generally considered the prosecutors to be adequate and only made negative remarks about one of them.

Defense Attorneys

There are three forms of representation available to people accused of criminal offenses in the Court of Common Pleas. If the arrestee is financially able, he may retain private counsel of his own choosing. If he is not, then he may either receive a court-appointed public defender (PD) at no expense, or seek out an attorney with the New Haven Legal Assistance Association (LAA). Arrestees may also go without representation, as did roughly half of all defendants in my sample. Of those in my sample represented by counsel, the public defender's office handled the lion's share (59 percent), with private attorneys accounting for 36 percent, and LAA attorneys 5 percent. Within each type of defense system there are great variations in experience and skill, as well as important institutional differences in the ways they obtain, deal with, and represent their clients.

Private Representation

New Haven is a lawyer's town. Almost 700 practicing attorneys are listed in the telephone directory, far more per capita than in Bridgeport, but substantially fewer than in Hartford.[12] There are several reasons for this. New Haven is the commercial center for central Connecticut, if not the entire state, and many businesses have offices there. It is also the central city for a much larger metropolitan area, and it is the home of Yale. The university and its law school draw attorneys to New Haven, attracting a disproportionate number of local students who remain in the area after graduation, and others who put down roots in the city during their school years.

Unlike many law offices in larger cities, New Haven firms are relatively small, and most engage in a wide range of practice. Consequently, a large number of attorneys handle cases in the Court of Common Pleas. Over thirty were involved in the 168 retained-counsel cases in the sample.

Another distinctive feature of criminal law practice in New Haven is the relatively high number of criminal law specialists with Ivy League educations and degrees from prestigious law schools. At the time of this study, there were over half a dozen such attorneys in town, partners in two- or three-person firms, who were engaged in general practice but preferred to handle criminal cases. Most were in their late twenties to mid-thirties, and had only marginally successful offices that were struggling to survive. Many were students in the 1960s during the heyday of the Warren Court and the civil rights and antiwar movements; after graduation they eschewed more lucrative practices to pursue careers either in smaller firms or on their own.[13]

Although attorneys with such credentials remain the exception rather than the rule and may be an anomaly of the 1960s, New Haven had none of the night-school–trained "schlock" lawyers whom observers report finding in other cities. There was no equivalent of New York's "Baxter's bar," Chicago's "State Street bar," or Washington's "Fifth Street bar," populated by lawyers who must split fees with jailers, bondsmen, and perhaps judges to earn their living. But such attorneys may be the fiction of elitist observers who want a convenient scapegoat for the ubiquitous chaos of American criminal courts. For instance, Blumberg's characterization of the "court regulars" in one New York City courthouse does not conform to the popular stereotype of the "Baxter Street" bar:

> . . . at least twelve [of seventeen] of these lawyers are persons of great intellectual and professional skills and political sophistication. In dress, speech, manner, erudition, and legal sophistication, they are more than a match for the Wall Street lawyer. In fact, they are often called upon by the "downtown" large firm lawyer who eschews criminal work and abhors those in it; he is usually terribly insecure in a courtroom—especially in a court like Metropolitan Court. The seventeen lawyers who appear in most of the trials in Metropolitan Court are reputed to possess the necessary skills for such activity. If so, their elaborate skills are underutilized, because their capacities for negotiation and the charismatic quality of their reputations are the real mainstays of their professional activity. And because they are so intricately enmeshed in the court organization, they cease being true professionals and instead function as "fixers for a fee."[14]

Perhaps the careless "copout artist" did once exist, but was put out of business by the rise of public defender systems. Or perhaps there were too many attorneys in New Haven; perhaps the city is not large enough to warrant such a high degree of specialization among the bar.

Whatever the reason, there apparently has never been a cadre of full-time criminal attorneys who obtained clients by haunting the corridors of the courtroom and splitting fees with jailers, bondsmen, and the like. The private attorneys who most frequently appeared in the cases included in my sample were reasonably well-regarded by other defense attorneys, prosecutors, and judges.[15] Those held in the least regard were not "court regulars," but a handful of lawyers who only occasionally handled criminal cases. They frequently came into court inexperienced, forgetful, and confused, then blundered their way through the complicated and unfamiliar processes in a way that often did their clients great disservice.

In my sample 60 percent of the identified retained counsel cases were handled by one of seven attorneys. These seven lawyers represented a wide range of personalities, backgrounds, styles of law practices, and according to the judgments of knowledgeable observers, legal competence. All were male. Two were in their early thirties, two in their mid-forties, and three were fifty or older. One was Black, three were Jewish, and three were WASP. Although a number of Italian attorneys occasionally handled cases in the court, none of these seven was Italian. One had a law degree from Yale, another from Georgetown, and a third from Boston University; the others were graduates of the University of Connecticut School of Law. All maintained comfortable private practices with annual incomes ranging from $20,000 to over $50,000. All belonged to small firms or practiced alone; the practices were general-purpose and criminal law was not their main specialty. The older they became, the less time they spent on minor criminal cases. As business increased, they preferred to take more lucrative or professionally rewarding civil cases and larger criminal cases.

The two younger attorneys were "movement" lawyers attracted to liberal causes in New Haven in the mid-1960s who remained to form a partnership. One was an attorney for LAA during its heyday,[16] and the other spent his first year after law school as part of the Bobby Seale defense team in the celebrated Black Panther case in 1970.[17] Both were politically conscious, and while one was a Marxist and the other a "classical liberal" (who saw himself so far to the right that he was on the left), they both supported liberal, left-wing, and civil libertarian causes. They had earned a reputation as troublemakers among prosecutors, judges, and many other defense attorneys. They were outspoken in their contempt for the police and the courts for tolerating, if not condoning, illegal and abusive police practices.

While they were known as outspoken critics and instigators of political and constitutional defenses, most of their criminal work involved "routine" cases, for which they were as rapid and perfunctory in their courtroom appearances as the most seasoned of public defenders. In their daily courtroom encounters they looked remarkably like most other attorneys, so that anyone unfamiliar with their reputations would not have singled them out. Although both had reputations for taking cases to trial, neither took one to trial in my sample of 1,600 cases, and one of them acknowledged that despite his reputation he had *never* taken a case to trial in the Court of Common Pleas. This does not mean that the reputations of these two attorneys are without foundation. The *occasional* trials, motions, and novel defenses are enough to set them apart.

Another attorney who regularly appeared in court was one of the city's few Black lawyers. A partner in a Jewish law firm, he specialized in criminal defense work, and almost all his clients were Black. He was a vocal and ambitious person, marginally active in New Haven Democratic politics, occasionally serving as an unofficial spokesman for the Black community and lending his support for Democratic candidates at election time. He had not ever run for elective office, although he was once rewarded with a part-time public defender position which he squeezed in between his private practice until it grew too burdensome.

There was little love between this attorney and the Chief Prosecutor. He thought the Prosecutor's Office was heavy-handed and unwilling to compromise, and the prosecutors viewed him as a second-rate lawyer lacking in professionalism. These differences reflected more than personal dislike; they also reflected the slow but steady changes that have transformed the

Prosecutor's Office and the nature of representation during the past decade. This attorney had practiced law in New Haven for a number of years, and recalled with fondness his dealings with the earlier prosecutors, men who were more informal and more willing to negotiate cases and "give breaks." He reminisced about his dealings with a former Chief Prosecutor:

[He] grew up in a black neighborhood—the only Italian kid in the neighborhood. When he was Chief Prosecutor there was a different attitude over there. . . . He empathized with Black people. He knew the pain they suffered. Prosecutors and judges used to give Blacks a break, but now they don't.

Somewhat older than the other attorneys who regularly appeared in the Court of Common Pleas, this attorney preferred the more casual negotiations and more cooperative relationships between prosecutors and defense attorneys of by-gone days. While he attributed the changes to increasing racism because of the rise of the Black population in New Haven, the reasons in fact appear to be more generalized, caused by an increased sense of professionalism and more formalism. Although the court is still moved by appeals to friendship and equity, it is more circumscribed by legalisms than it once was.[18]

Public Defense Services

Public institutions age rapidly and are quickly taken for granted; what is new and innovative at one moment becomes old, established, and entrenched the next. Many of those who write about such agencies do not have a historical perspective. This includes those who write about public defender organizations. These writers compare public defenders to successful private attorneys and contrast their practices with the full-fledged adversarial ideal. After tagging them with such labels as "copout artist," "cooperative," and "bureaucrat," they often assign public defenders major responsibility for the "twilight" of the adversary system. But it is dangerous to make such sweeping historical comparisons. Twenty years ago few people accused of misdemeanors were even represented by counsel, so that it is only fair to compare public defenders with an absence of counsel.

Many critical assessments fail to appreciate how new the right to appointed counsel and the rise of public defense organizations are. They were established under a constitutional mandate which is just a few years old. Prior to the Supreme Court's 1963 decision in *Gideon* v. *Wainwright*[19] most of those accused of felonies did not have a constitutional right to appointed counsel. It was not until 1972 that right to counsel was extended as a right to those charged with misdemeanors. Prior to these decisions in New Haven as elsewhere, an overwhelming majority of those charged with petty criminal offenses went without representation, and routinely threw themselves at the mercy of the court, personally requesting the prosecutor to drop charges, or more frequently pleading guilty and receiving a small fine or suspended sentence.[20]

Some expected *Gideon* v. *Wainwright* and later *Argersinger* v. *Hamlin* to cause a radical restructuring of the criminal process, replacing perfunctory "processing" with well-reasoned and vigorous adversarial proceedings. Others may have felt that the expansion of public representation would serve primarily as a screening function to discover and treat occasional "problem" cases who wanted full-blown adversarial proceedings. Whatever the expectations, the Supreme Court's decisions forced states to create public defense systems without waiting for agreement on answers. New Haven not only responded to, but also anticipated and helped create the climate for, the Court's decisions by experimenting with different types of public defense systems in the lower court.

New Haven Legal Assistance Association   One important experiment was the New Haven Legal Assistance Association. Early in the 1960s, a group of local lawyers and law professors, spearheaded by Yale professor Joseph Goldstein, envisioned a multipurpose law office to advise and represent people too poor to afford private counsel. They began to realize this vision through the New Haven Community Progress, Incorporated (CPI), a nonprofit antipoverty program established in 1962. CPI, the idea of New Haven's mayor Richard Lee and a handful of his closest advisors, was initially funded by the Ford Foundation. It was the "human renewal" equivalent of the city's earlier "urban renewal" program which in the 1950s had been proclaimed as the nation's most ambitious and successful public housing program.[21] This effort anticipated President Johnson's nationwide War on Poverty by several years, and served as one of the models for the federal effort.

CPI was conceived of as a self-help organization, one which could aid the poor in developing their own institutions and their own means for self-renewal. It was premised on the belief that the neighborhood was the natural unit around which to organize. This idea proved to be congenial with those whose particular interest was the provision of legal services, and one of CPI's first programs was to establish two neighborhood law offices—each staffed by a single recent Yale Law School graduate—housed in space provided by local schools.

From this beginning, the New Haven Legal Assistance Association evolved into an independent nonprofit legal corporation, which at its height had thirty attorneys attached to seven neighborhood offices. It became a model for the massive development of legal services sponsored by the Office of Economic Opportunity (OEO), and later received financing from federal and state antipoverty funds. The one major difference between it and other OEO legal services offices was that the New Haven Legal Assistance Association remained true to its original mission and continued to handle both civil and criminal cases. Unlike most other programs providing defense services for the poor, LAA patterned itself after a private law office. Its offices were located in neighborhoods, far from the courthouse, and it tried to give its clients a choice of attorneys. It allowed attorneys to keep their cases as they moved from one court to another or went up on appeal.

Several years after LAA was established, the state responded

THE PROCESS IS THE PUNISHMENT

to the requirements of *Gideon* v. *Wainwright* by creating a state-wide public defender system for the Circuit Court. Although some fought to keep the criminal defense function in New Haven located in LAA, the legislation as enacted did not provide for LAA to receive state funds for its criminal defense functions.

As the Public Defender's Office grew, state and local support for LAA's criminal staff waned. The drive for statewide organizational symmetry was the primary reason for this policy, although it was reinforced by rising antagonisms toward LAA attorneys. These attorneys were young, aggressive activists, strongly committed to equal opportunity, and independent of constraining local political, economic, and social ties. During their earliest years they were viewed as salaried competitors and did not enjoy good relations with the local bar. Once they were established and practicing in the criminal courts, they alienated both judges and prosecutors, who were unaccustomed to coping with defense attorneys of any kind and were wholly unprepared for the LAA's enthusiastic, vigorous defenses. Not only were the courts now dealing with large numbers of defendants with attorneys, but also these particular attorneys were neither familiar with nor deferential toward the traditional courthouse culture. One survey conducted in 1970 found that judges and prosecutors almost uniformly agreed that LAA attorneys were the most offensive and least effective lawyers appearing in court. However, the same study concluded that LAA attorneys were in fact more successful than either private attorneys or public defenders in obtaining preferred outcomes for their clients.[22]

Whatever the precise reasons, LAA had to make drastic cutbacks. At its height in 1969–1970, there were seven full-time attorneys on its criminal staff, but by late 1972 this number was reduced to just one full- and one part-time attorney. The lower court's Public Defender Office, nonexistent before 1965, expanded to include a staff of five full-time attorneys in 1972. LAA drew many young attorneys to the city who remained to enter private practice after it cut back. A number of them continued to handle criminal cases as private practitioners and special public defenders.

When I conducted my study, the one remaining full-time criminal attorney at LAA was a graduate of Yale College and Harvard Law School. His background and interests were typical of the highly motivated people recruited by LAA in the 1960s who at one time staffed all seven positions. He was the only hometown attorney at LAA, having returned to New Haven after graduation from law school with an intense desire to help poor people. His law school experience shaped his career choice:

Harvard permanently radicalized me. I found some of the biggest schmucks got the best grades and were filtered into the power structure. As a result I got involved in legal aid. I can't stand people being pushed around.

My survey showed that he was highly regarded by prosecutors, judges, and other defense attorneys, and enjoyed a reputation as one of the best criminal lawyers in the city.

In dealing with prosecutors, however, his style, manner, and presentations were only marginally different from those of most other attorneys. Despite LAA's general reputation as a group of litigation-hungry attorneys, he, like all the other lawyers in Common Pleas Court, relied almost entirely on negotiations and arguments laced heavily with appeals to equity and simple justice. Only upon rare occasion had he taken a case through trial, and he was not apologetic about this. The thing he most dreaded, he once said, was a "reformed" legal system with adequate facilities, expanded staff, and a rationalized system of administration for discretion-free "application" of law. He feared that this would result in substantially harsher penalties; in a system which is already overly harsh, he preferred the chaos and confusion which he believed could be manipulated to benefit the accused and avoid the time and expense of more drawn-out, formalized proceedings.

There were some marked differences which distinguished this attorney from other lawyers, especially the PDs. He had a much lighter caseload and was not as harried as they were. In the courtroom he was *always* prepared, while the others were not. He spent more time with his clients immediately after a court appearance, explaining to them what had just transpired and outlining the next step. He was also more vigorous in his efforts to reduce bail. If he was unable to secure a client's release on bail he sought a one- or two-day continuance rather than the standard one or two weeks. These occasional, small (but nevertheless significant) differences set him apart from the public defenders, and for that matter from most private attorneys as well.

Public Defenders At the time of my investigation, there were five attorneys in the Public Defender's Office, a chief and four assistants. Like the prosecutors, they were part of a state-wide system. Until quite recently they were appointed by the state conference of judges and were employees of the state Judicial Department. Despite this formal organization, the appointments of PDs, like those of the prosecutors, are controlled by local resident judges who apply essentially the same considerations in filling both positions. Successful applicants must have a local sponsor to intervene on their behalf. The Chief PD exercises little if any control over the appointments in his office. When an opening occurs as a result of a resignation or expansion, someone may simply show up in his office and announce that he is the new PD, having been interviewed, appointed, and sworn in without the Chief's ever having met him or even known about the appointment.

Each of the five PDs reached his position through a process similar to the one outlined above. The Chief was a middle-aged man who completed law school in the 1940s and spent twenty years with a family-owned business. When it was disbanded in the early 1960s, he took a position as a part-time clerk in the criminal court while he studied for his bar examination. After passing it he was named as the office's first Chief PD. His only experience with criminal law prior to his appointment was the few months he had spent clerking. But he had broad backing for the position, and at various times acknowledged that he was selected over another candidate with several years experience as a criminal defense attorney with LAA because of his support from the area's congressman and his longtime acquaintance with both the city's Democratic and Republican Town Chairmen.

Like the assistant prosecutors, the assistant PDs were young people who returned home after graduation from law school, and received their appointments through family connections. Two came from families who were longtime acquaintances of the resident judges, and another—although he claimed no direct connection—worked for a Connecticut congressman before receiving his appointment. Despite these connections, the assistant PDs had impressive credentials. The Chief graduated from Harvard Law School, two of his assistants graduated from Georgetown and Virginia law schools, and the other two received their legal training at the University of Connecticut.

The attitude of the Chief PD toward his office paralleled that of the Chief Prosecutor. He did not regard himself as an administrator, and preferred handling cases to running an office. Like his counterpart, this attitude stemmed from a combination of personal preference and resignation, a desire to appear in court and a feeling that there was little he could do to improve his office. While he was generally pleased with the quality of his assistants, he was openly critical about the quality of his support staff, and bitterly complained that he had little or no control over the hiring or firing of secretaries, interviewers, and investigators whose appointments were also part of the local system of patronage. He was also concerned about the PDs' heavy caseload, but contended that solutions lay beyond his control. On the whole, however, he felt satisfied with his work, claiming that the attorneys in his office did the best they could under the circumstances, and that on the whole his office provided service comparable to that offered by most private attorneys.

His younger assistants were more critical about the office, and much less content than their counterparts in the Prosecutor's Office down the hall. They complained about the poor quality of facilities and support staff, and the lack of opportunity for interesting legal work. In particular they were concerned about the lack of professional respect they were accorded. They felt that judges and prosecutors misused them, clients took advantage of them, and critics did not understand the obstacles they faced. In fact these problems did seem to exist, problems which were not shared by LAA or by private attorneys. Until the recent move to the new courthouse, the PD facilities were terrible, far worse than those of the Prosecutor's Office or any of the offices of private attorneys I visited. One report described them as follows:

There are four desks for six lawyers; there are four phones with only one outside line; whenever the Xerox machine is being used, the lights have to be turned off so as not to blow a fuse (this problem is often academic because frequently the machine does not even work); the temperature is a study in extremes—the Public Defenders have been observed wiping sweat off their faces with handkerchiefs one day and wearing gloves to keep warm on another. Privacy is some remote theoretical concept. A frequent sight is three lawyers interviewing six people in one room simultaneously.[23]

Midway through my study the PDs moved to more spacious and well-equipped facilities, but this did nothing to improve the quality of their support staff, and the PDs were still laboring with a group of nominal subordinates who had little interest in their jobs, and over whom they exercised little authority.[24]

The lack of resources symbolized the lack of opportunity for interesting legal work and the lack of professional status; these deficiencies are the most bothersome to PDs. Their entire caseload consists of criminal cases in the Court of Common Pleas. If they represent someone whose more serious case is bound over to Superior Court, they lose control of the case as soon as it is bound over. If a case is to be appealed, someone else handles it, which helps explain why there are virtually no appeals from the PD's office. If they discover that one of their clients has related civil legal problems, all they can do is advise him to go see another attorney who is not a public defender. Many perceive this limitation on their functions as evidence of their limited abilities, and PD clients often feel that they are being short-changed. The PD Office in New Haven has the same reputation among jailed inmates that public defender organizations have in most cities, that of second-rate attorneys.[25]

While this criticism is justified, it is overly harsh. PDs face a host of unique problems, not the least of which is the nature of many of their clients. People who seek private counsel express an intensity of interest by paying a fee, but many who have opted for a PD have done so because he is free and they "have nothing to lose from it." *As a group*, PD clients have much less intensity and interest than clients of private lawyers. They may have already learned that nothing too serious is going to happen to them, so that they do not always consider their arrest as serious as do other arrestees or their attorneys. In such cases PDs have trouble getting their clients to show up for court, let alone to meet them for interviews. And such cases constitute a sizable minority of a PD's caseload. The experience is demoralizing, for at a minimum, being an attorney implies having an interested client. If a client does not take his case seriously, how can his attorney? Casualness breeds casualness, and a harried PD can easily mistake a shy or confused client for a disinterested one, or begin to stereotype certain "types" of clients.[26]

Judges and prosecutors also unwittingly contribute to the PDs' second-class status. Because PDs are in court all day long, and handle cases in only one courthouse, it is easy for them to be taken for granted. Court officials expect them to make accommodations, to pass on their cases for the convenience of private attorneys and step aside for more "important" business.

Judges consider PDs interchangeable, and are quite willing to impress them into service to stand in for an absent colleague.

Because others view their work so casually, PDs have come to view it the same way. They see themselves as caught in a dilemma not of their own making, and cope with it in different ways. Some become openly cynical and condescending in their dealings with clients, others struggle to hold back their feelings while they look for other employment. There appears to be a rough relationship between the length of time a PD spends in the office and his degree of cynicism; the longer one has held his position the more likely he is to be openly cynical about it. This pattern is well-known in public defender and legal services circles, and has even been given a name: "burning out."

Comparing Types of Defense Attorneys

New Haven's three types of attorneys are distinguishable from each other in a number of ways. They have different backgrounds, they are recruited in different ways, they have different types of sponsoring organizations, and different kinds of clientele. They also have different reputations.

In an effort to examine this latter difference, I distributed questionnaires to all eight prosecutors and the thirty defense attorneys who represented the greatest number of arrestees in my sample of cases. These thirty-eight people were asked to rate each other on four different questions:

1. Does he take an adversarial stance in handling cases?
2. Does he advance all possible legal arguments in behalf of his clients?
3. Do his clients think he gets good results?
4. Do other lawyers think he gets good results?

Respondents were asked to rate only those attorneys with whom they were familiar and to locate them on a ten-point scale, ranging from "never" (0) to "always" (10). Fifty percent of the attorneys returned completed questionnaires.

The high rate of agreement among attorneys indicated that

there was a well-understood reputational pecking order. Furthermore, the relative positions of attorneys tended to be constant for each of the four scales. If someone was rated high on one of them, then he was likely to be rated high on all the others. There was but one exception to this pattern: almost all the respondents agreed that the clients of PDs rated them lower than they themselves would rate them. While the PDs consistently placed in the bottom quartile on all four items, they hit rock bottom in responses to the third question about clients' assessments. They fared somewhat better on the other three questions, sharing their low status with a handful of private attorneys.

Comparing the three groups of attorneys, present and past LAA attorneys had the highest average composite score, followed by private attorneys, and then by PDs in last place. But average ranking does not tell the entire story. While past and present LAA attorneys tended to cluster at the high end of the continuum and PDs at the bottom, private attorneys ranged widely across the entire spectrum, occupying the four top positions, but also crowding the PDs at the bottom end.

This distribution reinforced what I learned from direct observations and lengthy discussions with defense attorneys, prosecutors, and judges. While the very best of the defense bar are private attorneys, so are the very worst. Most of those held in lowest esteem are solo practitioners engaged in general law practice. They appear in criminal court so infrequently that they have forgotten or have never learned the rudiments of criminal law and the customs of the courthouse. They may come into court trying to bluff, to fake familiarity with the proceedings, making false appeals of warm friendship to prosecutors whom they would not recognize on the street, or frankly confessing ignorance and asking prosecutors for advice as to how to proceed. Prosecutors complain bitterly about these attorneys, feeling that at times they must not only serve as the prosecution but act as the defense as well.

The two types of public defense programs are a study in contrasts. Whereas LAA at its height had seven full-time attorneys serving a criminal court which handled fewer than 7,000 cases per year, at the time of this study the PD's Office consisted of five people who served a court with an annual caseload of over 10,000. Whereas LAA attorneys were located in neighborhood offices and obtained clients at their discretion from those who sought them out, the PDs were for all practical purposes an adjunct of the court, and had to take anyone whom a judge assigned to them. Whereas LAA had a well-stocked library, ample facilities, and a well-trained research and investigative staff, the PDs had cramped quarters, no library to speak of, and an all but nonexistent research and investigative staff. Whereas LAA was wholly free from the pressures of patronage, the PD's Office was part and parcel of the patronage system. Whereas LAA recruited attorneys from all over the country, the PD's Office had to accept whomever the local party organization and judges sent to it. Those who loafed at LAA did not have their contracts renewed, but no one in the PD's Office was ever fired. Whereas LAA radiated a spirit of ebullience and maintained a vigorous *esprit d' corps*, the PD's Office cast a pall of discouragement and disappointment.

It is not clear how important these dramatic differences are in accounting for variations in *actual* outcomes. Judgments on ability and interest focus on marginal differences. They may be based on an assessment of the rare and the exceptional rather than the typical or the routine. Such differences in ability and interest are real, but situations which present the opportunity for them to surface and make a difference occur only occasionally. For example, some defense attorneys are widely respected for their ability to keep clients from receiving jail sentences. But only a small handful of those convicted clients receive jail terms, and the talents of these exceptional attorneys are likely to be decisive in only a small number of borderline cases. Other attorneys are known for the frequency with which they file motions, but then very few motions are filed by anyone. The great majority of cases is handled according to a well-established routine, one which significantly blunts the importance of differences in personality, style, and interest. What holds for defense attorneys also applies to judges, prosecutors, and defendants. In short, norms of the courthouse workgroup and environmental factors are more important in accounting for practices in the courtroom than even the most striking differences among individual participants. I will return to this problem in chapter five, in which I will relate the characteristics of individual defense attorneys to outcomes at sentence and adjudication.

CHAPTER 4

Supportive Figures

Introduction

The court is a large and diffuse institution with a high degree of specialization and division of labor. Whenever a person is arrested, a dozen or so people besides the judge, prosecutor, and defense attorney are likely to shape the proceedings and affect the outcome. While the due process and plea bargain models focus on these three figures, the Pretrial Process Model emphasizes the decisions of a host of other, less visible people: bail commissioners, bondsmen, counselors, screeners, clerks, stenographers, sheriffs, investigators, and secretaries. These people decide on pretrial release, supply information to prosecutors, judges, and defense attorneys, and often dispense advice to arrestees which is unquestioningly followed. They facilitate the smooth functioning of an otherwise confusing and chaotic court. In short, these officials administer small doses of justice in their own right. Consequently, it is important to know who these people are and what they do.

Although most of the dozen or so people in these auxiliary positions might be characterized as functionaries or viewed simply as clerks—and some, like the bail bondsmen, are not even court officials—all occupy strategic positions in the court and significantly affect its processes. Several of them serve in "intake" positions, so that they define issues and label defendants for all those who subsequently handle them. Others have limited discretion to dispense sanctions in ways that have significant consequences at later stages of the process. Because the process is so informal and depends so heavily on oral communications, decisions made by the principal actors in the process—the judge, prosecutor, and defense attorney—are based heavily on the impressions, information, and recommendations passed on by these people. The sanctions imposed on defendants, particularly those dispensed during the pretrial process, are heavily influenced by these people's initial impressions. In turn, their desire to tailor jobs to fit their own interests and to administer their own sense of rough justice determine how they handle their responsibilities. In order to understand the organization and informal process of sanctioning in the Court of Common Pleas, we must look at these people's formal duties and how they are organized, what informal powers they have assumed, and how they are recruited.

These secondary officials can be grouped into three categories in more or less descending order of their importance to the principal participants in the criminal court system: those whose formal roles involve them in the early stages of pretrial release; those involved in the pretrial diversion programs; and those involved in the performance of auxiliary and administrative functions for the normal operation of the court and the officials in the primary workgroup. I qualified this ordering with "more or less" for two reasons. First, some whose formal powers may be severely limited or appear to be minimal and purely administrative can and often do exercise considerable informal powers that make them quite important. Conversely, some who appear to have considerable formal power exercise little if any actual power, and at times they are all but invisible in the process. Second, some of these officials are important only occasionally, when they exercise control over or decline to exercise control over certain types of cases that fall within their jurisdiction.

95

Pretrial Release Specialists

Bail Bondsmen

Most discussions of criminal courts give only cursory attention to bail bondsmen, presumably because they are peripheral figures who operate on the fringes of the criminal justice system, passively waiting in the wings to bail out those whom the criminal courts send their way. This is not an accurate characterization of their functions. In fact, they are active participants in the criminal process; but they have become so much a part of the landscape and their functions have become so familiar and accepted that they are taken for granted, and because they are taken for granted they are ignored.

Bondsmen help create norms, define operations, and structure alternatives in the court system. They do so because they want to perpetuate themselves, to remain in a low-risk, high-return business. In order to maintain themselves they perform substantial and useful services for the court and actively work with legislatures. Because they are active in promoting their own interests, they share responsibility for perpetuating the bail bonding system, a system which in effect places unneeded fines on a substantial portion of the criminally accused, fines which are levied against those who are eventually pronounced innocent as well as those who are found guilty. As we shall see, these fines loom very large in the eyes of the accused and usually overshadow the fines collected by the court as formal sentences.

While there is a sparse literature on the theory and practice of bail administration, there has been virtually no scholarly interest in the bail bondsman.[1] What few accounts there are tend to spring from the reformer's impulse to expose the corrupt practices of the bondsman as "an unappealing and useless member of society who lives on the law's inadequacy and his fellow man's troubles."[2] This neglect and perfunctory dismissal cannot be attributed to the bondsman's lack of importance. Despite momentum for bail reform over the past two decades, money bond remains a major condition of pretrial release, and bail bondsmen remain securely wedged between the court and the accused. It is because of this general neglect and their continuing importance that I deal with bail bondsmen at some length here.[3]

Although some claim that professional bondsmen are at best marginal businessmen and not well-organized,[4] it is clear that they benefit from a healthy business climate and exceedingly advantageous laws. In fact, a good portion of the professional bondsmen operate at or near their capacity.[5] There is little competition among them, since each tends to have his own territory carved out and can invoke a variety of sanctions to guard it effectively. Furthermore, the law requires bondsmen to possess a minimum of $15,000 in assets—and given the conservative appraising standards used by the state police, the face value of the assets is around twice this amount—which discourages entrepreneurs with limited capital.

Despite a host of bail reform legislation during the past decade, Connecticut law continues to preserve the interests of bondsmen. During the late 1960s, when the state assembly was considering bail reform legislation, several bondsmen in the state organized a lobbying effort and pooled their resources to retain a lobbyist. While it is impossible to assess the precise impact of this effort, bondsmen were not adversely affected by the resulting legislation which promoted release on recognizance (ROR) for those arrestees who previously had been released on low bonds. Some of the bondsmen even professed to applaud this expansion of ROR, claiming that there is too little profit in small bonds to make them worthwhile. But a 1976 proposal in the state legislature to introduce more substantial bail reform and to institutionalize a court-administered 10 percent bond program similar to those in several other states was actively opposed by many of the state's bondsmen and was killed in

97

committee. If it had been adopted, this proposal would have replaced the surety system with a 10-percent cash deposit system, whereby the accused could post a returnable deposit with the court rather than pay the same amount to a bondsman. Had this proposal passed, it could have put bondsmen out of business.

Bondsmen actively watch and react to administrative directives which affect their business. During the period my investigation was underway, the new state administrative judge for the Court of Common Pleas issued a directive which appeared to end the practice of "compromising" bonds by permitting bondsmen to settle forfeited bonds at less than their face value. The judge's initial memo was greeted with substantial opposition from bondsmen who urged prosecutors to intercede on their behalf with the judge. Several months later the judge issued a much toned-down clarification of his original memo, and prosecutors generally agreed not to issue any new policies instituting tighter control over compromises.

A bondsman needs little else besides initial capital to go into business. Most operate out of their homes or from small offices, or in some cases share office space with attorneys. While attorneys cannot advertise, bondsmen can, and the arrangement between them is mutually convenient. But the bondsman's real workplace is the courthouse. Bondsmen often appropriate space in a prosecutor's, a public defender's, or even a judge's office, and at times transact business from the clerk's table in the courtroom while court is in session.

Connecticut statutes restrict the fee or commission which a professional bondsman may charge; the limits are as follows: no more than $20 for the amount of bail furnished up to $300; not more than 7 percent of the amount furnished for amounts between $300 and $5,000, and not more than 5 percent of the amount on sums in excess of $5,000.[6] Insurance bondsmen may charge a flat 10-percent fee for bonds of any amount, with the company's share being about 3 percent and the bondsman-agent's fee 7 percent. Since several bondsmen do business as both professional and insurance bondsmen, at times there is an incentive for them to write insurance bonds in the larger amounts; despite the fee-sharing they are still able to make more money than if they handled the bond themselves.[7] Professional bondsmen claim that at times they accept commissions at less than the maximum rate, but some observers suggest that bondsmen have a strong incentive to report only a portion of their actual fee in order to understate their income for tax purposes.[8] Although no one knows the extent to which they actually do this, we do know that three bondsmen were suspended in the early 1970s after they were convicted for income tax evasion.[9] This practice may be particularly easy because the state agency which is supposed to regulate bondsmen is understaffed. By its own admission it is unable to audit bondsmen's financial reports and relies instead on self-reporting.

Although it is impossible for a bondsman to predict how long his money will be tied up in any particular bond, one study estimates that bond money is tied up for an average of ninety-five days,[10] and the data I collected show it to be much less for the lower courts.[11] An aggressive bondsman who regularly operates near maximum capacity may be able to turn his money over three to four or more times a year. Based on an average of 6 percent per bond and an ability to turn money around three to four times a year, a bondsman could gross from $18,000 to $24,000 for every $100,000 in assets posted as collateral.[12] This return would be increased by whatever additional income these assets might produce as investments in real estate, stocks, or savings certificates. In 1975, several bondsmen in the state, including one in New Haven, had licensed assets of over $300,000.

The bond business is relatively risk-free, can operate on a low overhead, and can be pursued on a part-time basis. The theory of suretyship holds that the bondsman has a direct financial incentive to see that the defendant appears in court, and

99

that if he fails to appear the bondsman must assume liability for him. But Connecticut law modifies this liability by providing that a bondsman can "compromise" with the prosecutor on the actual amount to be forfeited to the court in case of nonappearance. That is, the full value of the bond need not be paid, and in Connecticut it is standard practice to compromise bonds for around fifty to sixty cents on the dollar and often much less. Judges can also remit forfeiture of all or part of the bond, and at times do so.

In addition to compromise, there are other devices which relieve the bondsman of his liabilities if his client disappears. Some prosecutors and judges are quite willing to grant continuances when a bondsman's client fails to appear in court. Rather than call for a bond forfeiture or issue a warrant for rearrest, they hope that the bondsman will eventually be able to retrieve his client and secure his presence in court. Another device which may preserve more dignity in the open courtroom yet accomplish the same end is for the judge to issue a bond forfeiture but stay its execution pending the bondsman's effort to secure appearance. This allows the bond to be reinstated easily if and when the defendant eventually appears, at which time the bondsman may wish to withdraw from the case. Or the court may allow a bondsman to withdraw from a case and hence remove his liability for a client who has failed to appear. Some bondsmen have even successfully petitioned the court to reduce bond for their client who has failed to appear!

These devices allow the bondsman's business to remain financially attractive; they can collect commissions on all the bonds they write, avoid liability for most defendants who fail to appear, or make good on only a portion of the face value of bonds of those for whom they remain liable. While the initial failure-to-appear rate ranges between 10 and 15 percent in the lower courts, it is estimated that bondsmen eventually forfeit only about 3 percent of their gross commissions, and even this figure must be reduced by the amount that bondsmen are in turn reimbursed by their client's cosureties, an amount which may cut their actual losses in half.[13]

These practices belie the stereotype of a bondsman as a ruthless one-man police force who uses strong-arm tactics to assure his clients' appearance in court. These men operate relatively risk-free businesses; their occasional "losses" are met with sympathy from the court, and they can easily absorb the occasional loss that a nonappearance causes. The key to success in this business lies not so much in the employment of threats and strong-arm tactics to assure appearances, as it does in fostering friendly relationships with prosecutors and judges so that they will grant considerations when one's clients fail to appear.

As of 1975 there were four licensed professional bondsmen active in the New Haven area. Two of them were joined together in a loose partnership, which handled about 80 percent of the bonding business in the Court of Common Pleas. Together (and with an inactive third partner) they had posted assets of $435,000, and one of them also wrote bonds for an insurance company. In effect they had an almost unlimited ability to write bonds.

A third bondsman had posted assets of $85,000 and operated by himself. The other active bondsman was a salaried employee of the Wider City Parish Bonding Program, a nonprofit enterprise with posted assets of $40,000, which were to be used to serve the needs of minority-group arrestees charged with minor offenses and unable to post low bonds. The size of the licensed assets of these three enterprises hints at the proportion of business each of them did, although the first group did an even greater share of the business because it was much more aggressive, it was large enough to take more risks, and as we will see, it had securely established its presence in the court.

Despite some tension, there was no open hostility among the bondsmen, perhaps because there was little real competition among them. With his limited assets the small private bondsman could not afford to take many risks and was extremely cautious.

He accepted only those clients who were well-established in the community, had readily available collateral, and could produce financially secure cosigners. The salaried nonprofit bondsman was limited to low bonds and directed his efforts toward people of limited means, which often meant people from financially insecure families whose business the other bondsmen spurned. Rather than fierce competition, an informal division of labor had emerged, and bondsmen at times referred business to each other.

But such cooperation had its limits. When an occasional bondsman from out-of-town handled business in New Haven, he was not apt to be greeted with tolerance from local bondsmen, nor with understanding by the Prosecutor's Office. If one of his clients failed to appear in court, he was not always able to obtain a continuance or stay the execution of a bond forfeiture. And if eventually he was forced to forfeit a bond, he was probably not able to obtain as substantial a compromise rate as the local bondsmen. Prosecutors were open about their preferential treatment of local bondsmen, claiming that their credibility was established. This attitude seemed to prevail statewide, and effectively discouraged bondsmen from expanding their business into more than one area.

Because they handled 80 percent of the bail bond business in New Haven, the two "partners" were often thought of as the only bondsmen by many of the attorneys and staff around the courthouse. Like Hershey, Kleenex, and Coca-Cola, their names were virtually synonymous with their product. They maintained an office a few doors down from the courthouse, but did most of their business from a desk in the Public Defender's Office or while court was in session from a seat at the clerk's table immediately in front of the judge. Occasionally they transacted business in this location, bailing out defendants who had just been arraigned and pocketing the cash they had just received as a fee.

During the course of my study, these two bondsmen were in

constant motion in the courtroom, generating an aura of nervous energy as they darted about, keeping up with their various concerns, motioning to their clients waiting in the gallery to step forward, checking their own list of clients against the court calendar, and receiving new clients directed their way by the court personnel. They kept in contact with each other and their offices by means of penlight-sized beepers, and frequently rushed out of the courtroom to answer calls. All this activity conveyed a sense of their importance and efficiency, and they enjoyed a reputation based on these qualities with most of the city's defense attorneys and the court officials.

These bondsmen's tasks in the courtroom were not restricted to securing the appearance of their clients and receiving new business. The bondsmen often responded to inquiries from confused arrestees who wanted to know what was going to happen to them, and answered questions from prosecutors who wanted to know the whereabouts of a particular defense attorney or defendant. If a bondsman's client was not in court when his case was called, the bondsman would approach the bench and quietly prevail upon the prosecutor and judge to pass over the case until he could be located.

Judges and prosecutors were usually obliging, but some were less cooperative than others, particularly if they disliked the attorney whom the bondsman was representing, if the defendant had a history of nonappearance, or if the bond was several thousand dollars. In such instances the judge might insist on a bond forfeiture, although he almost always would agree to stay its execution to give the bondsman an opportunity to locate his client. This produced much the same result as a continuance; if the defendant was eventually found, then the order was vacated.

Rarely does a person out on bond attempt to flee the court's jurisdiction to avoid prosecution. Nonappearance is typically the result of a mistake, confusion, or simply lack of concern. Occasionally it is a convenient way to pay a fine.[14] Recognizing this, the prosecutors and judges are relatively tolerant of those who fail to appear, and grant bondsmen time to get defendants into court. And the bondsmen usually deliver.

Occasionally a defendant cannot be found, either because he has dropped out of sight completely or has simply moved to another state. This makes retrieval a complicated and expensive affair, and no one bothers with it if the charges are not serious. In such situations bondsmen are liable for the full value of the bond, but in practice they rarely pay full value. Some "withdraw" from the case. A bond is a private contract between the bondsman and his client, and if for any reason a bondsman does not want to continue to serve as a person's surety, he may appear in court with that person and announce his decision to withdraw, at which time the court must reimpose its original decision on release. Although withdrawal is supposed to take place in the presence of the accused, some of the friendlier prosecutors and judges are at times willing to allow a bondsman to withdraw from a case in the absence of his client, so that the bondsmen can escape all liability after it is obvious the client will not appear.

There are other ways to escape liability for nonappearances. Bondsmen can occasionally obtain nolles for missing clients. One defense attorney recalled such an instance in which he was a passive participant:

I had a case, a man from [out of state], who had a $2000 bond. He went back to his home and [the bondsman] was going to be out $2000. I was in chambers of Judge ——— and a prosecutor talking about another case when the judge suggested that the case be nolled, even though my client wasn't present. I said I wouldn't participate in the decision, although I wouldn't object to it either. . . . It was the funniest thing. Later the prosecutor called the case in court, and no one appeared before the bench, and then he announced he was going to nolle the case.

While technically legal, these devices for escaping liability for nonappearance actually cancel the wager after the hand has been played and the gamble lost.

More subtle ways of reducing the bondsman's liabilities for failures to appear are used much more frequently. A judge may substitute a substantially lower bond for the one in effect at the time of nonappearance. For instance, if a person with a $500 bond disappears, the judge may oblige the bondsman by reducing the bond to $50 or $25, an amount which the bondsman— or perhaps a cosigner—then forfeits to the court. Bondsmen have argued that their liability for clients who fail to appear should not exceed the amount of the fine they would receive if convicted. Perversely appealing, this logic has gained some adherents among prosecutors and judges, who at times cited it when they lowered bonds. But this same logic has not extended to benefit the defendants themselves. Prosecutors and judges see no incongruity in setting bond at $500 for cases in which the defendant is likely to receive a suspended sentence or a fine of $25 or $50.[15]

But the most common way to reduce the liability from bond forfeitures is by compromise. Connecticut law provides that "The attorney for the state . . . may compromise and settle bonds to the state after forfeiture . . ."[16] and it is standard practice in all the state's courts for bondsmen to be relieved of at least a portion of their liabilities in this manner. This practice is well institutionalized in New Haven's lower court. When bond forfeitures are ordered, they are allowed to remain dormant for periods of up to several months in hopes that the accused will eventually show up and the bondsman will be relieved of his obligation. Every few months the Chief Prosecutor will call the bondsman in and reduce "forfeitures for some bondsmen by as much as 75%."[17]

Judges and prosecutors are willing to go to great lengths to avoid forfeiture and to set aside forfeitures if the accused is found, so that the number of executed orders is relatively small, and the bondsmen's losses are minimal.[18] These losses are cut still further by the fictions sometimes devised to eliminate them, by the bondsmen's ability to recoup some of their money from the accused's cosigners, and through the practice of compromising. The risk for bondsmen appears to be so low that there is little need for them to expend resources to engage in strong-arm tactics or actively round up missing clients. Indeed, the process is flexible enough so that bondsmen do not have to be very aggressive in notifying their clients about their court dates. They simply wait to see who does not appear in court, then make an effort to round up the laggards.

Although these practices seem to undercut incentives for bondsmen to secure the appearance of their clients, both prosecutors and defense attorneys argue that insisting on full liability for nonappearance would make bondsmen more selective, and lead to an increase in the number of defendants in pretrial detention. Furthermore, prosecutors point out, compromising is analogous to "settling" in civil disputes, a practice deemed reasonable because it saves the state the costs of obtaining a civil judgment against the bondsman.

The practice of reducing liability, then, is a complicated system of exchange among the bondsmen and the judges, prosecutors, defense attorneys, and various auxiliary court personnel, rooted in self-interest and sealed in friendship, small favors, and flattery. Bondsmen find it advantageous to remain on the good side of the police who can direct business their way, and to ingratiate themselves with judges and prosecutors who can pass cases, grant continuances, stay bond forfeitures, and facilitate reductions through compromises. Defense attorneys do not object because these practices benefit their clients.

Why do all these people help the bondsmen? Why, despite the theory of bail, can bondsmen run a low-risk business, largely by getting other people to help them? The answer is that bondsmen provide desired services for these people. In New Haven I found the two busiest bondsmen to be gregarious and friendly, always ready with a friendly word and a pleasant smile. They frequently took court personnel to lunch, occasionally threw parties for the court staff and prosecutors, and regularly picked up the tab at a local bar on Friday afternoons. They also dispensed holiday presents and tickets to local sporting events to court personnel, prosecutors, some judges, and defense attorneys. One judge, when he sat in New Haven, was often driven to court by one of them.

These two bondsmen also contributed to the efficient operation of the court. Indeed, but for them the rapid-paced processes in the courtroom might have ground to a halt, an unpleasant thought for court officials who were anxious to get through the day as early as possible. Prosecutors, judges, and defense attorneys turned to these bondsmen for answers as to the whereabouts of other attorneys and defendants, which they knew because they were constantly moving about the courthouse during the day. A bondsman sometimes asked a prosecutor to delay calling a case because the defense attorney was still arguing a motion in another case across the street, or informed the court that an attorney or his client was home in bed with the flu. At least one defense attorney regularly relied on the bondsmen to keep tabs on his clients who were out on bail, to remind them of their court appearance dates, and to give them instructions as to which courtroom they should appear in. The two bondsmen also apparently extended favors to the police by bailing out risky persons whom the police were using as informants, and by refusing to write bonds for others whom the prosecutor or police wanted to summarily punish.

They also served as sources of information and at times as agents for arrestees without attorneys. As one prosecutor noted, "Bondsmen will frequently approach us and ask us to nolle a case or to 'take care of this guy.' Often these are their clients, but sometimes they are not. He's just around and listens to the guy's story and comes over to talk to us." Another prosecutor commenting on one of the bondsmen noted that "————'s good. He frequently comes back here and plea bargains for his clients. He does it a lot for defendants without attorneys and sometimes even for cases where PDs are appointed. He is pretty successful, and does a good job for his clients."

In contrast to the popular image of the bondsman as a pariah, a social outcast who sits stonefaced raking in money through a window gate, exploiting the human misery all around him, the two major bondsmen in New Haven were both naturally ebullient and gregarious men who obviously enjoyed their work and their association with the courtroom personnel, and in turn received friendship and respect from court personnel and criminal defendants, clients and nonclients alike. Their personalities served them well, for the bondsman's business involves a good deal of public relations and goodwill gestures. It is no small wonder that many spectators sitting in the gallery had the impression that these two busy men dressed in expensive suits, actively and authoritatively moving about the front of the courtroom, were important public officials. Unofficially, they were.

Bail Commissioners

Perhaps because the bail bondsmen have been so active, the Connecticut Bail Commission has been terribly moribund. Despite the boldness of the Bail Reform Act of 1967—hailed as one of the most liberal and thoughtful pretrial release statutes in the country—its primary creation, the Bail Commission has remained on the periphery of the pretrial release process.[19] In New Haven during my study bail commissioners were all but invisible.

The statute places an explicit burden on officials to state reasons whenever the accused is not released on his own recognizance, requires that conditions of release be related to the accused's ties to the local community, and creates an elaborate plan for pretrial release. Under the statute police officers in charge of detention facilities can initially set the conditions of release,[20] and if they do not immediately release the accused, an independent review by a bail commissioner is required. According to the statute the bail commissioner

shall be available at all times in each circuit to facilitate the prompt release of any person, regardless of his financial resources, pending final disposition of his case, unless custody is necessary to provide reasonable assurance of his appearance in court.[21]

If the arrestee is not released prior to arraignment, the bail commissioners are to be present in court, "to make recommendations on request of any judge, concerning the terms and conditions of release of arrested persons from custody . . ."[22]

The Connecticut Bail Commission, created by the second Bail Reform Act of 1967, was modeled after a widely heralded pretrial release experiment conducted by the Vera Institute in New York City, a program in which a "disinterested" third party based recommendations for release on the accused's ties to the community.[23] It was established to mitigate the hardships of obtaining money for bail, and to counterbalance the power of the police who many thought could not be relied upon to set *minimal* conditions for release.

The Commission also created a windfall of patronage positions for local party leaders. Like appointments to other positions in the nominally state-run court structure, appointments to these positions are controlled neither by the Judicial Department nor by the Chief Bail Commissioner, but by local resident judges and political leaders. One official of the Judicial Department recalls the appointment of the Commission's sixty bail commissioners:

. . . everyone who had a friend or a relative jumped on the big patronage bonanza. It was a wild thing to see, everybody jumping aboard. Since the salaries were pretty low, and no one really cared about getting arrestees out of pretrial detention anyway, nepotism ran wild. This seemed to be facilitated because there were no qualifications; virtually anyone could become a bail commissioner.

In a system steeped in a tradition of patronage, the Bail Commission resulted in so many "no-show" positions that it became a minor scandal, and two years after its creation the state assembly severely cut it back, from sixty to twenty-five commissioners, the level at which it has remained.

At the time of my study, the New Haven Court of Common

Pleas had two full-time bail commissioners assigned to it, one a retired police officer long active in Republican party affairs, the other a brother of a former mayoral candidate in New Haven, himself a low-level activist in the city's Democratic party organization. One of them was supposed to be available at the jail during late evening and night hours to review the conditions of those not immediately released by the police. The other was supposed to be present in court while it was in session in order to interview arrestees brought in directly, and to make recommendations to the judge on those not released before arraignment. This commissioner was also expected to keep a record of defendants who failed to appear in court and to send warning notices to them.

Except for the morning hours in court, both bail commissioners were all but invisible. Most pretrial release decisions immediately following arrest were made by the police, so that the commissioner assigned to the night shift had little to do and felt little need even to be present at "the lockup." Occasionally he dropped in at the detention facility for a few minutes around 10:30 P.M., but this was before most of the night's arrests occurred. Even then he rarely interviewed the arrestees. Instead he relied on police officers to complete the interview forms, simply placing his signature above theirs without bothering to search for additional information or complete the form. He rarely changed the amount of bond set by the police. Since the police officers were relatively liberal in their release policies, he considered this practice quite defensible. Those who were not released were being held for good reason, he claimed, and would be taken care of the next morning in court by the judge and the day-shift bail commissioner.

In fact, however, the day shift commissioner's morning "interviews" consisted of little more than stopping by the lockup to retrieve the interview forms which had accumulated over the night. Like his night counterpart, the "day man" simply put his signature above the police officer's, rarely talking to the arrestees or altering the bond amounts the officer had established.

For all practical purposes, the elaborate two-step process envisioned in the legislation—initial release conditions set by the police which are then reviewed more carefully by a "disinterested" bail commissioner—had been telescoped into a one-step process, with the primary release agents being the police and any additional review taking place in open court with a prosecutor or judge. The bail commissioner merely sat in court and signed, sealed, and mailed mimeographed letters of warning to defendants who did not appear.

The Bail Commission has not had much of an impact in New Haven. Those who are released without bond are almost always released by the police at the lockup; the balance of the arrestees remain in police custody until their appearance in court, where the prosecutor and judge rely on background information supplied by the police.

Pretrial Service Representatives

Many people view at least some criminal offenders as sick, troubled, or in need of "help" rather than adjudication and punishment, and the courts have instituted a host of "treatment" agencies to supplement or replace traditional methods of adjudication. Counselors for the Family Relations Office, the Pretrial Diversion Program, and various drug treatment programs all share this "treatment" perspective of the criminal process and are part of the extended courthouse workgroup. These officials consider those whom they admit into their programs "not really criminals," but rather people with social problems in need of help. Although the specific charges against his clients vary, the Family Relations Officer (FRO) specializes in domestic—usually husband/wife, sometimes parent/child—disputes referred to him by the court. The Diversion Program handles people charged with a host of different offenses, and is aimed at young and first-time offenders. If the accused satisfies certain conditions established by these alternative agencies, then the prosecutor is likely to drop charges against him. Those administering the drug programs, however, prefer to have their clients sentenced and paroled into their custody. Although they also consider their clients "sick," and hold to a "treatment" philosophy, drug program counselors prefer to have the threat of immediate incarceration to dangle over the heads of uncooperative clients.

Pretrial Diversion Program

The pretrial diversion program is supported on a year-to-year basis by funds made available under a grant from the Law Enforcement Assistance Administration (LEAA). Its objective is to divert from the criminal process young people with no serious record of prior arrests who are charged with relatively minor offenses. A screener for the program reviews the papers on all incoming cases, and contacts arrestees who seem to meet initial eligibility requirements. If the arrestee expresses an interest in participation, then the program's representative will contact the prosecutor and defense attorney (if any), and request a continuance until a full interview can take place. If the case is not too serious—and the representative can usually anticipate the prosecutor's decision—then the prosecutor will usually agree.

The philosophy of this program is based upon a version of the "labeling theory" of deviancy; its directors and staff of several counselors feel that a record of conviction is likely to have a stigmatizing effect which increases rather than decreases chances of future criminal activity. The program is relatively well-accepted by the prosecutors, who agree with its philosophy, although they are not as willing to extend it as broadly as the program staff. Prosecutors view the program as a way of handling some of their less serious cases, cases in which they do not want to press for a conviction, but ones for which some type of sanction seems appropriate.

Although requirements for participation are liberal, and roughly three out of four of all defendants brought into the court meet them, only about 2 or 3 percent of all defendants do in fact participate. The prosecutor prohibits a number of eligible and willing potential participants from entering the program, but there are a variety of other reasons that keep people from using this seemingly attractive way of avoiding a record of conviction. These will be explored in chapter seven.

Family Relations Officer

The Family Relations Officer (FRO) provides another non-traditional diversion alternative. A great many cases coming into the court involve incidents stemming from domestic disputes, either between husband and wife or parent and child. Although most such cases involve charges of disorderly conduct, breach of peace, or minor assault stemming from a physical confrontation between family members, some involve nonsupport, larceny, assault to a nonfamily member, or property damage outside the home. Either party in a case can ask the judge to defer action on charges and refer the case to the FRO, although the prosecutor, often upon the prior informal request of a defense attorney, usually suggests this course of action. Judges routinely grant the request.

Like the defendant whose case is diverted, the person referred to the FRO has his or her case continued for a period of up to several weeks, during which time the FRO will meet with the accused and members of his or her family in order to explore the basis of their conflict. At times this counseling is little more than one brief meeting at which the embarrassed spouses, already reconciled, indicate they want to drop charges. In these situations, the case is disposed of at first appearance, thereby saving all parties—the complainant, the defendant, and the court—the costs of a second court appearance. In other situations the FRO might put the family in touch with programs for drug addiction, alcoholism, or mental health, or with the state welfare or employment office, and then informally monitor the family for a short period. At times he may negotiate arrangements for a husband to resume support payments. As with the diversion program, if the FRO indicates at a second appearance that the defendants are "making progress" or trying to "straighten out their lives," the prosecutor may nolle the case or take this into consideration and recommend a lighter sentence. Unlike the pretrial diversion program, a substantial number of cases are directed to the FRO, probably 10 percent or more of all cases in the court.

Drug Treatment Representatives

The size and number of drug treatment programs depend largely upon the availability of federal money to run them. In the early and mid-1960s, when federal social welfare programs were in their heyday, New Haven, like many other urban centers, experienced a "drug epidemic," and with it came not only a special police narcotics squad, but also a proliferation of drug treatment programs. The 1970s saw a decline of interest in the drug "problem," stemming in part from a sense of futility in trying to "cure" it, as well as from greater tolerance for drug use and disenchantment with federal social welfare programs in general. Although heroin is still plentiful in New Haven, its presence is no longer considered a crisis, and the number of drug arrests has shrunk. But there are still several drug treatment programs in the city.

Rather than turning away applicants as they once did, they now vie with each other for those few defendants eligible and interested in their programs. Still, they prefer to accept as clients those who have been convicted and sent to them as a condition of probation. They have found, through long experience, that the threat of a jail sentence is helpful in securing a patient's "cooperation" and continued participation. In organizations whose funds depend in large part upon the number of *successful* participants, this sort of threat has proven to be an effective if not ideal way to maintain high "success" rates (usually defined in terms of participation for a specified length of time).

Auxiliary Personnel

In addition to the officials already discussed, there are a number of people who provide a host of support services for the court, people who occupy minor but usually necessary roles in the courthouse. They also perform a host of informal functions that make them vital to the smooth functioning of the court. Together they form an elaborate and highly complex and efficient communications system, one which allows more important and busier officials to use their time efficiently. They transmit important information to the accused, their friends, and family members. They reflect and represent the interests of the larger environment, providing a police presence in the courtroom and expressing the indignation and sympathy of the community at large as they come into contact with individual defendants. They are part and parcel of the patronage system, binding each other and other members of the court system to a common organization, which is often reinforced by ethnic and family ties. Some are conspicuous for what they do *not* do, secure in their positions because of patronage, not performance.

The collective portrait of the important officials in the courthouse is almost entirely white, in stark contrast to the many brown and black faces of those who appear before them. While this contrast is rarely spoken about, it goes unnoticed by no one.

Police Liaison Officer and Attending Officer

Police officers assigned to the court maintain custody of detainees who are making appearances. They keep their charges in the lockup in the basement of the courthouse and bring them up to appear in court for arraignment or their hearings. They also take custody of defendants sentenced to a term in jail for eventual delivery to the state-run correctional center. In addition, they are responsible for gathering information for Police Department files. They record the disposition of each case on a copy of the daily calendar and forward it to the Department's Records' Division, a task they perform casually and often inaccurately.

Like the bailiffs, these officers also have a lot of spare time and are willing to chat with defendants, answer their questions, and direct them to court officials and bondsmen. At times they bring defendants without attorneys to a prosecutor and act as his spokesman for claims of innocence or mistaken identity. Although it is reputed that the police officers sometimes obtain clients for private attorneys in town, the officers steadfastly deny it. Even if this practice does take place, it can happen only once in a very long while, since defendants who are not released on their own recognizance or post bond before the morning session of court are not likely to be able to afford private counsel. However, it is not at all uncommon for police officers to contact bondsmen for detainees in the lockup, and at least one bondsman expressed resentment at what he felt was their favoritism toward another.

Police in New Haven do not routinely appear at arraignments; and since there are few concerted investigations by the Prosecutor's Office, the little communication that does take place between the police and the Prosecutor's Office is usually over the telephone or occasionally in a brief conference out of court. But the Police Department does not altogether ignore what goes on in court, and the Department's permanent Court Liaison Officer occasionally affects the nature of dispositions. If the arrested person is someone whom the Department has been after for some time, its interest in securing a conviction will be transmitted to the prosecutors by the Court Liaison Officer. If the defendant is a police informer, this will also be communicated to the prosecutor, who may oblige with a low bond or a recommendation for a light sentence. Or, if the accused is a friend of an officer, or a friend of a friend, this information might be transmitted along with the request to "go easy on him."

Police are most concerned about charges of resisting arrest or assaulting a police officer. Although prosecutors privately acknowledge that policemen have a propensity to be overly liberal with such charges, they are reluctant to nolle them cavalierly. While none of these charges in my sample resulted in a conviction, they almost invariably meant that the prosecutor would insist on a guilty plea to the original charge which had provoked the arrest, and the presence of the police officer helped ensure this.

In general, the police are not deeply concerned with the outcome of their arrests in the lower court. In many instances they feel the purpose of intervention was served by the arrest itself. In others they see the bond—which they control to a large extent—as adequate punishment. Still, New Haven police share the feeling with police in a great many other communities that the courts are too lenient and do not back them up. But they seem to have responded to this situation by becoming cynical rather than by pressuring the Prosecutor's Office to adopt a tougher stance.[24]

Clerks and Stenographers

The Court of Common Pleas has a number of clerks and stenographers. When court is in session, each courtroom is required to have a clerk call the calendar, update the defendants' files, and maintain control of the court's records, and each courtroom must also have a stenographer recording the formal proceedings. In addition, there are a number of file clerks who maintain the court's files, receive payments for fines, and prepare daily calendars for the several courtrooms.

Although stenographers must be skilled in rapidly transcribing conversation, many of the clerkships require no specialized training at all, and many positions are filled through the patronage system. The son-in-law of the Chief Clerk of the statewide court system was for a time during this study the Presiding Clerk of the New Haven court, and his son worked there during one summer. The mayor's wife was a file clerk in the main office, and many other clerks have intertwining family connections with other court employees, public officials, or active members of the local Democratic political organization.

Despite the impression the title conveys, clerks, and particularly the Chief Clerk, can be persons of some importance. By tradition the Chief Clerkship has always been filled by someone with a law degree, and it can, in New Haven at least, be a stepping stone to advancement in the court system. Younger attorneys waiting for positions in the Prosecutor's Office to open up often receive appointments as clerks, which gives them exposure to and familiarity with courtroom routines. Both the Chief Prosecutor and Chief Public Defender at the time of my study began as part-time clerks before stepping up to their respective offices.

Despite the fact that clerks are employees of the state judicial department and formally responsible to the judiciary, they are for all practical purposes arms of the Prosecutor's Office. Prosecutors maintain no separate files and treat the court's records as if they were their own, keeping the files of open cases in their offices intermingled with their own private papers, notes, and privileged information. A defense attorney who wants to read a copy of a police report or see if the file of a current case contains a copy of his client's arrest record must often go to the Prosecutor's—not the Clerk's—Office to obtain it. Although prosecutors are generally cooperative with defense attorneys who want access to the files—at times they let them take files home overnight—they are also in a position to manipulate access to the files for strategic purposes, occasionally denying access to "uncooperative" attorneys.

In theory the clerks organize and order the daily calendar, but in fact again they take cues from the Prosecutor's Office. The Prosecutor's Office has adopted an informal rule to call the cases of private attorneys first, followed by cases of public defenders, and finally by cases of those not represented by counsel. However, if a private attorney cannot get to court until late in the morning, his case may be passed or placed toward the end of the list, or if a defendant without an attorney is knowledgeable enough to request it, he may be able to have his case called earlier in the morning so that he will not have to miss a full day's work. But scheduling of cases is largely at the whim of the prosecutor, and if one is irritated with a particular defendant or defense attorney, he may instruct the clerk to hold off calling the case, forcing the irritated defendant or attorney to cool his heels or accede to an offer proposed by the prosecutor. The clerk's passivity allows prosecutors considerable freedom to manipulate the docket to their own purposes.

Secretaries, Aides, and Investigators

Both the Prosecutor's and the Public Defender's offices have a number of assigned secretaries, aides, and investigators. Like the prosecutors and PDs, most of these people were appointed through the patronage system, so that there is a tension between professionals and members of their support staff who have no strong or continuing loyalty to the office, and whose tenure depends not upon satisfactory work, but rather upon their sponsors outside the court.

But at the time of my study, the prosecutors were relatively satisfied with their two secretaries, one investigator, and several file clerks who were on loan from the clerk's office. In sharp contrast, the public defenders were extremely dissatisfied with both the size and the quality of their support staff, which consisted of two secretaries, one investigator, three court aides, and one service coordinator. To a person, they complained that their investigator was unresponsive to their needs, cared little for defendants, and refused to go out in the field to interview witnesses and visit sites of incidents. In fact, they complained, he was often not even around, and there were allegations that he was driving a taxicab during normal working hours. In response this investigator claimed that he did not investigate because he was not reimbursed for use of his own automobile, did not have access to an official one, and felt unsafe in Black neighborhoods. In any case, none of the public defenders relied on him to handle investigations; what little investigation there was the attorneys conducted themselves.

The PDs' court aides also posed some difficulties. Aside from assisting in investigations, they were formally responsible for interviewing arrestees applying for court-appointed attorneys. Most of this work took place in the morning, and they often left early in the day, leaving the PDs themselves to handle any applications which came later in the day. The PDs deeply resented this but apparently were unable to do anything about it.

Like other officials whose duties require them to be present in court for much of the day, investigators and court aides have also assumed the role of informal advisers to and sources of information for defendants. During spare moments—at recess, in the hall, or in the room to the side of the arraignment courtroom—they frequently give advice to defendants who ask what courtroom they should be in, what the judge is like, where they can find a prosecutor or public defender, what is likely to happen to them if they plead guilty, and when their case will be called. Like the bailiffs and clerks, these aides and investigators are usually free with information and advice. Their advice seems to be good, for large numbers of defendants go without representation, and as a group they fare no worse in sentences and nolles than those who do have attorneys to represent them.

Bailiffs and Sheriffs

Each courtroom is assigned a bailiff or sheriff whose formal duties are to announce the arrival and departure of the judge and maintain order in the courtroom. Most attempt to do both, keeping in mind that he is presiding over an organization whose survival depends on being able to process cases rapidly. But the primary functions of the bailiff and sheriff are unrelated to their formal responsibilities for maintaining quiet in the courtroom. By local custom they act as messengers for lawyers and court officials. At recess they often fetch coffee for the "regulars," and while court is in session they keep track of prosecutors, defense attorneys, and bondsmen, calling them from the hall, their offices, another courtroom, or across the street in Superior Court just before their cases come up.

These officials also serve as an information source for defendants, who regularly ask them what courtroom they should be in, who their attorney is, what he looks like, where they can find him, and when their case will be called. Defendants also pump the bailiffs and sheriffs for information about what is likely to happen to them and how they should plead. Like most of the other court personnel who are asked similar questions, the bailiffs and sheriffs are usually obliging, providing rough estimates of the type and size of the sentence the defendant is likely to receive if he pleads guilty, informing him of the procedure for paying fines, outlining the need for additional appearances if he wants to plead not guilty, and perhaps directing him to a prosecutor who might provide him with more detailed and authoritative answers.

Many defendants and their friends and family are also quite eager to talk about their cases, to explain their side of the story to whoever will listen. The auxiliary personnel—many of whose duties require frantic spurts of activity interspersed with long periods of idleness—usually prove to be a receptive audience.

They are fascinated by what they consider to be the strange and bizarre lives of many of those brought into court. They frequently probe for more details, laugh and express amused incredulity; although helpful in answering inquiries and providing information, they often make defendants the butts of jokes among themselves. After such encounters, staff members sometimes make comments among themselves about "them" or the "coons," although more generally they merely express exasperation because they feel the people are so different from themselves. As one official put it, "These Black kids are simply different. They walk differently, they talk differently, they have different values. Nothing we do fazes them."

This casual communication between defendants and officials serves to highlight an important feature of the courtroom. Authority is almost all white, while those dependent upon the court—accused and victim alike—are disproportionately Black. Much of the innocent bantering between court officials and defendants reinforces racial stereotypes, and the occasional racist remarks only serve to dramatize the fact that two quite different worlds populate the courtroom. The manner in which much of the communication takes place reinforces the prevailing feeling among Black defendants and many whites that the court treats Blacks more harshly than whites. As we will see, it is a feeling more apparent than real, but it nevertheless persists.

Conclusion

In this and the previous chapter, I have tried to present a collective portrait of the important officials in the criminal court system. I have described their formal powers and informal functions, how they view their work, how they are organized, and how they relate to one another and their environment. In the process, I hope that the reader has begun to see how their separate offices and roles function as a system, how they balance against one another, accommodate individual interests, promote common interests, and how they have adapted the ideals of the adversary system to the realities of their own institutional needs and community pressures.

By examining those who administer justice, I hope that the reader has also caught a glimpse of *how* and *why* justice is administered as it is. These are the issues I will explore at greater length in the following pages. What might appear as pathological if presented by itself can begin to be seen as normal.

CHAPTER 5

Outcomes: Adjudication

and Sentencing

Introduction

This chapter reports on my efforts to account for outcomes at adjudication and sentencing in terms of three sets of factors: legal considerations; social characteristics of principal decision makers; and structural characteristics of the system itself. A great many social scientists have focused on one or another of these sets; my initial goal was to integrate them into a single model and then examine the relative importance of each one. Figure 5.1 depicts this task.

But during this effort my research strategy changed, and what I once envisioned as the core of a full-length study has now been reduced to a single chapter, a chapter which reports mostly negative findings. As I immersed myself in the operations of the court, first to collect data and later as a participant-observer, I came to appreciate the ways in which organization and attitude affected the handling of cases, factors which are not easily captured in quantitative analyses and which are most visible *during* rather than before the research process. I also began to question the value of quantitative analysis in developing explanatory

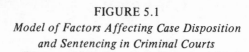

FIGURE 5.1

Model of Factors Affecting Case Disposition and Sentencing in Criminal Courts

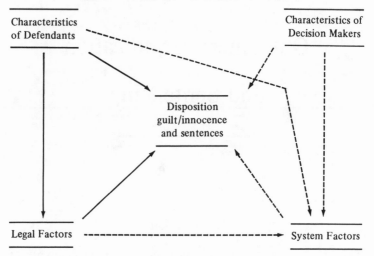

analyses of criminal courts, particularly lower criminal courts in which official records are notoriously unreliable and important outcomes are often distinguished by subtle differences not easily captured on a close-ended data collection form.

Quantitative analysis, particularly multivariate analysis, of the factors identified by previous social science research continued to serve a useful purpose in this study, although more in relation to negative than to positive findings. The results caused me to examine conventional explanations and at times to alter my questions, to ask why these conventional explanations are so often believed, even by participants in a system in which they obviously do not apply. The negative results also constitute indirect evidence for the argument that the more subtle factors of organization and attitude are most likely to provide satisfactory explanations of the criminal process.

The discipline of developing a data collection form leads one, as nothing else can quite so convincingly, to appreciate the complexities of the criminal process. Trying to untangle and understand the labyrinth of the court and the vast array of alternatives and options open to participants, to trace the tortured paths of the accused through the court, served as a sobering introduction to the complexities of the subject. It forced me to map out the case-handling process systematically, an exercise of inestimable value. It alerted me to alternatives and practices I could not easily have discovered by questioning even the most cooperative of informants or deduced from the most thorough direct observation, since certain practices are taken so much for granted by those who employ them that they become all but invisible. Many of the subtleties I probe in detail in the next chapter were suggested by the analysis summarized in this chapter. In short, quantitative analysis launched rather than wrapped up the investigation.

The Variables

Traditional legal analysis emphasizes the importance of *legal factors*, suggesting that strict application of the rule of law determines the outcomes of criminal cases and the severity of sentences. It also suggests that factors such as strength of evidence should play a dominant role in determining guilt or innocence, and that the seriousness of the charge in combination with the offender's prior record should be the main considerations in sentencing decisions.

In contrast, social scientists have typically sought to account for outcomes in criminal cases in terms of the *social and personal characteristics* of the people involved in the process. This emphasis stems from traditional sociological concerns with stratification and organization, and focuses on such factors as the defendant's age, race, sex, social class, and dress; and on the characteristics of court officials, such as party affiliation, and age.

A third approach focuses on *system factors* or structural influences. This approach suggests that the way cases are handled is shaped by the court's own interests and the ways structural factors are manipulated for strategic purposes. The interests of organizational maintenance account for the practice of plea bargaining and for differences in sentences between those who are convicted after trial and those who plead guilty for consideration.[1] Other structural factors count as well. For example, delay often benefits the accused because witnesses grow disinterested, prosecutors lose enthusiasm, and the case becomes "stale."[2] But there is a consensus among students of the subject that if the accused cannot make bail before a trial, then there is a compounding effect at later stages of the criminal process, an effect which increases the likelihood of conviction and a stiffer sentence.[3]

After I had established these three broad approaches—legal, social, and system—I searched the literature on criminal case outcomes and catalogued factors which this research suggested were particularly important in explaining variations in outcomes. I grouped them—as far as possible—into one or another of these three broad categories. This introduced over thirty different factors into the analysis, although the number was reduced considerably after I eliminated those which covaried with other variables or did not produce even a minimal trace of a relationship. I then considered this smaller number of independent variables (see Table 5.1) in more detail, using several different techniques and obtaining the same general results each time. Because stepwise multiple regression provides a convenient way to summarize the findings, I will use it here to discuss the independent contributions of each variable. Each variable was introduced separately into the equation, first in the order of its importance in accounting for the total variance, and later by experimenting with forced orderings.

In this way I tried to account for two distinct decisions: case outcome and, for those who were convicted, sentence. First I looked at case outcome. Establishing guilt is itself a significant sanction, and because there were so few trials, the central questions I considered were: Who pleads guilty and who obtains a nolle? What factors affect this choice? Next I looked at sentences. I constructed an index of severity of sentences ranging from a conditional discharge to a jail term of up to one year, and sought to determine what factors accounted for severity of sentences.

Adjudication Alternatives

In the Court of Common Pleas, most cases are disposed of in one of two ways: either the accused pleads guilty or he receives a nolle. (Or if he fails to appear in court, his case may be terminated through a bond forfeiture.) Fully 96 percent of all the closed cases in my sample were formally disposed of in one of these ways. Fifty percent of the defendants pleaded guilty to one or more charges; 38 percent had their cases nolled, and 8 percent forfeited their bonds without making a court appearance. The remaining 4 percent were disposed of through a number of other little-used alternatives, such as dismissals, bindovers to Superior Court, transfers to other jurisdictions, and civil commitments for medical or mental reasons. Not one case was resolved by trial. Setting aside the practice of closing out cases by bond forfeitures, we must ask, Why do some defendants obtain nolles and others plead guilty? What accounts for this decision? What factors explain it? But before we pursue these questions, we must define the two alternatives.

The Nolle   Under early British common law the decision to prosecute was a private matter, left largely to the victims of a crime. If for whatever reason the victim did not wish to prosecute, there was no public authority to pursue the matter inde-

TABLE 5.1
Major Independent Variables

Variable

Legal Factors

1. Weapon in Possession
2. Seriousness of Initial Charge

3. Type of Charge
   property
   person
   morals
   order
   justice
4. Number of Charges
5. Seriousness of *Final* Charge

6. Indication of a Prior Arrest
7. Date of Last Arrest
8. Seriousness of Prior Arrest

9. Number of Prior Convictions

Social Factors

10. Sex
11. Race
12. Age

13. Type of Victim
    individual (no acquaintance)
    individual (acquaintance)
    other victim
14. Type of Defense Attorney
    public defender
    private attorney
    no defense attorney
15. Reputation of Defense Attorney
16. Type of Prosecutor
17. Reputation of Prosecutor
18. Party Affiliation of Judge

TABLE 5.1 *(continued)*

Variable
Structural Factors
19. Number of Court Appearances
20. Police Intervention
21. Arrest Made on a Warrant
22. Initial Release Condition
23. Final Bail Status
24. Initial Charge Reduced

pendently. This practice was rejected in early American law, and the authority to prosecute was transferred to a public official, the prosecutor. The discretion *not* to prosecute was also vested in the prosecutor. With few exceptions and qualifications, these powers have remained securely in the hands of the public prosecutor, entrenched by both common law and statute in all American jurisdictions. The term for the decision not to prosecute charges formally brought to the prosecutor's attention is *nolle prosequi*, or more colloquially *nolle*, which literally means "not willing to prosecute."

In Connecticut the prosecutor's common law discretion to nolle remains intact and undiminished. Prosecutors retain complete authority over the decision and can exercise discretion without obtaining concurrent approval from the court. This absolute power notwithstanding, the Connecticut Practice Book provides that whenever a nolle is entered the "prosecutor shall make a statement in open court of the grounds for the nolle," and this practice generally holds in court.[4] But judges have never made any serious attempt to use this requirement to closely supervise the process, and invariably accept a prosecutor's reasons for a nolle without question.[5]

The Plea of Guilty   While those accused of crimes have a right to trial, they also have a right to plead guilty, and roughly one-half of them do so. In practice prosecutors almost always negotiate guilty pleas with the accused or their attorneys, and judges almost always accept their arrangements. Like the decision to nolle, the guilty plea is typically a decision arranged by the prosecutor without active participation of the judge. This is not to suggest that these practices constitute a denial of due process, an abrogation of the rights of defendants, or an abdication of duty by defense attorneys or judges. Prosecutors have a full right to nolle charges and defendants have an unrestricted right to plead guilty. These practices do suggest, however, that the exercise of unsupervised discretion rather than the application of rules under the close scrutiny of a judge characterizes the process of adjudication. If this is the case, then in order to understand the administration of criminal justice we must determine how this important exercise of discretion works and what the consequences are.

Determinants of Adjudication

I used several different techniques to explore both the direct effects of and the interactions among these variables. Each technique was based on a number of assumptions, not all of which readily conformed to the types of categorical data with which I worked. After considerable experimentation, I settled on multiple regression analysis, in large part because standardized coefficients (beta weights) provide a convenient way of comparing the importance of a number of independent variables. While the discussion of the results presented below is based on an analysis which introduced variables into the equation in order of their contribution in explaining the variance, other orderings did little to change the overall picture. In addition, other techniques which I describe later in this section yielded surprisingly similar results.

TABLE 5.2
Regression Results for Adjudication Outcomes

Variable	B	Beta	Std. Error B	F
Legal Factors				
1. Number of Charges	0.24	0.53	0.02	123.79*
2. Indication of Prior Arrest Record in Police Files	0.30	0.26	0.08	8.62*
3. Weapon in Possession	0.80	0.05	0.06	1.70*
4. Indication of Prior Arrest Record in Court Files	0.12	0.18	0.06	4.14
5. Seriousness of Initial Charge	0.00	0.06	0.00	1.59*
6. Defendant on Probation at Time of Arrest	0.22	0.02	0.46	0.23
7. Seriousness of Prior Arrest	0.00	0.02	0.00	0.22
8. Time Since Last Arrest	−0.00	−0.02	0.01	0.14
9. Indication of Prior Treatment for Drug Use	0.03	0.01	0.11	0.09
10. Number of Prior Convictions	−0.00	−0.02	0.01	0.08
11. Number of Witnesses	0.00	0.00	0.02	0.02
Social Factors				
12. Age of Defendant	−0.00	−0.07	0.00	2.96
13. Defendant Not Represented	0.08	0.08	0.04	3.39
14. Race of Defendant	0.03	0.03	0.04	0.42
15. Sex of Defendant	0.03	0.03	0.05	0.39
16. Complainant Was Acquaintance	0.18	0.18	0.16	1.31*
17. Victim Was Acquaintance	0.16	0.16	0.15	1.02*
18. Type of Prosecutor	−0.01	−0.01	0.04	0.05
19. Party of Judge	0.00	0.01	0.00	0.04
Structural Factors				
20. Final Bail Status	−0.17	−0.14	0.05	10.44*
21. Arrest Made on Warrant	−0.17	−0.12	0.06	8.45*
22. Number of Court Appearances	−0.02	−0.07	0.01	1.20*
23. Time to Disposition	0.00	0.04	0.00	0.35
24. Arrested While Out on Bail	−0.04	−0.03	0.08	0.32
25. Indication of Failure to Appear on These Charges	0.03	0.02	0.07	0.19
26. Police Intervention	−0.03	−0.03	0.05	0.31
27. Warrant Issued for Rearrest	0.01	0.00	0.10	0.01
Constant	0.12			

Multiple correlation squared $(R^2) = .36$

*Significant at the .05 level.

Initially I introduced thirty-two variables into a stepwise multiple regression equation, and twenty-seven of them were eventually incorporated into the analysis. I rejected the others because of problems of collinearity or because of their inability to contribute even a bare minimum to the total variance. The results of the multiple regression analysis presented in Table 5.2 were disappointing. The R^2 for all twenty-seven of the variables was only .36, not an impressive figure. One factor stood out as especially important; others were moderately important. Several were of interest precisely because they did not yield the expected results.

Legal Factors Three of the eleven legal factors yielded statistically significant independent effects. Defendants with records of prior arrests (beta = .26), who had weapons at the time of their arrest (beta = .05) and were charged with more serious offenses (beta = .05), all had higher conviction rates than their counterparts who had no records and no weapons. While each of these three factors is statistically significant at or below the .05 level, only the first—prior arrest—accounts for anything more than a minute trace of the variance. This suggests that the decision to press for a conviction is based not only on the incident which prompts the arrest, but also on the accused's past association with the court.

Social Factors Four of the social factors were significantly related to the nolle/guilty plea outcome. Two of them—the complainant's relationship to the defendant (beta = .18) and the victim's relationship to the defendant (beta = .16)—were moderately related to the outcome. But both had high standard errors. The other two factors were presence or absence of a defense attorney (beta = .08), and defendant's age (beta = .07). Each of these statistically significant relationships conforms to expectations; those who had some prior acquaintance with the complainant or victim, were represented by attorneys, and were younger, were all more likely to receive nolles than their counterparts.

Several social factors I originally thought were important produced insignificant results. Neither the defendant's race or sex nor the judge's party affiliation was even statistically significant. Finding that race was unimportant (beta = .03) at this stage was consistent with findings at the sentencing stage.[6] It was also understandable that the judges' party affiliations were insignificant; judges play virtually no role in the guilty plea/ nolle process. My finding that the defendant's sex is unimportant calls into question the results of others' studies.[7]

Structural Factors   Four structural factors were significantly related to case outcome: the number of charges (beta = .53); whether or not the defendant was detained or free at the time of disposition (beta = −0.14); whether or not the accused was arrested on a warrant (beta = −0.12); and the number of court appearances (beta = −0.07). Each of these factors relates to the intensity of official interest in prosecution. The number of charges is at times a function of the interest of the police in sanctioning an arrestee, and at other times the result of more than one incident. Whether or not a defendant is released prior to adjudication is based in part upon police, prosecutorial, and judicial assessments of the seriousness of the alleged offense.[8] The number of appearances is at times an expression of the intensity of the defendant's interest in avoiding conviction, and at others an expression of the prosecutor's intensity of interest in obtaining a conviction.

The relationship between the number of charges and the case outcome bears detailed comment since it is by far the single most important of these relationships and accounts for most of the variance. Its singular importance illustrates an important feature in the dynamics of case settlement. In his study of limited warfare, Thomas Schelling showed that the forces of compromise were constantly at work among adversaries. Hills, rivers, and other geographical divisions provide natural boundaries and form the basis for implicit cooperation—even in the midst of combat—and tacit bargaining even among the most bitter of enemies.[9] This same phenomenon seems to take place in the Court of Common Pleas as well. If the accused is charged with two or more offenses, the "natural" solution is to split the difference, to plead guilty on one charge in exchange for a nolle on the other. If this observation is correct, then it is the single-charge cases—seemingly the most simple situations—which are likely to produce the most difficult problems for the court. Since there is no "natural" solution as there is in the multiple-charge case, resolution is less predictable and more difficult to achieve. Even though charges can be reduced and sentences bargained over, the symmetry of a sense of joint victory is not there.

The pretrial status of the accused is also important to the eventual outcome of a criminal case. A number of studies have concluded that those unable to obtain pretrial release have difficulty obtaining counsel and potential witnesses, and therefore have a strong incentive to plead guilty in order to get out of jail or into better prison facilities.[10] Although the findings here are relatively weak, they reinforce those of other studies; pretrial detainees are slightly more likely to plead guilty than those who are released.

Warrants are also related to the rate of guilty pleas. Those arrested on a court-ordered warrant are more likely to plead guilty and less likely to have their cases nolled. This is not surprising, for a warrant indicates that the arrestee has had a prior history with law enforcement officials who have made a special effort to sanction him.

The last important structural variable is delay, operationalized as the number of court appearances—instead of as the elapsed time between arrest and final disposition—because repeated appearances cause the most problems for the court. Despite a general belief by defense attorneys that delay works to their clients' interests—expressed around the courthouse in the aphorism that a "speedy trial is a denial of due process"—delay was not significantly related to outcomes favoring defendants. If anything, the opposite may be true; delay is inversely related to the likelihood of receiving a nolle.

Additional Analysis

After looking at the direct effects of the three sets of variables, the next step was to determine whether the relationships would hold up under closer scrutiny and whether the interactions among any of the variables might suggest a more complex model and yield more substantial results. Again, I considered only the more theoretically intriguing variables in this additional analysis. I used two additional techniques: Goodman's log-linear analysis and analysis of variance. When I examined only the direct effects of these variables, the patterns suggested by the regression analysis reported above were replicated. But once I took interactions into consideration, the substantive significance of even these few relationships came into question. The findings cast doubt on the importance of the direct effects, and the resulting patterns of interaction were weak and difficult to interpret.[11] Rather than suggesting a more complex explanation of the court's decision-making processes, the more intensive analysis yielded even more theoretically confusing results.

But the additional analysis did reinforce two important findings. The importance of both the number of charges and the type of attorney remained undiminished. In particular, the results of the test for interaction suggested that private attorneys outperform PDs in cases in which there is no victim, and in which the defendant has no prior conviction. This last pattern is particularly significant because it suggests that private attorneys do better than PDs in what is perhaps the most important group of cases, minor ones for which the court is in a position to create a first-time record of conviction and thereby formally label a person a criminal for life. However, there are two competing explanations for this finding. The conventional interpretation would argue that PDs are less interested and less capable than private attorneys in pressing for their clients. The finding might also be considered along with the suggestion made earlier that on the whole PD clients do not have as intense an interest in *maximizing* their gains *at this stage* of the criminal process as do the clients of private attorneys. The differential effects of this disparity in intensity of interest and willingness to invest time, effort, and money are explored more fully in the following chapter.

Conclusion

In this criminal court system the adjudication process for all practical purposes is limited to two alternatives: either the prosecutor nolles the charge or the accused pleads guilty. The process involves virtually unsupervised discretion, subject to a host of legal and extralegal factors. No explanation for this apparently open-ended decision process was suggested by the several variables examined here. Only one strong and consistent pattern emerged (although several much weaker tendencies were also suggested): in multiple-charge cases the standard practice is to "split the difference," exchanging a nolle on one charge for a plea of guilty on the other. This relates to the desire to compromise and the norm of reciprocity, common features of the nominally adversarial process, ones which are explored at great length in the next chapter. The other more intriguing findings deal with the relative importance of type of counsel, a factor that will also be explored later.

Sentencing Alternatives

The Connecticut penal code classifies almost all offenses according to seriousness. There are four classes of felonies and three classes of misdemeanors. Each class is defined by its maximum sentence. Class A felonies specify a maximum of life imprisonment, imprisonment for class B felonies may not exceed twenty years, that for class C felonies cannot exceed ten years, and class D felonies may call for up to five years imprisonment. Misdemeanor sentences range from a maximum of one year for the most serious class A offenses, six months for class B offenses, and three months for class C offenses. The code also provides for a sliding scale of maximum fines which can be imposed either in addition to or in lieu of imprisonment. They range from $1,000 to $500. Because the code says virtually nothing about how a judge should determine a proper sentence within the permitted range, the judge has almost unfettered discretion. The question is, How is this discretion exercised?

The Range of Sentences Of the 1,648 defendants in the sample, 843, or just slightly more than half, were eventually convicted. Sentences ranged from largely symbolic unconditional discharges to jail terms exceeding one year.[12] Most of the sentences fell toward the lenient end of the range. Figure 5.2 shows the distribution of the major types of sentences for the sample.

Unconditional discharges, which are in essence determinations of guilt without even a formal slap on the wrist, and *conditional discharges,* usually coupled with a suspended sentence and a warning, are the most desirable sentences; 14.7 percent of all sentences were of this type. A suspended sentence coupled with *probation* is another penalty assessed by the court, and 13.3 percent of all sentences involve some combination of probation and suspended jail sentence. In theory this outcome could involve significant punishing effects, but in fact probation rarely involves much more than an initial interview and an occasional meeting or telephone call to a probation officer. Over 45 percent of all sentences are *fines,* the overwhelming majority of which are less than $500.

Jail terms account for slightly less than 5 percent of all sentences. Sentences vary from five days to over one year in jail, although most of them (75 percent) are for ninety days or less. Only four of the forty people sentenced to terms in jail received sentences of one year or longer.

There are other sentencelike alternatives which should be

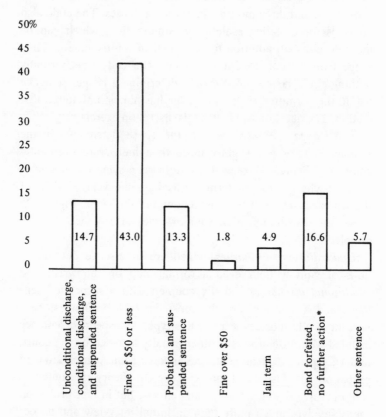

FIGURE 5.2

Distribution of Sentences in Circuit Court

(N = 843)

*These are bond forfeitures, cases in which defendants failed to appear and the judge called their bond and closed their cases. Although there is no determination of guilt, bond forfeitures are usually regarded by the prosecutor and judge as the functional equivalent of a fine. Despite this, these cases have been discarded in the subsequent analysis.

mentioned in passing, but which I did not consider in my analysis. One is *bond forfeiture*. If a defendant fails to appear in court, the judge has two alternatives: He can issue a warrant for rearrest for failure to appear, or he can call for forfeiture of bond and close the case. Although there is no plea of guilty and no formal sentence in the latter alternative, prosecutors and judges consider it the equivalent of pleading guilty and paying a fine. It is a standard device for "paying fines" in many of the nation's traffic courts, and is used to dispose of over 15 percent of all cases in this criminal court. Although most of the bonds that forfeited were low ($5 to $25) several of them were over $200, higher than most of the fines levied by the court.

There are still other alternatives for those who have been judged guilty. About 5 percent of all convicted offenders are released into the custody of some type of "total" institution other than a jail, usually a program for alcohol or drug reform. But such cases are too few in number and too varied to be included in this analysis.

Determinants of Sentence Severity

A comparison of the statutory maximum and the actual sentences suggests that judges are lenient. While the court is empowered to impose sentences of up to one year, it rarely sends anyone to jail for any length of time, and while fines could exceed $1,000, they rarely exceed $25. But there is a wide range in the classification of offenses with which defendants are charged and found guilty. Class B, C, and D felonies accounted for 16 percent of the sample, class A misdemeanors for 20 percent, class B misdemeanors for 33 percent, and class C misdemeanors for 24 percent. The clustering of sentences at the lenient end of the continuum cannot be attributed to any corresponding clustering of charges.

The same techniques used to explore outcomes at adjudication were used here to examine the direct effects of and interactions

TABLE 5.3
Regression Results for Sentence Severity

Variable	B	Beta	Std. Error B	F
Legal Factors				
1. Weapon in Possession	−0.04	−0.01	0.18	0.06
2. Seriousness of Initial Charge	0.03	0.03	0.07	0.17
3. Type of Charge: Order	−0.38	−0.19	0.12	10.59*
4. Number of Charges	0.07	0.03	0.15	0.21
5. Indication of Prior Convictions	0.44	0.03	0.13	0.11
6. Seriousness of Prior Arrest	0.18	0.10	0.13	1.99
7. Number of Prior Convictions	0.11	0.18	0.04	6.94*
Social Factors				
8. Sex of Defendant	0.31	0.12	0.14	5.15*
9. Race of Defendant	0.09	0.04	0.11	0.66
10. Age of Defendant	−0.02	−0.03	0.05	0.29
11. Victim Was Acquaintance	−0.17	−0.08	0.13	1.64
12. Defense Attorney Was Private	0.15	0.05	0.16	0.93
13. Defendant Not Represented	0.12	0.07	0.11	1.25
14. Type of Prosecutor	0.17	0.09	0.09	3.45
15. Party of Judge	−0.19	−0.11	0.09	4.77*
Structural Factors				
16. Number of Court Appearances	0.06	0.13	0.03	5.18*
17. Police Intervention	−0.11	−0.01	0.12	0.01
18. Arrest Made on Warrant	−0.17	−0.06	0.15	1.28
19. Initial Release Condition	0.11	0.09	0.07	2.32
20. Final Bail Status	0.12	0.04	0.15	0.64
21. Type of Guilty	0.14	0.06	0.16	0.74
Constant	2.27			

Multiple correlation squared (R^2) = 0.127
*Significant at the .05 level.

TABLE 5.4
Sentence Severity

Sentence Severity Scale*	
Unconditional discharge	= 1
Suspended Sentence Conditional Discharge or both	= 2
Fine: Under $50 Conditional Discharge to Specific Treatment Program Suspended Sentence plus Probation	= 3
Fine: $50 or more	= 4
Jail Sentence Jail plus Probation	= 5

*I experimented with further breakdowns within these categories and assigned higher values to them—up to 20 for jail plus probation. Expanding the categories and altering the values of these few cases, however, did not significantly alter the R^2.

among variables on sentencing. Initially I included thirty-two variables in the analysis, but after testing for multicollinearity and eliminating variables which did not produce even a trace of a direct relationship, this number dropped to twenty-one. This smaller group of variables is presented in Table 5.3.

The dependent variable is, of course, the severity of sentence. Unlike most of the dependent variables, which are either natural interval or nominal scales, there is no obvious classification scheme for sentence severity. I experimented with several different indices and weighting systems to determine how they affected the R^2 in the regression equation.[13] Overall, I found that altering the weighting system produced no substantial differences in results, so I contented myself with the index in Table 5.4.

The results of this exercise were discouraging. Relationships which *appeared* to be strong in two-way cross-tabulations disappeared in the multiple regression analysis. In experimenting with the ordering of the variables, the highest percent of variance which could be explained by all twenty-one of the variables was less than 13 percent ($R^2 = 0.127$). Furthermore, no single variable stood out as especially important. This failure to account for much of the variance may be attributable to the limited range of the sentence continuum. No doubt the variables would have been more important had the sample contained a greater range of charges and sentences.

Despite these slim and rather desultory results, the analysis did yield some insight into the sentencing process. Most obviously, it showed that several variables often thought to play a central role in sentencing are not terribly significant. In addition other variables produced interesting, although weak, relationships.

Legal Factors   Only two of the seven legal factors yielded statistically significant results. Those convicted of charges against the public order received more lenient sentences (beta = .19) than those convicted on other types of charges (against persons, property, and justice). Coupled with the fact that the seriousness of the charges mattered little, this suggests that the *substance* of the act may be the most crucial factor in the eyes of the court. The other factor which produced a significant independent effect was the number of prior convictions (beta = .18). As the number of prior convictions increased, so too did the severity of the sentence, a finding highly consistent with most "legal" notions of punishment. Despite their statistical significance, however, it is impossible to breathe much theoretical substance into these findings, since these two factors account for only a minute trace of the total variance. With respect to two other legal factors which are usually regarded as central to the sentencing decision—seriousness of charge and seriousness of prior record—I found not even a minimally significant relationship. Taken together, these findings indicate that while legal factors alone cannot explain why people are sentenced as they are, there is at least minimal evidence to suggest that they are not wholly insignificant.

Social Characteristics The *social characteristics* variables, like the legal factors, accounted for little more than a trace of the variance. Only two of the seven social characteristics were even statistically significant. The most positive of the findings showed that women were sentenced slightly more severely than men (beta = .12), and that Democratic judges were slightly more lenient than their Republican counterparts (beta = −.11). The first finding contrasts with other studies which argue that, on the whole, judges, who are predominantly male, are more likely to be more lenient to female than to male offenders.[14] The second finding is consistent with those of a number of other studies of appellate courts, although it is puzzling because the judges in this court usually do little more than follow the recommendations of prosecutors in sentencing, and for the latter there was no hint that party made a difference. Again, I was cautious about drawing conclusions, since neither of these two variables accounts for more than a minute fraction of the variance (less than 1 percent), and little of substance can be read into the findings.

Numerous students of the criminal process have argued that there is a strong racial bias in the criminal courts which manifests itself most invidiously in the sentencing process,[15] but my results do not support this conclusion. Although the direction of the relationship is consistent with this view, the beta weight for race and sentence severity approaches zero (beta = .01), and the relationship is not statistically significant. Although the number of Blacks arrested and taken to court is clearly disproportionate, once in the system, Blacks appear to receive more or less the same treatment at sentencing as whites.

Because of its importance, defense counsel was examined in several ways. Despite a common belief in the indispensability of an attorney in criminal proceedings and despite the court's provision of free counsel, almost one-half (49 percent) of the defendants who pleaded guilty in my sample were *not* represented by counsel. Of course, many of the offenses in this sample were petty ones, so that this figure may not be terribly surprising. However, a closer look at the data shows that those who went without counsel were not limited exclusively to those charged with the least serious classes of offenses. While 78 percent of those charged with class C misdemeanors—the least serious class of offenses—went without counsel, well over 20 percent of those who pleaded guilty to felonies were also unrepresented. Furthermore, those without counsel received sentences which ranged across the entire spectrum of possibilities. Fully one-third of all those who received jail sentences did not have formal representation. In short, defendants without counsel were confined neither to those charged with minor offenses nor to those who received more lenient sentences, and the presence or absence of an attorney made *no measurable impact* on the severity of the sentence.

As noted earlier, New Haven has three types of defense attorneys: private attorneys; public defenders; and LAA attorneys. Each type has its own distinct method of recruiting, history, and institutional reputation.[16] I tried to determine whether there were any significant differences in sentences which could be attributed to the type of attorney, and if so, to see if they corresponded to conventional beliefs about that type. Public defenders represented the bulk (198 of 299) of all convicted defendants with attorneys, while private attorneys handled most of the rest (LAA attorneys handled too few cases for meaningful analysis so I will not include them here). The comparison between private and public attorneys yielded a beta weight of only .05, and a relationship that was not statistically significant.

These conclusions should not be taken to mean that counsel is not important at other stages of the criminal process, nor that the presence of defense counsel is altogether unimportant to the operation of the court. For instance, defense counsel may establish norms which are generalized to all defendants. These findings do suggest that *overall*, for this sample, defendants who went without counsel or who had public defenders did not receive appreciably harsher or more lenient sentences than those who had counsel or who were represented by a private attorney.

Structural Factors Turning to the third set of variables, only one of the six factors—the number of court appearances—was significantly related to sentence severity. As the number of court appearances increased, so did the severity of the sentence. There are two possible interpretations for this. Perhaps more difficult cases—i.e., those in which the stakes seem high, the participants more intense, or the evidence more fuzzy—take longer to resolve. Or, as some have suggested, defendants who impede the court's normally rapid pace of disposition may meet with an unsympathetic court organization that retaliates with harsher penalties.[17] Neither of these practices seems to take place very often or to have much effect, since this variable, although statistically significant, accounts for less than 1 percent of the variance.

Again, what is most interesting about these structural factors is their relative unimportance. For instance, plea bargaining is usually considered crucial in accounting for sentence disparity; yet the reduction of charges does not appear to be a significant factor (beta = .06).

Additional Analysis

Multiple regression analysis allows a researcher to examine the direct effects of a relatively large number of variables. It can not only determine the *existence* of a relationship between the dependent variable and each of these independent variables, but it can also provide a measure of the strength of these relationships. It provides a dramatic advantage over many earlier studies of sentences which relied on simple two-way cross-tabulations, physical controls, and tests of statistical significance.

But while regression analysis provides a convenient means for examining relationships among a large number of variables in a parsimonious way, as it is conventionally used, it cannot easily cope with the problems of interaction effects. Two or more variables might be important only in combination, so that examining the direct effects of each in isolation may obscure their importance. Furthermore, regression analysis is based on a set of assumptions which many statisticians argue are not realistic for the type of data I used. Therefore, I tried other methods to probe for possible interaction effects and to further test the importance of several variables. These included analysis of variance and Leo Goodman's log-linear analysis,[18] considering several variables whose importance was suggested by the regression analysis or by others' discussions. This additional probing yielded results which were by and large consistent with and as disappointing as those produced by the regression analysis. None of the variables had a strong direct relationship to the sentence, and efforts to establish interaction effects generally led to weak and confusing results. No compelling model of the sentencing process emerged, and the interaction effects were difficult to interpret. For instance, "bail status" in interaction with "seriousness of charge" produced weak but nevertheless statistically significant effects on the sentence, but only when seriousness of charge took on one of three values. When the charge was a class B misdemeanor or less, and when the accused's condition of release was a citation, a promise to appear (PTA), or low bond, then the accused was likely to receive a lenient sentence. But when the charge took on other values, this relationship dissolved. In the absence of a compelling model for sentencing, the various combinations of just a few variables presented so many alternatives that they could not be examined or interpreted easily and none of the variables in interaction with others produced any strong, compelling relationships.

Conclusion

Although some people receive harsher sentences than others, and there is considerable variation in the seriousness of charges, there is no convenient explanation for this variation. Observed differences in sentences are *not* attributable to the seriousness of charge, the defendant's record, race, sex, or age. Nor are they attributable to the practice of plea bargaining. It is tempting to infer that sentencing is an irrational or idiosyncratic process, subject to nothing more than the whim of a judge, but this would be premature. The variables tested above are relatively crude, and capture neither the subtleties of individual cases nor the peculiarities of particular personalities, factors which I examine in the following chapter.

Reflections on a Quantitative Approach

It is a disheartening but not entirely disillusioning truth that social science is at its best when it is puncturing myths and challenging conventional wisdom, and to this extent negative results and findings that support null hypotheses are of value. For example, a great many people have argued that Blacks are treated more harshly by the courts than whites; yet the results of my analysis do not support this claim. It has also been argued that an attorney is indispensable to a defendant at sentencing, but in fact neither type of counsel nor presence or absence of counsel seemed to make much difference at sentencing and only a slight difference at adjudication. Many discussions suggest that reductions in charges result in sentence advantages to those who plea bargain, but this claim was not borne out by my data. And finally, it is often argued that prior acquaintance between complainant and defendant reduces the likelihood of conviction and the severity of the sentence; yet my data showed otherwise.

The data did show several positive relationships that were consistent with others' findings. But only one variable provided a strong positive clue to the nature of the court's decision making. On multiple-charge cases, one charge is often nolled in exchange for a plea of guilty on the other(s). This pattern was consistent, regardless of the seriousness of the charges, the type of case, the type of attorney, and a host of other factors. There appears to be an implicit rule of thumb which says compromise in order to reach a quick conclusion.

Above all, this chapter suggests that the set of variables with which social scientists have conventionally sought to generate models of criminal court decision making may be incomplete. It also suggests that the ways in which the questions have been formulated may be inadequate. While it is dangerous to generalize from only one study, particularly an investigation of a *lower* criminal court with a severely limited jurisdiction, the general lack of predictive power generated by the variables considered here gives pause for serious reflection about approach and method.

In addition, careful examination of a great many other studies reveals results similar to mine. John Hagan examined twenty of the more widely known and well-regarded studies of criminal sentencing, and found that most of them had serious deficiencies which caused their authors to inflate the importance of statistical significance and draw spurious relationships. "While there may be evidence of differential sentencing," Hagan concluded, "knowledge of extra-legal offender characteristics contributes only relatively little to our ability to predict judicial dispositions."[19]

Does this mean that the decision-making behavior of judges, prosecutors, and defendants is entirely idiosyncratic, irrational, random? Is there no consistency in their behavior and no pattern to the actions of courts? While the findings presented here and elsewhere might tempt one to draw these conclusions, there is another set of not-so-easily measured organization and attitudinal factors that may account for the court practices, and unless or until these variables can be identified and systematically measured there is little chance of developing convincing quantitative analyses. Moreover, researchers may not be asking the right questions. As I argued earlier, the criminal process is a complex and interrelated series of sanctions, and the severity of punishment at any stage may be determined in part by what preceded and what may follow it. To look at each stage as a wholly separate and distinct decision in isolation from the others may fragment the process beyond recognition and in turn account for the failure of quantitative studies to explain outcomes at any one stage. All of these problems lead us to question the usefulness of a quantitative approach in studying the courts for reasons summarized below.

1. Quantitative studies using sophisticated statistical analysis require large sample sizes. For this reason many students of the criminal process have had to turn to official court records—rather than direct observation—for their data. While this enables them to examine a large sample of cases, *it also restricts examination to those factors which are recoverable from the official files.* This means that other crucial factors cannot be recorded easily or examined systematically. For instance, while type of charge is one measure of the seriousness of the offense, it does not always reflect the *actual* seriousness of the incident. Although such information may be contained in a police report or passed on orally by the arresting officer, it is not often made available by merely reading the charge or the arrest report. In addition, in many jurisdictions prosecutors develop a "feeling" about the reliability of individual police officers, and this affects how they respond to their arrest reports.

In "petty" cases there are still other factors that make systematic collection and coding of important variables especially difficult. Prosecutors are sensitive to external pressures and adjust their policies accordingly. If the arrestee is a police informer, he may—as a favor to the police—receive a lenient sentence. If the suspect is charged with shoplifting, it may depend which department store is filing the complaint. Vigorous prosecution may be a temporary response to a well-publicized arrest or a public outcry for a "crackdown." While information on such factors is fairly easy to obtain, it is not easy to relate it in a systematic way to outcomes in particular cases.

Although the problems raised here can in principle be over-

THE PROCESS IS THE PUNISHMENT

come—the data are amenable to discovery, measurement, and codification—the identification of these more subtle factors is likely to emerge as *part* of the research effort from direct observation, not prior to it. But this approach undercuts the researchers' ability to obtain a large enough sample size to permit sophisticated data analysis and multiple controls. A purely technical problem may in fact lead to important methodological and theoretical choices.

2. A criminal case rarely flows down a straight and narrow path from arrest to conviction. The criminal court system is a labyrinth in which cases get waylaid, joined with other charges, delayed, and complicated. People arrested on one charge often have outstanding warrants for arrest on others. Defendants out on bail are often rearrested on new charges. Prior offenders charged with one offense may be charged with violating probation as well. Many defendants fail to appear, and their cases drag on endlessly. Clerks misplace files for long periods and occasionally lose them altogether. Pretrial service programs generate long delays and circuitous routes to disposition. All of these factors not only complicate the progress of cases through the court, but they also affect the strength of the case and the types of dispositions a prosecutor is willing to seek.

3. Typically each stage of the judicial process is viewed as a separate and distinct outcome. In fact these stages overlap and intermix with each other; they are part of an interdependent whole. The pretrial process model outlined in chapter one shows that at each stage of the criminal process there are a host of sanctions at the disposal of court officials; it is impossible to understand sanctioning at any one stage without considering the system as a whole. For instance, charges may be nolled not only because the case against the accused is weak or the prosecutor is soft-hearted, but also because the prosecutor feels that the accused has suffered enough from a period of pretrial detention. Or a judge may pass a lenient sentence on a serious charge, knowing that more severe punishment will be meted out on other charges pending in another court. It may be especially

important to recognize these connections in considering "petty" cases for which sanctions at each of several stages are of roughly the same magnitude.

4. Prosecutors and defense attorneys organize their work so that much of it is done under frantic conditions; they must rely extensively on memory, hurried summaries, and oral recapitulations. They peruse case files rapidly, often skipping pages and overlooking important details. As a consequence cases are confused and facts are forgotten or never learned. Material collected from files and considered by researchers under relatively leisurely conditions may not be the same "facts" which were important in shaping a courtroom decision.

5. A host of organizational factors which influence case outcomes are difficult if not impossible to trace by reading case files. For instance, many argue that sentence practices are directly affected by the availability of space in prisons. But feedback in the criminal justice system is delayed and erratic, and the prosecutors' and judges' perceptions of this consideration may be most important. These perceptions in turn may be shaped by the media. In Connecticut judicial and prosecutorial perceptions of crowding problems in jails may be shaped more by reading *New York Times*' articles about the Tombs than by direct knowledge about conditions in local jails.

Reciprocity and exchange are common features of complex organizations, and they appear in courts as well. Conversations between prosecutors and defense are filled with allusions to exchange: " . . . I can't give you any more nolles today, you've had your quota," ". . . after all I've done for you today—give me a break," " . . . look, I haven't asked for a thing today, it's not too much for you to give him a nolle." I have also seen prosecutors and judges fall into a response set, routinely handling each case as they have the one before it. This is most visible in sentencing, where a judge might automatically impose a fine of $25 on all offenders who come before him during a particular session.

6. Many sociological studies of criminal case disposition have

treated officials as "black boxes," seeking to account for outcomes in terms of the sociological characteristics of the participants. Yet decisions in criminal courts are presumably *purposive* and *principled*. Perhaps decision making is best explained by examining the attitudes, values, and goals of the decision makers themselves. For example, John Hogarth found that variation in sentences was best accounted for not in terms of the judges' social characteristics, but rather in terms of their attitudes and values on punishment.[20] This may be the case for prosecutors and defense attorneys as well.

7. The interests of the accused can also shape the outcome of a case. Many defendants are intense, and willing to do whatever is necessary to avoid conviction or minimize their sentence. They are open and frank with their attorneys, responsive to their suggestions, and anxious to make a good impression on the court. Other defendants have little interest in prolonging contact with the court. Many do not even bother to appear at their hearings, and others are content with a perfunctory plea of guilty at the earliest opportunity. While representation by counsel may leaven the impact of the levels of interest of individual defendants, it does not altogether dispense with the problem. An attorney is likely to be able to do more for a highly motivated client than he is for someone whose sensibilities have been dulled by alcohol, drugs, and a lifetime of failure. To get beyond these problems may require interviews with large numbers of defendants, which is much more difficult than interviewing a handful of officials.

Clearly, researchers must go beyond official records and identify more subtle variables about organizational pressure and the attitudes of major participants; John Hagan's review article and John Hogarth's, Eisenstein and Jacob's, and Leslie Wilkin's pioneering studies did exactly that.[21] But in order to overcome the many problems posed above, a different research strategy may be necessary. Participant observation and ethnographic methods which yield descriptive analyses of the process of decision making may be preferable to quantitative analyses of outcomes. As Karl Popper is said to have remarked, there are times when one may learn more about the nature of a product by focusing on the process of making it rather than the product itself.

I am not suggesting that quantitative analysis cannot be used to examine such issues as equal administration of justice; if the goal is to determine if disparities exist, quantitative analysis is indispensable. As long as adequate controls are introduced, there is no need to develop a comprehensive theory of decision making to conclude that such factors do or do not play *some* role in the outcome.[22]

Quantitative studies also produce rewarding descriptions of the process. Tracing a sample of cases through the criminal courts from arrest to final disposition is an invaluable exercise which sensitizes researchers to the complexities of the criminal court, complexities which may elude even the most helpful of informants.

For this study at least, the quantitative data analysis proved to be the beginning point rather than the end result of the investigation. It helped shape the investigation which is reported in more depth in the next two chapters.

CHAPTER 6

The Process of Adjudication

and Sentencing

Introduction

At 10 A.M. each day the bailiff calls the main courtroom into session. In one five-second breath his voice above the continuing din announces:

Oyez, Oyez, Oyez! ThishonorableCourtofCommonPleasfortheSixth GeographicalAreaatNewHavenisnowopenandinsessioninthisplace/ Allpersonshavin'causeofactionpendin'orhavin'beendulysummonedare boundtoappearhereinandtakeduenoticethereofandgivetheirattention accordin'tolaw/TheHonorableJudgeMancinipresidin'/Kindlybe-seated/Notalkin'orwalkin'whilehisHonor'sonthebench.

This manner of speech and delivery capture well the court's preoccupation with speed and efficiency. With the arrival of the judge the court goes into formal session, but the intense sideline activity continues. Defense attorneys hold whispered conferences with their clients and prosecutors, badger the clerk for a preferred position on the day's calendar, or dart about trying to locate clients whose faces they can barely recognize. After they finish this business, they gravitate to the never-used juror's space, exchanging gossip as they wait for their cases to be called. The bondsman, in his customary seat next to the clerk of court, may be writing bonds for people arrested the night before. A secretary sits in the seldom-used witness box to the right of the judge taking applications for public defenders. Late arrivals continue to file in, and the gallery which often overflows into the hall is peppered with noisy children made restive by the strange scene and crowded conditions.

But after the judge enters the room, a new activity is added to the hubbub, a ritual before the bench, a ritual which might easily remain wholly unintelligible if not overlooked entirely amid all the other activity to a visitor watching from the gallery. A clerk mumbles out a name and a long series of numbers (identifying numbers for relevant sections of the criminal code) and someone (a defense attorney) springs forward. At the same time someone else (a prosecutor) peers up at the judge as he begins shuffling through a set of papers which has just been thrust into his hands by the clerk, and announces to the judge what he is going to do with the case—whether he will continue it for another week, nolle the charges, or urge the accused to plead guilty.

This preliminary business is completed at just about the same time the defendant has finished moving forward from the gallery and crossing the courtroom floor, until he arrives in front of the bench between the prosecutor and his defense attorney. He might arrive just in time to hear the resolution of the case. If it is a continuance, either the prosecutor or the defense attorney instructs him to show up again at the same time and place a week later. If it is a nolle, they point to the door and tell him he is free to go. If it is to be a plea of guilty, he makes the plea and the clerk then recites the charges anew, after which the prosecutor interjects his sentence recommendation to the judge, usually a fine of $10 or $25 or a suspended sentence. If it is a suspended sentence, the judge tells the defendant not to get in trouble again. If it is a fine, the prosecutor points out the bailiff who will instruct him as to how to pay the fine. If the defendant has any questions, it is unlikely that they will be answered because the prosecutor and defense attorney have already turned their attention to the next case.

Off to the side of the main courtroom—in the "backroom" as it is called—another drama is unfolding. Sitting at a table with a handful of case files spread out before him is a prosecutor. Seated across from him are several defense attorneys waiting to talk to him about their cases which, if all goes well, will be sent out to the open courtroom a few minutes later. After each attorney in turn takes up his cases with the prosecutor, he may carry the case file out to another prosecutor in open court for disposition. The following is a typical backroom exchange.

The prosecutor holds out the arresting officer's report so that both he and the defense attorney can read it for the first time. The defendant is charged with receiving stolen goods and larceny (theft). The prosecutor argues that the case is cut and dried, but the defense attorney counters by claiming that the report is filled with ambiguities and that there are serious questions about the strength of the evidence. This, he suggests, is cause for leniency.

The prosecutor refuses to acknowledge this line of reasoning, saying, "The defendant knew that they were stolen; two TV sets, stereos, and all that other stuff for fifty dollars!"

The defense attorney protests, "Yea, but a black-and-white TV may not be worth very much."

The prosecutor shrugs off this line of reasoning, but does concede, "I'll give the guy a suspended sentence because the goods were recovered—I'll give you a suspended on the larceny and nolle the other charge."

The defense attorney pleads, "My client has no record and he's only nineteen years old. Give me a break."

The prosecutor returns with, "This is a good deal. I'm giving you a break because of no prior and because the stuff was recovered."

Whereupon the defense attorney asks, "How long is the suspended sentence?"

The prosecutor replies, "Three months."

And the defense attorney backs down: "OK, I'll take it."

After the attorneys reach this agreement, the case file is carried out to another prosecutor doing duty in "the pit," as the main courtroom is known, and placed in line to be called later in the day. In the interim the defense attorney scans the gallery looking for his client, then holds a brief conference with him in the corridor, explaining what the terms of the arrangement are and instructing him on what to do when his case is called.

Most cases are closed after one or two appearances, after a consideration about as detailed as the one described above. But in the event that a quick settlement cannot be reached, the prosecutor will readily agree to pass over or continue the case. The defense attorney may want to talk further with his client, try his luck with a different prosecutor, or simply stall, hoping for a better deal later. Because judges usually accept the prosecutor's recommendations, the continuance is rarely sought to avoid or obtain a particular judge. The prosecutors who periodically rotate in assignment to this courtroom are more than willing to postpone decisions, transferring work and responsibility to one of their colleagues and allowing them to finish their day's work earlier. If the case is especially serious or if there are substantial differences between the prosecutor and defense attorney, then the latter may have the case placed on the jury list, which means automatic removal to the other, less crowded courtroom. It does not mean, however, that the attorney has any serious intention of going to trial, nor is the move necessarily born of a desire to get the case before another prosecutor. Instead it allows for a protracted period of delay during which the defense attorney may expect to obtain additional information on the case, or "work on" the prosecutor or his client.

During this interim there is often little if any consideration of the case, and it resurfaces on the agenda of the prosecutor and defense attorney the morning of its appearance on the jury room's calendar. At this time the two adversaries move off again into the backroom of this courtroom and discuss the case under less hectic conditions. No matter where the issues are finally resolved, however, the decision process remains essentially the same, and this process is the main subject of this chapter.

Establishing the Worth of a Case

The court is a reactive institution. Others outside its direct control determine its workload and define the problems it must process. Occasionally cases may result from an action initiated by a prosecutor, but almost all in the Court of Common Pleas are brought there by police officers who have made a street arrest on their own or a citizen's initiative. But police and prosecutors have different perspectives. What the former perceive as trouble serious enough to warrant official intervention and arrest the latter may not consider serious enough to warrant prosecution and conviction. Like members of all organizations who depend upon someone else to supply them with work, those who receive the arrest must first "redefine" or translate another's—the arresting officer's—definitions to suit their own understanding and purposes. This process begins at the station house with the setting of bail, and continues at the first appearance and throughout the life of the case. Officials are continually evaluating the "seriousness" of the case from the information at hand and fashioning options and sanctions accordingly.

There is no clear line which distinguishes sentencing from adjudication. In deciding whether to seek a jail term, ask for a fine, recommend a suspended sentence, press for a plea of guilty, or grant a nolle, the prosecutor goes through essentially the same process. He attempts to establish the "worth" of the case, which in turn dictates how he will treat it. This concept of the worth of a case has considerable significance for criminal justice officials. By establishing the worth of a case, both the prosecutor and defense attorney know how to treat it. If it is "serious" or "heavy" the arrestee may have to plead guilty and even serve time in jail, but if it is "not worth very much," or if, in more colloquial terms, it is "garbage," "bullshit," or a "meat-ball," then the defendant may receive a nolle because all agree that it is not even "worth" the time to prosecute.

Although prosecutors and defense attorneys tend to become inarticulate when pressed to specify how they evaluate the "worth" of a case, they claim to know it intuitively. And there is a general consensus in their respective offices as to who among them can quickly assess the worth of cases. For instance, part-time prosecutors are not as adept at determining worth as are full-timers. Public defenders quickly become adept at it, but many private attorneys who appear in court only occasionally never do.

The worth of a case is established by considering a host of factors, and different types of cases call forth different rules of thumb, so that there is no single checklist against which to compare all cases. A breach of peace case involves a set of factors not germane to a shoplifting incident. One prosecutor offered the following statement:

. . . You have to know the witnesses and the potential for sym-pathy for the defendant. You've got to know how the complainants are going to react, the priority of the prosecutor's office, and the prior history of the defendant, and the problems of introducing evidence, how your witnesses will appear on the stand. The priority of the complainants themselves is important—we are, for instance, reluctant to get involved in an intrafamily fight and don't want to give mothers-in-law a new forum for harassing their daughters-in-law.

Some prosecutors simply don't have common sense, and end up giving things away. Some are too soft and others are pricks who want to prosecute everything. With experience, however, you learn and begin taking all these factors into consideration in coming up with a solution to the case.

I think the legal factors probably come into play in about one in every twenty-five cases, although they do set the outer boundaries. Clearly if you have an ambiguous police report or confused state-ment about evidence, the defense knows you don't have a strong case and you're going to treat it accordingly. But still most of the appeals are sort of common-sense assessments of the situation, mixing both problems of evidence and appeals for simple justice.

What this prosecutor suggests and what is abundantly clear when listening to prosecutors and defense attorneys negotiate settlements is that it is difficult to articulate the factors considered in assessing the worth of a case, not because decision making in the court is arbitrary, *ad hoc,* or embarrassingly simple, but because it is extremely complex. The process is subtle, complicated, and finely tuned to consider a host of factors which cannot be reduced to a convenient set of rules of thumb.

The single most important factor in determining how much care will go into reviewing a case to determine its "worth" is the official description of the charges. Felonies are likely to be treated more seriously and involve more time and effort than misdemeanors; crimes against persons are regarded more seriously than crimes against public order; and a charge of rape is taken more seriously than a charge of breach of peace. This is dramatically obvious from the police department's "bail schedule" which ties the minimum amount of bond to the classification of the charge.[1] However, official crime categories are not in themselves reliable indicators of the worth of a case. Many arrestees charged with seemingly serious offenses are released on recognizance (ROR), while others with low bonds are not. Within each offense category about one-third to two-thirds of all defendants eventually receive nolles, which indicates that official crime categories are not accurate predictors of how a case will eventually be treated. The charges against a defendant are simply the first and most obvious of many considerations that establish the meaning of a case and shape its outcome.

A charge is an abstraction, and while participants in the process are willing to characterize the "type of person" likely to commit such an offense, there is nevertheless a desire to look beyond the charges, to respond directly to the incident itself and to the character of the defendant. For a charge to assume meaning it must be given substantive content supplied by a description of the incident and information about the defendant's character, habits, and motivation. A variety of factors can make a case seem less serious than it did at the time of arrest or an initial reading of the arresting officer's description of the incident. Some have to do with *who* is making the judgment, others with the *changing assessment* of the incident and the defendant's character.

On the whole the court has a higher tolerance for "trouble" than do those who determine its business, the police. A loud and threatening arrestee for whom the police or bail commissioner may purposefully set a bond that is beyond reach may appear quiet and unassuming in court the next day so that the prosecutor may downgrade the worth of his case and reduce the bond or even nolle the case outright. Ironically, one cause for differences in assessment may be police professionalism. Traditional police practice encourages officers to administer rough justice on the street in lieu of arrest, but modern police professionalism dictates that an arrest should be made whenever there is any basis for doing so. An arrest transfers responsibility for handling the case to a prosecutor, who must then assess the "seriousness" of it and dispose of it. Practices which minimize police discretion may simply shift the burden for informal dispute resolution away from the police and to the court. For example, prosecutors regard some arrests as so trivial that they may even resent police pretrial release practices which *encourage* defendants to appear in court. It may be that many of the benefits of reduced police discretion are offset by increased prosecutorial discretion, with the added costs of court appearances being paid by the accused and the public.

The court also receives a host of minor cases which at the time of arrest may have appeared to be quite serious. When police intervene in family disputes or barroom brawls they may find an injured victim, damaged property, an outraged wife, or a proprietor anxious to be rid of an unruly patron. Police are well aware that homicides and serious assaults frequently stem from "petty" incidents involving domestic disputes or arguments among acquaintances stimulated by alcohol; arrest and high bond are sure ways to prevent the immediate incident from escalating.[2]

The court does not respond to the immediate circumstances of an arrest, but rather to a recounting of the incident tempered by hindsight, and more restrained principals. Despite clear evidence of a violation and an initial label of "serious," prosecutors view many of these cases as "minor," and often nolle them or treat them "leniently."

Other factors besides the charges and revised perceptions of the offense contribute to an understanding of the seriousness of the case. These factors have to do with the defendant's attitudes, relationships with complainants, assessment of damage or injury, and the court's evaluation of the defendant's background and potential for the future.

The court has a keen interest in the defendant's character, and the prosecutor's assessment of his "responsibility" may significantly affect the outcome of a case. Responsibility for provoking an incident may be shared among several persons, which might serve as an acceptable "excuse" for a defendant. A prosecutor may nolle a case because the defendant "had been drinking with the complainant and they got into a quarrel." Such an explanation does not relate directly to the strength of evidence nor the degree of responsibility, but it still suggests a belief in shared responsibility for the incident. But an uneven division of responsibility may work to the detriment of the codefendants. If a prosecutor can infer that primary responsibility falls upon one of them, then the seriousness of the case may decrease for the others. For instance, if several young persons are arrested in connection with the same incident, an older one may be singled out for the greatest "blame" because he should have "known better."

Another factor which contributes to the understanding of the worth of a case is a defendant's *subsequent* relationship with the complainant. If the defendant has made a sincere effort to express remorse or restore property to his victim, then the seriousness of the case may be downgraded.

The defendant's history and reputation in the court can also affect the way he is treated. Although the injury or damage may have been slight, the prosecutor may consider the charge particularly significant because it is the latest in a *series* of troublesome acts. If the prosecutor has been lenient on this defendant in the past or if he learns that the arrestee has a bad reputation, then the prosecutor may decide that the defendant's time has come, and will treat an otherwise "minor" case as "serious."

A case may become more serious because the prosecutor discovers there is a warrant outstanding for a defendant's arrest. This occurs with some frequency, since if a defendant fails to appear on one set of charges, prosecutors make little effort to retrieve him, and wait until he is rearrested on other charges. He then faces not only current charges, but also the prior charges plus an additional charge of "failure to appear." In such instances the entire group of charges is treated as a whole.

A prior record is likely to increase the seriousness of a case, although the *type* of record makes a difference. Has the defendant ever served time? If not, the prosecutor may be reluctant to mark him for life. Has the defendant been arrested on these charges before? How recently? If the record indicates a prior history of similar behavior, the prosecutor is likely to view the case more seriously, particularly if there are recent entries on the rap sheet.

The defendant or his attorney may use a clean record to argue that the current incident is an aberration, a mistake—as opposed to a "real" indication of character—which should be treated leniently. The "fact" of no prior record, however, can cut two ways. While a prosecutor might respond with leniency in one case, in another he might decide to follow a harsher strategy, believing that "a firm hand" at an early point might be the most effective deterrent against future misconduct. For

most, the lack of a prior record is likely to reduce the seriousness of the case and its outcomes, although at times the effect is
quite the opposite.

Ironically, a serious prior record can reduce the worth of a
case. If a defendant charged with a "minor" offense has a past
record of "serious" offenses, a prosecutor may regard this as an
"improvement" in his behavior and treat the case less seriously
than he would for another defendant. For example, if a defendant is on drugs (although the charges may not reflect this), he
may admit that he cannot control himself and in doing so may
be able to enter into a drug treatment program rather than
receive a jail sentence.

If concerned family members or friends come to court, officials may take this as an indication of stabilizing forces in the
defendant's life and may "downgrade" the worth of the case.
Parents, clergymen, teachers, counselors, and employers also
promote this move. Normally, however, friends do not come to
court. If the defendant is employed, in school, or has ambitious
career aspirations, this is taken as a sign of stability and contributes to a downward revision of the seriousness of the case.

Such considerations raise ethical dilemmas which some of the
prosecutors, judges, and defense attorneys feel quite sharply,
since they are biased toward middle-class defendants. For instance, defense attorneys will occasionally approach a prosecutor and plead for a nolle, explaining that a conviction will
injure his client's chances of getting into college, law school, or
some other self-enhancing program. His appeal is usually
punctuated with a rhetorical question of the following sort:
"You wouldn't want to louse up this guy's whole life for this
measly prank, would you?" The prosecutor is faced with a
paradoxical situation: If he treats similar cases equally, then he
will cause unequal injury. A factory worker likely to remain in
unskilled or semiskilled jobs will not lose his position as a result
of a conviction, while a middle-class student may have his entire
future jeopardized. By a perverse but compelling logic, the

prosecutor is forced to provide a preferred outcome to the more advantaged person and justify it in the name of equality.

The degree to which a court relies on family and community ties is also an indicator of how effective it thinks it is. Prosecutors, defense attorneys, and judges readily acknowledge the limited impact of *whatever* they do and are happy to accept the support of these other potentially more influential agents in their limited effort to instill a sense of civility in defendants.

At times the character of the arresting officer enters into the assessment of a case. When interpreting an officer's arrest report, prosecutors may adjust their response in light of their assessment of the particular officer's character. While they never criticize police practices in open court, they have a high regard for some officers and an extreme distaste for others, and adjust the reading of their reports accordingly. Although they are responsive to pressures to "support" the police, prosecutors will often quietly nolle or downgrade a charge if they feel the arresting officer is unreliable or unfair.

One plea bargaining incident I observed involved charges against three men in their late teens or early twenties, two whites and a Black friend. The three of them had entered a bar in a white working-class neighborhood, whereupon some of the patrons—including an off-duty policeman—began taunting the two white men for bringing a "nigger" into the bar. As the three men attempted to leave, a fist fight broke out. When another officer responded to a call he arrested the three men and charged them with breach of peace and, upon the insistence of the off-duty officer, with assaulting a police officer. In discussions with the prosecutor, defense attorneys for the three men pressed for nolles, saying that the officer involved in the incident was an outspoken racist, a known drunk, and should have been arrested himself.

While the prosecutor was sympathetic to this position, he expressed reservations about nolle-ing the charges and did so only after considerable badgering and after checking with the

Chief Prosecutor, who informed him that this particular officer was not well-regarded by others on the force. One of the other reasons the prosecutor gave for not nolle-ing the charges was that he thought the defendants were partly to blame for the incident. Anyone stupid enough to take a Black man into that bar, he reasoned, ought to be arrested. This was not said entirely in jest, and it illustrates the contextual notions of "responsibility" and "causation" that prosecutors employ when assessing the actions and motivations of the accused.

The Prosecutor's Office is responsive to other interests as well. The large downtown department stores have pressed the Office to prosecute shoplifting cases vigorously, which the prosecutors might otherwise not do, particularly if the items are recovered or if they are of low value. These stores, concerned about losses from shoplifting and fearful that they might be liable for charges of false arrest by suspects whom their security staffs have detained, press the prosecutor to seek conviction rather than nolle the charges outright or allow defendants to participate in diversion programs leading to nolles. Although it is possible to obtain a nolle on shoplifting charges, defense attorneys—not used to the recently increased worth of these cases—first have to obtain permission from the department store and have their clients agree to a waiver against charges of false arrest. Defendants without attorneys in such cases and defendants with private attorneys who do not regularly appear in court are not likely to benefit from these exceptions because they are not aware of the unpublicized "loopholes."

Other community group pressures may also affect the "worth" of cases. Prostitution is concentrated in one area of New Haven, a racially transitional neighborhood comprised of a mixture of older low-rise apartments, single-family homes, and small businesses. Prostitutes position themselves on the street corners and solicit business from passing motorists who slowly cruise the streets looking them over. Pimps and a variety of "street people" are also attracted to the neighborhood to over-

THE PROCESS OF ADJUDICATION AND SENTENCING

see their business interests and to buy and sell drugs. Residents of the neighborhood, older poor whites, younger but also poor Blacks, and a sprinkling of college students organized and visited the Chief Prosecutor to press for more vigorous enforcement of the law. While he was sympathetic to them, the prosecutor viewed the problem as insoluble, and privately expressed a preference to have a whore house somewhere in the city, something he claimed worked well in a neighboring community because it kept prostitutes off the streets. While the Chief Prosecutor obliged the group with an office policy "upping the worth" of a prostitution charge, he is skeptical of its effects: "Even a sentence of thirty days or sixty days . . . doesn't deter. It's still good business. There have been a couple of murders there but they keep coming back."[3]

The Inherent Ambiguity of the Process

Despite a loose consensus among prosecutors as to what factors are important in assessing the worth of a case, outcomes are far from predictable. They vary because of differences in personality, variations in incentives to obtain information, the elusive nature of "facts," and a structuring of the decision process in a way that fosters mistakes. Various prosecutors aggregate these factors differently, giving them slightly different "weights" which at times lead to different outcomes.

Personality   The defense attorneys I sampled were in general agreement as to which prosecutors were especially "reasonable" and which were particularly "difficult," and their ranking correlated highly with the proportion of nolles each of the prosecutors granted.[4] But because the prosecutors' reputations are so well-known, many of the problems that these differences could cause are anticipated and avoided.

Only in rare cases in which the case involves something about which the prosecutor is known to be especially sensitive will an

attorney go to the trouble to avoid him. For instance, one prosecutor had family ties to a member of the Board of Police
Commissioners, and some defense attorneys felt this made it
difficult to deal with him in cases involving challenges to the
integrity of the arresting officer. Attorneys who regularly appear
on behalf of defendants may be aware of occasional idiosyncra-
cies and make adjustments accordingly, but those defendants
who do not have attorneys or who are represented by attorneys
who only occasionally handle cases in the court do not enjoy
this benefit—a situation that on occasion leads to harsher
treatment.

Mobilizing Facts   The "facts" of a case are *not* self-evident;
they must be *mobilized*. A case is a continually evolving process
up until the moment of final disposition. Additional bits of information continue to emerge and shape its "worth." A victim
may be released from the hospital or fail to appear in court, the
defendant may obtain a job, the defendant's parents may appear
in court, a priest may telephone the prosecutor or public defender, a drug sample sent out for testing may be lost, or a
diversion program may accept the defendant. "Facts" must not
only occur, they must be "observed," marshaled, and brought to
bear as evidence in a case.

Despite the near consensus among prosecutors and defense
attorneys on how to assess the "worth" of a case, the process of
decision fosters error. Because they feel that the consequences
in most cases are so minimal, prosecutors and defense attorneys
have little incentive to scrutinize their cases carefully. This
casualness leads to a great many errors, which if not caught can
have significant consequences for the defendant. The following
story by one prosecutor illustrates this problem.

This morning I had a case—a young guy charged with criminal
mischief. He had been sitting in the backyard of a church when
people came out trying to follow someone who had burgled the
church. He was arrested there, but he didn't have anything from
the church, so was charged with criminal mischief. I had talked to

THE PROCESS OF ADJUDICATION AND SENTENCING

[a PD] about it, and would have been willing to go easy on him, but when the case came up, [another prosecutor] handled it. [The PD] and I had agreed to a plea and although we had not agreed to a sentence recommendation, it was assumed that it would be light and that the guy would not do any time [in jail]. The other prosecutor read the charge and the defendant pled guilty. Then he summarized the police report for the judge. In doing so, he stated that the defendant had been *inside* the church and had taken something from it. I would simply have said that the defendant had been found sitting outside on the wall and let him go at that. As a result, the judge sentenced him to thirty days in jail. It all depends on how the facts are presented. I would have presented them significantly differently. [Implying that the defendant would probably not have done any time at all.]

Prosecutors also occasionally confuse case files or neglect to read second or third files in a multiple-charge case. Information about cases is often transmitted orally, and in the process can be lost, distorted, or confused. Defense attorneys too are susceptible to this, especially those like the PDs, who often arrange to handle several different cases at a single appearance.

Prosecutors and public defenders readily acknowledge that this rapid and often perfunctory reading of case files results in frequent mistakes, but argue that these errors tend to benefit the accused and at any rate are usually corrected by challenges from opposing counsel. The bias in favor of the accused tends to justify the process which gives rise to error.

Moreover, questions which seemingly could be answered with a simple yes or no can become extremely complex. Because of poor recordkeeping, the question of whether or not a defendant has a prior record can become tangled in a complicated reasoning process, as an example drawn from my notes indicates.

A private attorney and a prosecutor are engaged in an argument as to whether the defendant has a prior record. The prosecutor seems willing to count as a prior record charges for which there is no entry for a disposition. The defense attorney, in turn, argues that an arrest without a subsequent entry of conviction is no record at all. The prosecutor's argument is that if the case were nolled, it would have been erased since it is over a year old. However, he concludes his argument by stating that this is only the New Haven record, implying that he is certain that the defendant must have a record of conviction *someplace* else.

Sometimes information on prior records is obtained from an unreliable source, and on numerous occasions I observed prosecutors asking defense attorneys if their clients had prior records. Defense attorneys often learned about their clients' records from the clients themselves, not always reliable sources of information. A prosecutor described another situation which had profound consequences for the defendant.

I was handling the files in the main courtroom and ————'s file came up. She was charged with assaulting her landlord and breach of peace. Nothing too serious—she had slapped him and broken his glasses in an argument over rent. There was no record in her file, and I assumed she had none. I was getting ready to plead her out for a $75 fine when another prosecutor came into the room and informed me that he thought the defendant had a record, that he recognized her name. He remembered that she had been in court before and we checked. Among other things, she had been convicted of manslaughter in 1969 and was still on probation. As a result, we wouldn't bargain so much and insisted on six months in jail. Her attorney wouldn't take it, and eventually went to trial. He did a lousy job—for instance, he allowed her prior record to be introduced, and it took six minutes to read it into the record—and she ended up getting one year and three months—all the time left on her probation. I almost pled her out for $75!

This is a dramatic case with extreme consequences. Nevertheless, it illustrates the extent to which "hard" facts are not always obtained or can be overlooked. Most cases do not have such dramatic implications, and it is precisely because they do not have that information about so many cases and defendants can be gathered and reviewed in this casual and haphazard manner.

Malleable Facts Facts are *malleable*, and can be presented in ways which either enhance or downplay the seriousness of a case. Defense attorneys have a variety of devices to mold facts around their client's interests. Although a defendant may have a prior record of arrests, he may not have been convicted on any offenses, and the record may not indicate what the disposition was. And even if he does have a prior conviction, he may not have served any time in jail. Defense attorneys point out that the record was a "minor" one, that none of the prior convictions involved personal injury or use of dangerous weapons, or that a client's last arrest was "sometime before."

Other factors also thought of as serious can at times be blunted or used to a defendant's advantage, turning weakness into strength. Even though most studies on the subject have found that detained defendants are treated more harshly than their released counterparts, pretrial incarceration can at times be turned to a defendant's advantage.[5] Some defense attorneys are particularly skilled at this, as the following exchange between a prosecutor and defense attorney illustrates.

The defense attorney argued: "He's already done eighteen-days pretrial," and suggested a suspended sentence. The prosecutor agreed, saying he would recommend six-months suspended plus one-year probation. Later I asked the defense attorney about this, and he suspected that his client might have received thirty days if he had bargained the case out earlier or if the defendant had been released.

But such skill is the exception. More typical are cases in which after pleading guilty, people are sentenced to "time served," a sentence which defense attorneys witnessing the proceedings often agree is a feeble and perhaps even unwitting attempt to justify the time the defendants had already spent in pretrial detention.

For many defendants, arrests and convictions are, if not routine, at least not unfamiliar occurrences. It is not at all unusual for a defendant to be charged with several offenses stemming from more than one incident, and defense attorneys make a concerted effort to consolidate these separate files and charges because they think they can get a better deal for the defendant by treating them as a whole. Prosecutors like to consolidate cases because it facilitates negotiations and reduces their workload. Typically the most serious charge "defines" the case and determines the sentence, so that the lesser charges get a free ride on the coattails of the *defining* charge. This was illustrated most dramatically in the following case:

A private attorney appears before Judge ———— and begins to tell a complicated story. After questioning by the judge, the story and request are finally untangled:

Two weeks earlier the defendant had pled guilty to several charges and had fines totaling $650 levied against him. At that time, the case was continued for two weeks—until today—for final sentencing in order to allow the defendant time to obtain the money. Since then, the defendant has been arrested on still other charges, and today he is pleading guilty to them. These new charges require under the new law a six-month mandatory minimum jail sentence. (This is the defendant's sixth conviction for driving while intoxicated and his fourth for driving while under suspension of license.) The defense attorney is now asking the judge to revoke the earlier fine and sentence his client to a jail term to run concurrently with the current sentence. The prosecutor indicates to the judge that this is acceptable to him, and the judge agrees to set aside their earlier fine.

Some defendants become chronic repeaters, and if the charges are minor, their long records may be discounted. No one quite knows what to do with these nuisances, so they often do nothing.

A PD approaches a prosecutor and says he has three cases he wants to discuss. The first involves a defendant with three files and several charges. The PD opens the discussion asking for nolles in all of the charges, arguing that they are all criminal mischief, breach of peace, disorderly conduct, and are related to the defendant's drinking problem. He continues, "The defendant is a drunk and prosecution or a jail term serves no useful purpose here." The PD concludes, "What can we do with this guy?" The prosecutor replies, "Hang him." They end the conversation without reaching an agreement, although the PD has learned that the prosecutor is reluctant to nolle all the charges but, on the other hand, is relatively sympathetic to his plight. After reflecting on it, and perhaps after the PD has talked to the defendant, he will come back and make a final agreement on sentence.

Manufacturing Facts   In the interval between arrest and conviction, the future quickly becomes the past. During this period facts can be *manufactured* and become part of the record. Between the time of first appearance and disposition of a case, a defense attorney helps his client create a favorable record, one which might convince the prosecutor and judge that the defendant is on his way toward reform and rehabilitation. He wants to show the court that the defendant is helping himself, and may encourage him to get a job, go back to school, or get into a drug counseling program. As one defense attorney put it:

Help the defendant begin his rehabilitation as soon as possible. Get a job, make restitution, get him involved in social service programs, thus by the time sentencing comes up, the judge is likely to accede to the plan the defense attorney presents.

Several weeks after hearing this attorney give this advice, I watched him put it to work in a case for which he was afraid that his client would receive a jail sentence.

(Defense attorney tells the prosecutor he wants to talk about the ———— case. She is charged with breach of peace and resisting arrest.) He argues: "She has a real drinking problem. She is twenty-one and looks thirty-five. Another prosecutor let her out PTA even though her mother wanted her committed and indicated she wouldn't put up any bail. By fighting for her on this, I think I gained her trust and confidence. My feeling is that she should try an out-patient program at Connecticut Mental Health. CVH [Connecticut Valley Hospital] is a joke and jail wouldn't do her any good. Look, how she pleads on the charges are the least of her worries. We have to try to straighten her out. I want to impress on her how serious the charges are and try to get her into this clinic. I hope you'll go along with the idea. The clinic is willing to take a chance with her."

These strategies can become quite elaborate, as another attorney suggests.

If the charges involve theft or property damages, arrangements for restitution are advantageous. You want to start restitution before sentencing but you don't want to finish paying. Then you can argue: "Don't send my client to jail—he's now working and paid 75 percent of the damage back and can pay the remainder if he's not sent to jail."

While some facts can be created deliberately during the interval between arrest and adjudication, others evolve naturally. A great many charges stem from disagreements among persons who know each other—many of them husbands and wives—and in such instances time may at least dull the intensity of disagreement if not heal the wounds entirely. This situation is so common in domestic disputes that the prosecutor refers most cases routinely to the Family Relations Officer (FRO) for "counseling," and many are later nolled. Time allows wounds to heal, and complainants who may come to court for their first appearance on crutches, or who may have been altogether unable to come to court because they were in the hospital, may recover fully by the time the case comes up again. Delay not only provides an opportunity for defendants to make themselves look better, it also puts distance between the incident and the defendant which diminishes the seriousness of the event in the eyes of the complainant and the court.

A complainant's diminished interest in pressing for a conviction does not always ensure that the case will be treated leniently. If the accused is known to have been arrested several times within the recent past for similar incidents, the prosecutor may ignore a reluctant complainant-spouse and insist on a plea of guilty. At times the prosecutor may suspect that the complaint's change of mind is attributable not to a forgiving heart but rather to intimidation and fear. When the prosecutor does press for a conviction in such situations, he tries to protect the complainant by stressing to the accused that he—the prosecutor —and not the complainant is responsible for insisting on the conviction. Or the prosecutor may insist on a guilty plea in a "minor" case in an effort to put a stop to a recurring pattern in which a person—usually a wife—calls the police to have her husband arrested and then later seeks to have the charges withdrawn. If the prosecutor feels that the wife is too quick to involve the police, he may insist that the husband plead guilty in hopes of putting a stop to what he feels is a frivolous use of his and the Police Department's time.

The prosecutor must be knowledgeable enough about the defendant's recent past to be able to discern a "pattern" in it. In an office with a part-time staff and no fixed functions, the prosecutor can do this only if he happens to handle the several cases that produce a pattern, or if he happens to trade enough information with his colleagues and the court staff.

Delay Despite the popular image of defendants being unwillingly drawn into a seemingly endless process, delays are usually a consequence of deliberate planning by defense attorneys bent on achieving more advantageous outcomes. Requests for jury trials are one sure way to obtaining delays of several weeks or months. But a simple request for a continuance is a more common way to obtain an automatic one- to three-week hiatus in the case. Like so many other practices, this is tolerated by prosecutors and judges who find it easier to adopt a blanket policy of not objecting to requests for continuances than to take the time and trouble to distinguish between legitimate and concocted reasons.

Delaying in order to improve the defendant's position is not just a shrewd defense attorney's trick; it has also been formalized by the court. There are several well-institutionalized programs based on the premise that adjudication should be delayed in order to grant the accused time to "pay for his mistake" or make progress toward rehabilitation. If the charges are minor, if the defendant has no record of serious offenses and appears "promising," then the Prosecutor's Office may agree to recommend that the judge continue the case for an extended period of time, during which the accused will participate in any of several programs designed to "help" or "rehabilitate" him. The least formal such arrangement is known by the euphemism "prosecutor's probation" and usually entails the accused's agreeing to read for the blind, work part-time at a local hospital, or perform similar charitable services. If after several weeks he has performed satisfactory work, then the prosecutor may agree to nolle the charges. A similar arrangement called "accelerated rehabilitation" allows for a dismissal after a period of unsupervised "pretrial probation." The largest and most formal of these alternatives is a pretrial diversion program which maintains a staff to counsel those whom the program has accepted and whom the Prosecutor's Office has agreed to let participate. If the participant appears regularly at these sessions for the period specified, one of the program's counsellors will appear in court and recommend that the court nolle the charges or impose a suspended sentence with no additional conditions.

While imbued with a rehabilitative ideal, each of these alternatives imposes restraints upon the accused which in essence mean that if the accused is willing to undergo a regime of social control *prior* to adjudication, then he or she can avoid a determination of guilt and possible sentence after adjudication. Prosecutors rely on these programs to impose some type of restraining influence on people against whom the case may be weak but whom they think are in need of a "lesson." Although these programs do not impose heavy burdens on most of the participants, neither do most of the court's sentences, and the impositions placed on those who may have entered a program under the false impression that it was the *only* alternative to a term in jail may quickly come to outweigh the burden of the sentence that would have been imposed had they pled guilty. Diversion treatments, then, can only be understood as a form of sanctioning administered *prior to* adjudication, without a formal determination of guilt.

All of these alternative programs are relatively small and only several years old; none is well-known, especially not to private attorneys who appear only infrequently in court. Unfamiliar with the informal practices of the court, some of these attorneys may guide clients into one of the programs thinking that it will be a substantial benefit while in fact it may produce a more restrictive outcome than a guilty plea or a request for a nolle. Other attorneys miss opportunities which might benefit their clients. For instance, I observed a situation in which a defendant awaiting sentence chanced to remark to the judge that she was going to lose her job as a result of conviction. The judge paused for a moment and asked her private attorney and the prosecutor if either of them had considered accelerated rehabilitation as an alternative to conviction. Neither indicated they had, whereupon the judge directed the woman to withdraw her guilty plea and then postponed decision on the case, urging the prosecutor and attorney to "get together" on the terms for accelerated rehabilitation.[6]

While delay is often beneficial to the defendant, it can also be costly. Prosecutors and judges often take this into consideration, as shown by the following attorney's appeal to a judge:

Your Honor, my client has already been punished enough. He has made six separate appearances in court and each time his case has been continued. If he had pled guilty the first time, his sentence would have caused fewer problems than those encountered by his having to come down here so often.

Other factors such as pretrial detention, attorney's and bondsmen's fees, and lost jobs are also taken into account in deciding the case outcome and sentence. Such considerations lead to the blurring of the formally distinct and sequential stages of adjudication and punishment.

Prosecutor–Defense Attorney Relationships

Contrary to popular opinion, the prosecutor is relatively passive in the criminal process. But his is a peculiar type of dynamic passivity. Once a case has been set in motion—and this is activated by the arresting officer, not the prosecutor—the prosecutor proceeds on the case as if his path were clear and obvious. On arraignment or first appearance he will announce charges to the court and "expect" the defendant to plead guilty. This is implied in the standard question the prosecutor addresses to the accused: "Do you want to get your own attorney, make application for a public defender, or dispose of your case today?" The implications are clear: If the defendant wants to get an attorney it will be complicated for him, but if he pleads guilty the whole matter will be over within a few minutes. The prosecutor is clearly communicating his preference and it is up to someone else—the defendant or his attorney—to suggest *another* course of action. While the prosecutor is prepared for and accedes to other courses of action, he does not actively seek them out, nor does he screen the cases to weed out "bad arrests" or to channel defendants to other available alternatives. Someone else must initiate these other possibilities, and then the prosecutor will respond.

But the prosecutor will readily deviate from his "normal" course of action. He expects to be contacted by defendants and defense attorneys who will offer "explanations," fill in details, point out weaknesses, or recommend alternative courses of action. For the sake of convenience, he presumes that the accused should plead guilty; this shifts the burden of decision away from him and places it on someone else. In theory, the prosecutor knows where he wants to go and is moving toward that goal; it is up to others to convince him to depart from it.

This passive stance is also reflected in the way prosecutors develop—or perhaps more accurately do not develop—their cases. Only in rare cases that involve a particularly serious charge, a well-known "bad guy," or a serious injury will the prosecutor carefully read through the file before arraignment or first appearance. Even then, he will probably read the file just before court convenes. It is not at all uncommon for the prose-

cutor to read through the file for the first time while the defendant is standing next to him before the bench, and he may even
have to rely on the defendant or his attorney to supply details
on the incident or information about the defendant's prior
record.

In contrast, the defense attorney or defendant is often the
aggressive person. The defense must persuade the prosecutor to
"deviate" from the normal course of action.[7] While this places a
burden on the defense attorney to convince the prosecutor that
his client is not guilty or marshal convincing mitigating factors,
this task is made easier by the fact that the prosecutor usually
has little incentive to construct a "strong" case against the defendant in the first place. His initial judgment of the worth of
the case is usually based upon a hurried reading of the police
report and little more. The defense attorney then is in a good
position to amplify or expand on this report in ways that benefit
his client. While the prosecutor develops a rough notion of a
"normal" crime and places a value sentence on each such offense, the defense attorney must break down this stereotype
and individualize the charge and the defendant. In essence, he
does this by providing reasons why the case should not be
treated "normally," so that even though cases begin their journeys through the court as "routine," they rarely leave that way.

Plea bargaining often consists of little more than the defense
attorney calling the prosecutor's attention to ambiguities contained in the prosecutor's own file, and in doing so convincing
the prosecutor that the case is not worth as much as he originally thought it was. The defense attorney does this by pointing
out complicating, contradictory, or mitigating factors in the police report; by fleshing out—explaining—the setting and circumstances of the incident; or by telling the prosecutor something about the defendant's background or relationship to the
complainant.

The defense attorney often suggests what charges might be
nolled or what the sentence might be. For example, after both a

PD and a prosecutor silently read through the police report, they had the following conversation:

PROSECUTOR: His story is nuts. I simply don't believe it. He's crazy.
PD: It's so crazy it must be true. No one would make up such a dumb story.
PROSECUTOR: Look, if we had a charge for stupidity, I'd charge him with it. He's crazy.
PD: I know. But what can we do with him?
PROSECUTOR: What do you want?
PD: How about a twenty-five-dollar fine?
PROSECUTOR: OK.

The prosecutor and defense attorney assume an adversary relationship, but it is not like those in popularized versions of jury trials or plea bargaining. The process is not so much a negotiating session as it is a discussion to develop a *common understanding* of the case. It usually has to do with disputed facts or shades of understanding of those facts, not with assurances of leniency exchanged for agreements to plead. But the prosecutor is likely to emphasize factors and interpretations favorable to the state and the defense attorney to emphasize factors favorable to his client. This session may proceed with a joint reading of the police report, both parties reading it for the first time. The seated prosecutor will hold the report and read it silently while the defense attorney stands, reading over the prosecutor's shoulder. The prosecutor will often read passages aloud which are damaging to the defendant—"kicked the complainant . . ." "threatened complainant with a stick . . ." "pounded on the door . . ." and so on. The defense attorney often counters by reading out loud other portions of the report which soften the charge—"both arrestee and complainant had been drinking together . . ." "arrestee claimed complainant owes him money . . ." "complainant also arrested . . ." Most often a settlement can be reached, but at times a session can drag out.

Although prosecutors are usually passive in bringing a case to a close, they are not without considerable power, which they exercise from time to time and which hovers in the background of all their dealings with defense attorneys. They control the docket and can punish recalcitrant defense attorneys by placing their cases last on the daily calendar, denying easy access to the court's files, and manipulating the jury trial list. For instance, one device defense attorneys use for delay is to place their cases in the jury trial calendar, even though they have no intention of going to trial. Because almost all cases placed on the jury trial calendar are eventually settled through negotiation, prosecutors schedule many more cases on any given day than could conceivably be tried. Knowing this, defense attorneys rarely come to court prepared for trial; they expect instead to discuss the case further with the prosecutor, and if they cannot reach an agreement, to have the case continued. But because the prosecutor rather than a disinterested clerk or judge calls cases for trial, a hard-driving defense attorney may be met with an unexpected demand to go upstairs immediately to begin trial, an action which is usually enough to force him to agree to the prosecutor's conditions for settlement. Although such showdowns occur infrequently, the possibility and an occasional hint of them are usually enough to draw lingering cases to a close.

Defendants Without Attorneys

Many defendants do not have attorneys to intercede and negotiate for them. How then do they obtain a nolle? How do they learn about the possible consequences of pleading guilty? When this question was put to several public defenders, judges, and prosecutors, the most frequent response was that defendants without attorneys are usually charged with minor offenses, are rarely treated harshly by the court, and are usually repeaters who because of their prior experiences in the court know what to expect. But my sample of cases suggests quite a different picture. Fully 40 percent of all defendants had no representation and were charged with a wide variety of offenses, ranging from very minor to very serious. Some had long histories of contact with the court, but many others had no prior record of any sort. Some obtained nolles, but many others were convicted and received suspended sentences or fines. A few were even sent to jail. In short, people *not* represented by counsel are *not* confined to a few types of habitual offenders whom the court dealt with in a tolerant, routine manner.

One of the reasons why court officials underestimate the number of defendants without attorneys is that these defendants tend to be invisible, often slipping through the court quietly by pleading guilty at first appearance or failing to appear altogether. Fully 15 percent of all defendants do not return to court, and a disproportionate number are unrepresented. Many of these arrestees prefer to forfeit small bonds rather than appear in court to pursue a plea of not guilty, or to plead guilty and recieve a small fine or suspended sentence.[8]

Although people without attorneys go through the court unnoticed, they still must learn about the consequences of their actions and be guided in their movements through the complicated maze of the legal processes. I gave special attention to the ways in which these defendants passed through the court, how they arrived at their decisions to seek a nolle or plead guilty, and how they learned of the likely consequences of these decisions. As a group these defendants are remarkably resourceful in obtaining information about how to handle their own cases.

For the prosecutor's convenience, defendants are routinely instructed to be in court at 10 A.M. on the day of their scheduled court appearance. Because he cannot handle all the cases at once, the prosecutor responds to pressures about sequencing by calling private attorneys first, then public defenders, and finishing with defendants without representation. This means that the latter must while away a good portion of the day waiting for their cases to be called, but that they also have time to observe proceedings, compare notes with others in a similar situation, and discuss their cases with the court's auxiliary personnel. Because they are anxious, they often pursue several of these courses of action simultaneously. From these encounters, they learn that they can talk directly to a prosecutor about their case either at recesses or after court has adjourned for the day. At times they can be seen queuing up in the "attorneys' line" before court convenes.

Although defendants are usually less articulate and more hesitant than defense attorneys, those who do approach the prosecutor to "find out about my case" frequently raise the same points that an attorney would. One prosecutor, comparing dealing with attorneys and directly with defendants, observed:

> All the attorneys do in so many cases is to repeat the story of their clients. The attorneys don't know the technical legal rules to raise elaborate defenses. Most defenses are common sense anyway, so if the defendant repeats his side of the story, it often raises adequate defenses we take into consideration.
>
> There are a lot of them who have strong incentive to come down here and tell us their own story . . . and we listen.

But because defendants are easily intimidated, prosecutors are likely to be aggressive and blunt with them, as the following example indicates.

> A prosecutor is talking to a defendant who is not represented by an attorney. He is speaking very rapidly and forcibly, asking the defendant, "Why do you want to go to trial? Don't fuck around. Take a small fine. Why come back again or perhaps two or three times? Why miss a few days' work and end up with a stiffer sentence than you would get from me? If you go to trial, you may go to jail." (He continues to almost berate the defendant, not giving him an opportunity to respond.) Finally, he asks, "Do you have ten dollars on you?"
>
> For the first time the defendant has an opportunity to respond to the rapid-fire questions of the prosecutor. He nods affirmatively, indicating that he has that amount on him and will plead guilty.
>
> The prosecutor then says, "Look, I'll recommend a ten-dollar fine, and that will be the end of it. You can get out of here and you don't need to fool around with this any more."

The defendant nods approvingly, and the prosecutor tells him to go outside and wait until his name is called, and the case will be concluded.

But only particularly enterprising defendants argue with a prosecutor; most limit their contact with him to a quick exchange before the bench and turn to other courtroom officials for information and advice. Most of these officials are easy to identify because, in contrast to defendants and their families, they wear coats, ties, or uniforms, and are engaged in purposeful—although perhaps vague—behavior. In contrast to defense attorneys, most of these people are quite willing to give off-the-cuff advice. Bondsmen are among those who give it most frequently and freely, especially to clients not represented by counsel. Other courtroom advisers include bailiffs, sheriffs, police officers, and investigators, whoever happens to be free at the moment. I was approached for advice numerous times when I was conducting research in the courtroom.

Most of the advice given to defendants without attorneys is delivered in a casual way, and generally advisers provide accurate and helpful information. Court routines remain fairly stable, and like the prosecutors and defense attorneys, the auxiliary personnel soon learn how to sort through facts and excuses to establish the crucial elements and worth of the case.

The examination in the preceding chapter showed only slightly more favorable nolle rates and sentences for defendants with counsel, and one might be tempted to conclude that overall these informal "advisers" are just as effective as attorneys. In one sense this statement may be correct most of the time, but in another it is subject to important qualification. It is precisely because so many defendants do have attorneys that the differences between those with and those without is so slight. By pressing their client's interests, occasionally raising legal defenses, and pressing for openness and trust between themselves and the Prosecutor's Office, defense attorneys have helped carve out the factors which enter into the assessment of a case and helped define the court's relationship to the defendant. Once they are established, these norms and sense of rough justice are applied more or less equally to all, even to those without attorneys who nevertheless benefit from the "common law" which has been shaped in part by defense attorneys. To suggest that there is little difference between outcomes in cases with and without attorneys does *not* imply that the outcomes would be the same if *no one* at all had an attorney.

Plea Bargaining

Almost all convictions in the Court of Common Pleas follow guilty pleas. The court's records for the past several years showed that on the average, fewer than 1 percent of all criminal cases went to trial. Nationwide figures indicate that in most jurisdictions anywhere between 90 and 98 percent of all criminal cases are resolved by some means other than trial.[9] Officials in New Haven and most other observers point to these figures when documenting the prevalence of plea bargaining, which they assert is the dominant means of disposing of criminal cases in modern American courts.[10]

Plea bargaining is based on the premise that a defendant will exchange the uncertainties and costs of going to trial and the possibility of a lengthy sentence for the certainty of a fixed outcome which guarantees a less severe sanction than would have been imposed if he had been convicted after trial. In return, the argument continues, the state saves the time and expense of having to mount a trial. The lack of trials, most observers feel, is a clear indication of the pervasiveness of plea bargaining. The simple logic of plea bargaining is compelling, so much so that perhaps it is now taken for granted and has not been subjected to careful scrutiny or empirical examination under varying conditions. Because plea bargaining has come to be understood as the nearly universal means for resolving criminal cases, the term may have become so inclusive that its value as an explanation for the process may be diminished.

In the conventional view of plea bargaining, the defendant

extracts concessions, either the elimination of charges or an agreed-upon sentence recommendation, in exchange for pleading guilty. This view is based on the assumption that in the absence of such concessions the defendant will go to trial. However, few defendants in lower criminal courts even seriously contemplate this option, and even fewer actually invoke it. The question is why? The virtual absence of trials in New Haven's lower court may be partially attributable to the *quid pro quos* suggested above, the press of public defender's heavy caseload, or the private attorney's desire for quick financial gain.[11] But consider the sole LAA lawyer's trial record in lower court. Unlike the PDs, the LAA attorney was able to regulate his caseload and turn away potential clients if he felt he would be overloaded; unlike private attorneys, he was on salary and had no financial interests at stake. Still, only upon rare occasions did he take a case to trial. Despite this, he was generally regarded as one of the most able adversarial attorneys in town. In fact, because of the lack of financial constraints, he complained that at times there were pressures for him to go to trial needlessly.

Those guys [private attorneys] simply have to inform their client how much it will cost them to pursue their claim of innocence at trial. This causes a lot of defendants to sober up. I have guys whose stories are crazy but still maintain their innocence. While I never try to pressure anyone out of a trial, by the time I explain what a trial will involve, most are willing to drop their stance and level with me. We can then bargain.

In order to avoid economic coercion, some private attorneys charge a flat rate for their services regardless of the method of disposition or the amount of time they spend on a case. The name of one such attorney was included in my survey, and despite the fact that he was rated the most adversarial and aggressive lawyer in New Haven, he had *never* taken a case to trial in the lower court.

About 46 percent of those who are brought into court have their cases nolled, and over 90 percent of those who are convicted do *not* receive a jail sentence. In comparison, the time, effort, and expense of going to trial are overwhelming. A private attorney may charge $200 a day to conduct a trial; yet few fines exceed $50. For all practical purposes, a defendant's most vehement threat to go to trial is a hollow one; prosecutors know these threats will only be carried out once in a great while. In fact, trials are so rare that some prosecutors and judges regard them as a welcome change of pace, and at least one judge is rumored to lobby the Prosecutor's Office to send him cases for trial to relieve his boredom. A trial is a rare opportunity to allow the principals to "feel like lawyers." For the overwhelming majority of defendants, however, trial is simply *not* a viable alternative, and the key incentive in the orthodox notion of plea bargaining is not present. The more common question among defendants in this court is not whether to go to trial, but whether to show up in court at all.

If the key ingredient of the plea bargain is not present, or if it is only partially present in a very few cases, then how can we describe the process of negotiating cases more accurately? Why do participants continue to characterize the process as plea bargaining? And what functions does this language serve?

Discussions of plea bargaining conjure up images of a Middle Eastern bazaar, in which each transaction appears as a new and distinct encounter, unencumbered by precedent and past association. Each transaction involves higgling and haggling anew, in an effort to obtain the best possible deal. American lower courts have a different reality. They are more akin to modern supermarkets in which prices for various commodities have been clearly established and labeled. Arriving at an exchange in this context is not an explicit negotiation and bargaining process—"You do this for me and I'll do that for you"—designed to reach a mutually acceptable agreement. To the extent that there is any negotiation at all, it is debate over the nature of the case, and hinges largely on establishing the relevant "facts" which flow from various interpretations of the police report, and only occasionally involve independent investigation by a defense. In a supermarket customers may complain about prices, but rarely "bargain" to get them reduced. But an alert consumer may try to convince a store that an item has been mislabeled and "mispriced." This type of "bargaining" characterizes most of the negotiations in the Court of Common Pleas; for this reason cases in which one side—the prosecutor—gives up everything and nolles the case can still be characterized as plea bargaining.

This does not mean that there is never plea bargaining of the more familiar type. Although in the modern American supermarket prices are labeled and there is little bargaining over them, market forces still operate. Prices are not tested and adjusted with each and every retail purchase, but occasional changes in wholesale prices eventually lead to adjustments in consumer prices. Likewise, an occasional "real" plea bargain or a sentence after trial may reaffirm or revalue the "worth" of a certain type of case. Once this is established it will prevail until it is slowly eroded or challenged by another key case, and a new "price" is established. There is a kind of "plea market," so that a case which has been vigorously bargained over or decided at trial can establish a new "going rate" for all subsequent similar cases.

This has been true for drug possession cases. Within the past few years, marijuana and heroin have become "familiar" to the court and the community, and tolerance of drug use, especially marijuana, has increased. One result is that the court has become progressively more lenient in its handling of these cases, and in essence the "worth" or "going rate" of this type of case has declined.

This decline has been precipitated by changing social mores, but it received impetus in the court from the occasional actions of defense attorneys who have not been pleased with the "going rate," and have threatened trial—in classic plea bargaining fashion—unless their positions were accepted. A few such confrontations resulted in trials in which prosecutors found that judges were not as harsh at sentencing as they had expected. Other reductions in going rates have been occasioned when attorneys for college students vigorously pressed for "better" deals for their clients, whom they argued would face a lifetime of lost opportunity if they were convicted for possession of marijuana. But once such exceptions were made, then attorneys for other defendants began to press for the same treatment, and eventually a new lower price for this type of case was established. Because communication is so rapid in the small world of the courthouse, it only takes a handful of such key cases—perhaps only one—to establish a new "going rate." But although the classic process of plea bargaining does not take place very frequently, it is not unimportant. On the contrary, it is extremely important precisely because one case may have widespread and lasting effects.

The Symbolic Importance of Plea Bargaining

Although most of what prosecutors and defense attorneys refer to as plea bargaining is actually a type of normative endeavor—a joint assessment of the incident and the accused's actions and character—many of the trappings of the classic plea bargaining process still exist and serve important symbolic functions. They provide the illusion of a bargain and provide a prop for attorneys anxious to provide tangible evidence of service to their often skeptical clients. In a classic plea bargain, defendants attempt to secure reductions of charges or guarantees of reduced sentences in exchange for their pleas of guilty. Both of these reductions take place with great frequency in the Court of Common Pleas. Defense attorneys regularly approach their clients to report that the prosecutor is willing to nolle one charge, or to recommend what appears to be a lenient sentence in exchange for a plea of guilty. For those without attorneys, the prosecutor may himself make such suggestions directly to the defendant.

Whether they are proposed through an attorney or directly by the prosecutor, these "offers" are often phrased in a way that makes them appear to be exceptional, "deals" which are too good to pass up. Criminal offenses are characterized in minute detail in the criminal code and each offense can easily fit into one of several different classifications. For instance, there are four classes for larceny and four for assault, each gradation distinguished by the value of the items stolen or the amount of damage. In addition, two or three different charges are so closely related that they can easily be applied to the same action. Assault might reasonably be labeled a threat; shoplifting, a trespass; and a breach of peace, disorderly conduct. By dropping one of two closely related charges or substituting one for the other, prosecutors can convey the impression of a bargain, while in fact they may simply be offering the standard rate under a slightly different label.[12]

Defendants are singularly concerned with their case outcomes. If they cannot have charges dropped entirely, then they want a minimal sentence. The seeming harshness of the penal code facilitates acceptance of whatever the defendant actually receives. A defense attorney or prosecutor may describe a defendant's predicament to him in terms of his "theoretical exposure," calculated by determining the maximum possible sentence for all charges and then treating them additively. One charge of second-degree larceny and one of breach of peace have a total theoretical exposure of eighteen months: twelve for the larceny, a class A misdemeanor, and six for the breach of peace, a class B misdemeanor.

The prospects of an eighteen-month sentence are quite sobering to a defendant, and an attorney or prosecutor who can arrange to obtain one substantially less than this is likely to be greeted with appreciation. For instance by dropping the larceny charge, theoretical exposure is reduced to six months, knocking off 67 percent of the jail time. The same benefits can be produced by offering to recommend a sentence substantially below the "maximum," again emphasizing that it is a bargain. And almost invariably the reduction is so dramatic that it would be difficult for the defendant to pass it up.

It is the salesman's stock-in-trade to represent a "going rate" as if it were a special sale price offered only once. The gap between theoretical exposure and the standard rate allows defense attorneys and prosecutors to function much the same way, making the defendant think he is getting a special "deal" when in fact he is getting the standard rate. Together prosecutors and defense attorneys operate like discount stores, pointing to a never-used high list price and then marketing the product at a supposedly "special" sale price, thereby appearing to provide substantial savings to those who act quickly.

In addition, this makes the attorney appear to have been of service. Criminal law is a difficult practice. Being accused of a crime is a humiliating experience, and few people come away from court feeling good about it. Clients are usually hostile and suspicious, especially if they are being represented by a public defender. The time, service, and skill an attorney invests are not always visible to them. As a consequence attorneys, like doctors, must not only make an effort to render services, but also *appear* that they are doing so. Securing a sentence substantially below the "theoretical maximum" is one way of doing this.

Plea bargaining is also an important way of measuring success for defense attorneys and prosecutors. In assessing their own and each others' skills, defense attorneys and prosecutors spoke in terms of their ability to secure reductions in *theoretical exposure*, although when pressed they acknowledged that such reductions probably did not translate into any actual reductions in sentences. *Theoretical exposure* functions as a way of magnifying something that is invisible to the naked eye, and provides a more dramatic way of measuring one's own and one's colleagues' abilities.

Theoretical exposure is a concept with more symbolic than actual content, but it does perform important functions. It serves as an index of success for both defendants and their attorneys. It provides a sense of at least partial victory for the defendant. It dramatizes his attorney's efforts and magnifies his benefits, thereby facilitating the guilty plea process. And it provides a rough measure of competence for attorneys who desire some basis for assessing and comparing their skills as negotiators. It may have more parallels with a game than most think.

My findings run counter to those in much of the literature on plea bargaining. But they are based on intensive study of only *one* court, although they have been reinforced by my impressions of others. And the process I have explained applies to relatively minor criminal offenses, *not* major felonies. In chapter one I pointed out that discussions of the criminal justice system often do not provide a clear indication of the types of cases and offenses to which they refer. This is especially important with respect to plea bargaining. The transaction costs for a person accused of a major felony are relatively small in comparison to the possible sentence he may receive. In contrast, transaction costs loom large in minor cases for which suspended sentence or fine is a likely outcome.

Negotiation as a Process of Exchange

Although cases are usually resolved through a mutual agreement as to the "worth" of a case, we have seen that there is a clear adversarial stance which pits prosecutors against defense attorneys, one which usually focuses on the meaning of "facts" in the case. Both sets of attorneys take pride in their jobs and neither wants to be "taken advantage of." This adversarial stance, quite proper when considering individual cases, "spills over" to affect relationships between distinct cases. It generates a subtle but still detectable process of exchange which weights actions in one case against actions in others.

This process becomes most apparent when a prosecutor and

defense attorney sit down to negotiate several cases at one time. After they have discussed a few, the prosecutor might say rhetorically, "Jesus, I've already given you three nolles today, do you want me to go out of business?" Or, he might urge, "That judge is tough; I can't give you any more nolles today." Conversely, the prosecutor might hear a defense attorney plead, "You've put me through the wringer this morning; give me a break on this one!"

Language in other settings also points to this process of exchange. Prosecutors, defense attorneys, and other courthouse officials are constantly asking each other to "Do me a favor. ..." This is a standard introduction to many types of requests (e.g., "Do me a favor, find me a bondsman; . . . give me a continuance; . . . give me a nolle"). Occasionally the request is punctuated with a reminder of a particularly favorable or unfavorable treatment in an earlier case. A prosecutor might retort, "Christ, I gave you the moon on the ——— case; I can't do it here too. The guy has got to do some time in jail." Or a defense attorney might press, "You've been screwing me all week. Give me a break for the weekend." Much of this language is exaggerated bantering characteristic of courthouse discourse in general; it smoothes the rough edges produced by the fast pace of the courtroom and the constant clashing of interests. Yet the very use of this language suggests a subtle equilibrium which can only be maintained by a give-and-take not only within but *between* cases.

Evidence of exchange is also manifested by the elaborate efforts some attorneys make to avoid it. Defense attorneys give considerable care to the order in which they discuss cases with prosecutors. Knowing that prosecutors are unwilling to "give away" too many cases at any single session, they may postpone discussion on some cases in order not to cluster requests together or call attention to themselves. Or they may introduce their most difficult request first, pressing hard on it and hoping that the "obvious" ones will take care of themselves later.

Prosecutors are well aware of this practice, and acknowledge that they feel under pressure not to nolle "too many cases." It is not their chief but the judges who exert this pressure. While judges generally pay little attention to the prosecutor's recitation of reasons for a nolle, if the judge has heard the same set speech several times in a row, he might ask rhetorically why the police are doing such a poor job or why the prosecutor is nolle-ing so many cases. While the judge may not even pause for an answer, and only upon rare occasion does a judge "refuse" to accept a nolle, still prosecutors seek to avoid such criticism. At times they too order their cases so as not to call attention to the number of nolles they are requesting.

These maneuvers by both defense attorneys and prosecutors are usually successful. Prosecutors have few fixed functions, often change positions (from discussing cases in the "backroom" to presenting them in open court) during their day's work, and they liberally grant continuances. Both these practices provide defense attorneys with the leeway they seek. Similarly, judges do not police their professed concerns very vigorously. If they conclude that there are "too many nolles" —never did I see them conclude the reverse—judges are usually responding to what has just occurred in the preceding few cases, not to a shift in the prosecutors' policy or a trend based upon inspection of court records. Because they rotate and have little interest in the administration of the court, their judgments are limited to off-the-cuff remarks based on immediate impressions, and in all but the most unusual of circumstances can easily be avoided by a prosecutor.

While this ease of adjustment no doubt blunts the impact of exchange, the process persists in subtle and, upon rare occasions, blatant form. In borderline cases, a very problematic outcome might unwittingly or only half-consciously hinge on what transpired in preceding cases. Only a handful of private attorneys have gained reputations among prosecutors for their willingness to try to promote "package deals."[13] Whereas prosecutors report that they scornfully reject these offers, and point to this as evidence that such exchanges do not occur, the very fact that such offers are ever made suggests that there is a norm of reciprocity which involves more subtle types of exchanges.

In its more subtle forms, the reciprocity depends upon the amount of business a defense attorney brings to court. Even though private attorneys concentrate their courthouse appearances into one or two days a week, they are likely to have only two or three cases to discuss with a prosecutor at any one time. In contrast, while public defenders may not have as heavy a *total* work load as a successful private attorney, all of their work takes place in one courthouse, and they may handle as many as ten or more cases a day. Because they handle so many cases and because these are compressed into such a short span of time, public defenders are most vulnerable to the pressures of exchange. If a PD feels that he received a good deal in one case, he may ease off on the next; if he feels irritated that he did not press hard enough on one case, he may redouble his efforts on the next. The pressure to handle a large number of cases rapidly invites this effort at adjustment. If public defenders are to be especially faulted for this practice, then it is more the product of the structure of their job than of personality.

Trials and Sentences

If a prosecutor is intent upon securing a conviction, most defendants have no real choice but to plead guilty. Even if they have free counsel, the time and effort necessary to mount a defense can quickly come to outweigh the magnitude of the sanction that the defendant is seeking to avoid. But this alone is not a complete explanation for the almost total absence of trials. For by going to trial, the defendant risks a substantially harsher sentence than if he pleads guilty.

Although trials are infrequent, there are enough of them to

serve as constant, vivid reminders of this risk. Most trials occur after unsuccessful efforts to plea bargain; both defense attorneys and prosecutors agree that defendants who are convicted often receive sentences that were harsher than the prosecutor's proposed sentence recommendations during negotiations. This was borne out in the trials I observed. In one case a defendant was convicted on two charges and received a combined sentence of fifteen months, in sharp contrast to the six months she had been offered as a "sentence rec" by the prosecutor before trial.

There are several explanations for this two-tiered sentencing policy. As one judge argued:

A trial may expose a certain gravity of the case. The development of the facts, the victims' description and appearance, and the presentence report may all bring the gravity of the offense in a way that discussions between counsel and prosecutor do not, and so sentences are likely to be stiffer.

Other officials concurred with this opinion, adding that when defendants in trials take the stand, as they often do, they usually perjure themselves, which also contributes to the harsher penalties.

While they do not disagree with these observations, defense attorneys emphasize still a third factor. They tend to view the harsher sentences as an unwritten but nevertheless strictly enforced threat by judges to intimidate defendants. One defense attorney who was especially indignant about this practice felt that most judges are basically lazy people who "do nothing and prefer to do nothing." This view was echoed although in a more diplomatic manner by many of the prosecutors, public defenders, and some of the more candid judges. One judge claimed that many of his colleagues viewed their positions on the bench as rewards for past services to their party and sought to avoid the hard work of presiding over a trial. Another felt that many of his colleagues resented "obviously guilty" people, forcing the state to bear all the expenses of proving them guilty at trial. "Many judges," he suggested, "are likely to be harsher because the defendant has made the state take the time and go to the expense of a trial."

During my research the issue of stiffer sentences after trials emerged as a minor statewide controversy. In a concerted act of civil disobedience, a large number of motorcyclists courted arrest by openly defying the law requiring them to wear helmets, and at arraignment insisted on jury trials. The judge hearing the cases indicated that he would follow the prosecutor's recommendation for suspended sentences if they pleaded guilty, but that he would levy the maximum penalty if they were convicted after trial. Since this penalty was only $100, and the cyclists were intent on preserving their right to appeal and interested in publicizing their opposition to the law, they were not deterred from trial and welcomed support from the Connecticut Civil Liberties Union on behalf of their right to trial. The state's law was eventually repealed before these cases were called; yet the incident does highlight what prosecutors and judges are reluctant to state publicly, that there is a likely surcharge for going to trial that deters those few people who might wish to have one.

Summary

Decision making in the court focuses upon a concern for substantive rather than formal justice. Although the relationship between prosecution and defense is somewhat adversarial, they are actually engaging in a decision process to reach a consensus about the "worth of the case." But the outcomes of each and every case are problematic, in part because of personality differences, but more because the facts are elusive. Much of what passes for plea bargaining is really negotiation over the meaning of facts, and the adversarial roles of prosecution and defense may be crucial. Facts are malleable. They must be mobilized, and often they are manufactured. It requires time and effort to deal carefully with facts, but the court is structured to offer rapid substantive justice, through processes that invite carelessness and error.

Other features of the court's decision-making processes also make outcomes problematic. There is a subtle process of exchange which suggests that at times the disposition of one case is dependent upon the outcomes of the cases which immediately preceded it. The two-tiered sentencing structure is more apparent than real because there are so few trials, and it diminishes whatever little incentive there is to take a case to trial almost to the vanishing point. Even without this deterrent, the costs of the pretrial process are usually not only sufficient to discourage most from ever seriously contemplating a trial, but they also give rise to the impulse to offer *rapid* substantive justice rather than more deliberate and more costly formal justice.

CHAPTER 7

The Process Is

the Punishment

Introduction

The last two chapters examined sentencing and adjudication,
two stages of the criminal process which are featured in most
research on criminal courts. This chapter returns to a third
concern which I characterized as the pretrial process model in
chapter one. It develops the argument that in the lower criminal
courts the process itself is the primary punishment. In this chapter I identify the costs involved in the pretrial process, and
examine the ways they affect organization, as well as the way a
defendant will proceed on his journeys through the court. This
examination should help explain why lower courts do not fit
their popular image, and why cases are processed so quickly in
the Court of Common Pleas.

The first set of factors I examine deals with the consequences
of pretrial detention and the problems of securing pretrial release. The second explores the costs of securing an attorney.
There are obvious financial outlays involved in retaining a private attorney, but there are also hidden costs associated with

obtaining free counsel. A third set of factors deals with the problem of continuances. While delay often benefits the defendant, its importance for the defendant is often exaggerated, and it is crucial to distinguish defendant-induced delay from continuances which are arranged for the convenience of the court.

By themselves these costs may appear to be minor or even trivial in a process formally structured to focus on the crucial questions of adjudication and sentencing. However, in the aggregate, and in comparison with the actual consequences of adjudication and sentencing, they often loom large in the eyes of the criminally accused, and emerge as central concerns in getting through the criminal justice system.

These pretrial costs account for a number of puzzling phenomena: why so many people waive their right to free appointed counsel; why so many people do not show up for court at all; and why people choose the available adversarial options so infrequently. Furthermore, pretrial costs are part of the reason why pretrial diversion programs designed to *benefit* defendants and provide alternatives to standard adjudication do not receive a more enthusiastic response. The accused often perceive these programs as cumbersome processes which simply increase their contact with the system.

The relative importance of the pretrial process hinges on one important set of considerations. Students of the criminal courts often overlook what many criminologists and students of social class do not, that the fear of arrest and conviction does not loom as large in the eyes of many people brought into court as it does in the eyes of middle-class researchers. While I did not systematically interview a sample of defendants, I had informal and often extended discussions with dozens of defendants who were waiting for their cases to be called, and I watched still more discuss their cases with attorneys and prosecutors. While there were obvious and numerous exceptions, I was nevertheless struck by the frequent lack of concern about the stigma of conviction and by the more practical and far more immediate concerns about what the sentence would be and how quickly they could get out of court.

There are several reasons for this. First, many arrestees already have criminal records, so that whatever stigma does attach to a conviction is already eroded, if not destroyed.[1] Second, many arrestees, particularly young ones, are part of a subculture which spurns conventional values and for which arrest and conviction may even function as a celebratory ritual, reinforcing their own values and identity. In fact, they may even perceive it as part of the process of coming of age.[2] Third, lower-class people tend to be more *present*-oriented than middle-class people, and for obvious reasons.[3] Many defendants are faced with an immediate concern for returning to work or their children, and these concerns often take precedence over the desire to avoid the *remote* consequences that a (or another) conviction might bring. This *relative* lack of concern about conviction is reinforced by the type of employment opportunities available to lower-class defendants. If an employee is reliable, it may make little difference whether or not he pleads guilty to a minor charge emerging from a "Saturday night escapade." Indeed, an employer is not likely to find out about the incident unless his employee has to arrange to miss work in order to appear in court.

If the stigma of the criminal sanction is not viewed as a significant sanction, the concrete costs of the pretrial process take on great significance. When this occurs, the process itself becomes the punishment.

Pretrial Release: An Overview

A quick reading of relevant Connecticut statutes, case law, and administrative directives conveys the impression that the state has an unswerving commitment to prompt pretrial release. There is an elaborate multi-layered system for decision and review, there are a variety of pretrial release alternatives, and assurance of appearance at trial is the sole criterion for establishing release conditions.[4]

The police are empowered to make the initial release decision and can either release a suspect at the site of the arrest or take him to the central booking facility. Once the suspect is booked, police retain the power to establish release conditions, and they may release suspects on a written promise to appear (PTA) or on bond, which they set. If they do not release the arrestee, at this point, the police are then required to notify a bail commissioner who in turn is supposed to "promptly conduct [an] interview and investigation as he deems necessary to reach an independent decision." If after this the accused is still not released, then the bail commissioner "shall set forth his reasons . . . in writing."[5] The accused has a third opportunity to seek release at arraignment and all subsequent appearances, at which time he can request the judge to consider a bond reduction or release on PTA.

This liberal release policy is reflected in practice as well. Table 7.1 indicates that 89 percent of those arrested were released prior to the disposition of their cases, and that 52 percent of them were released on nonfinancial conditions, by police field

TABLE 7.1
Release‧Detention Rates

Condition Immediately Prior to Disposition	N	%
Released on Citation	244	16%
Released on PTA	565	36
Released on Bond	567	37
(Subtotal released)	(1376)	(89%)
Detained	166	11
TOTAL	1542	100%

citation or PTA. Thirty-seven percent were released on bond, and only 11 percent were detained until disposition. Although the proportion of arrestees released pending trial is typically regarded as the most important measure of a jurisdiction's "liberality," it is far from a complete picture. Two additional questions must be answered. First, at what point in the process do people secure release? To identify as "released" only those who were free at the time their cases were disposed of is to overlook those who were held in detention for a while before eventually securing release. And if a person is released on bail, at what price was freedom purchased?

Length of Time in Pretrial Custody Table 7.2 provides a breakdown of the length of time defendants in my sample were in custody before being released. Seventeen percent were released almost immediately on police citations. A much larger group—44 percent—was released within three hours after being taken to the "lockup," and a third group was released within a period of thirteen to twenty-four hours after arrest.

TABLE 7.2

Length of Time in
Pretrial Detention

Length of Time	N	%
none	244	17%
0-3 hours	624	43
4-7 hours	82	6
8-12 hours	92	6
13-24 hours	308	21
2 days	31	2
3 days	10	1
4-7 days	12	1
8-20 days	18	1
over 20 days	17	1
	1438	99%*

*Rounding error.

Many of the people in this group were released in court the morning after their arrest, at which time they were able to secure reductions in the amount of bond or contact a bondsman or family member to post bond; some pleaded guilty and were discharged from custody. However, 6 percent of the sample remained in pretrial custody for a period of two days or longer, and a small number were held three weeks or more.

A small but nevertheless substantial number (142 of 1,151) of those eventually released prior to trial secured a delayed release only after their bonds had been lowered. Eighty-three of them eventually had money bonds reduced to PTA. In a number of instances this change took place after several days. (Seven of the eighty-three who were eventually released PTA spent a week or longer in jail before being released.) Another forty-six people had their bonds reduced but still could not afford to post the smaller amount, and consequently remained in detention until their cases were disposed of.

Many of these delayed releases were the result of police-applied situational sanctions, of trying to cope with a potentially explosive problem or to teach an arrestee "a lesson." As a group, people who have just been arrested are not in a pleasant mood. All are hostile, many are belligerent, and some are even threatening. A few are frightened, timid, and remorseful, but many have just been dragged abruptly and unceremoniously from a barroom scuffle or a domestic battle, and continue to curse their absent adversary, threatening to return to continue the fight or redirecting their hostility toward the police. The police are usually able to calm arrestees down by being quite formal and "correct" in their interviews, ignoring the insults and threats. However, if the arrestee remains belligerent, the police may place him in a cell and let him "cool down," and only later complete the charging process or reduce the high bail they initially set. Most of those who are released after between eight and twelve hours (see Table 7.2) are people whose bonds were subsequently reduced to PTA after police judged them cool-headed enough to be safe.

Other arrestees secure delayed release because the lockup facility becomes overcrowded. On Saturday evenings police may "weed out" the lockup by granting PTA's to Friday evening's arrestees in order to make room for new arrivals.[6] Women are housed in a separate facility in another location and are generally more likely to be released earlier on lower bond.

Detention Until Disposition Whether they are detained for a few hours or several days, people who are held in custody until disposition are at a special disadvantage. Research has consistently shown that those unable to post bond are more likely to be convicted than those who have been released prior to trial, and if convicted they are more likely to receive harsher sentences.[7] These studies have concluded that those who are detained do not have easy access to their attorneys and cannot aid in the development of their defenses. They are at a disadvantage when they enter a courtroom, often dressed in prison garb and always under the watchful eye of a guard who views them as "convicts." These studies suggest that someone who is detained is more likely to plead guilty, in hopes of either being transferred to a prison which has better facilities, or of being released altogether. The findings in my sample supported these general arguments. Detainees were less likely to receive nolles than those who were released (30 percent to 49 percent). These figures still held up even when controls for the seriousness of the offenses and other factors were introduced.

Daniel Freed has observed that "of the many paradoxes which beset the criminal justice system, few surpass the picture of judges and jailers imprisoning more accused offenders before their trials than after conviction."[8] This paradox is certainly demonstrated by these data. Of the 102 people who were detained until disposition and pleaded guilty, only a small handful of them received substantial jail sentences. Even excluding those arrestees whose cases were disposed of at arraignment shortly after their arrest, this imbalance persists.

During my court observations I paid especially close attention to the guilty plea process in an effort to supplement this assessment of the impact of detention on pleading and sentencing. Whenever a detained person was sentenced to "time served" or received an additional jail sentence, I sought out defense attorneys who were familiar with the case and solicited their opinions on the consequences of detention. Their responses often indicated a strong belief that many sentences to "time served" were the judge's attempt to justify pretrial detention. In cases which involved additional jail time, they also often concluded that the sentence was overly harsh, and that had the person been out on bond he would not have had to serve any time in jail.

Although it is impossible to know how many of those detained until disposition would have received nolles had they been released, it is certain that had any of them refused to plead guilty and insisted on a trial, most of them would have had to spend more time in jail. While there may be some doubt about the precise magnitude of the effect of pretrial detention on inducing detainees to plead guilty, there is no doubt about its *chilling effect*. When the choice is between freedom for those who plead guilty and jail for those who want to invoke their right to trial, there is really no choice at all.

Conditions for Release Although many people are released without financial conditions, many others must buy their freedom. In my sample 37 percent of all arrestees secured their pretrial freedom only after they put up a cash or surety bond, and another 11 percent were detained because they could not raise the needed money.⁹ What differentiates members of these groups from one another? What accounts for variation in the conditions of release? Who is released on citation or PTA and who must pay for their pretrial freedom?

Connecticut law is unambiguous about the purpose of bail— to secure appearance at trial—and the Bail Commission's interview form identifies factors commonly believed to be indicators as to whether or not someone is likely to appear. They are: the accused's ties to the community as indicated by length of residency in the area; employment status; and family ties. Table 7.3 contains the results of a regression analysis which examines the direct effects of a group of eleven "legal" and "extralegal" variables on the conditions of release (nonfinancial/financial). Only five of the eleven variables were statistically significant at the .01 level, but of these, three relate to legally permissible considerations—length of time in New Haven (beta = .33), employment status (beta = .14), and arrest on a warrant (beta = .14)—all of which were related in predictable directions. In contrast, two extralegal factors were also statistically significant. They are "race of the defendant" and "number of prior convictions." Although they were not strong, they were in the predicted direction.[10]

Amount of Bond   Table 7.4 shows that bonds range from a

TABLE 7.3

Regression Results for Selected Characteristics of Arrestees and Conditions of Pretrial Release

Variable	Regression Coefficient	Std. Error of Coeff.	Standardized Coefficient	T-Test	Sig.
Length of Time in New Haven	.08	.01	.32	6.25	.001
Employment Status	.14	.05	.14	2.72	.007
Race	.15	.05	.15	3.09	.003
Arrested on a Warrant	−.01	.00	−.14	−2.90	.004
Number of Witnesses	−.56	.20	−.13	−2.83	.005
Marital Status	.06	.04	.08	1.59	.113

Multiple correlation (R) = .50
Multiple correlation squared (R^2) = .25

TABLE 7.4
Bond Amounts

Bond Amount	N	%
1. Cite	249	15.2
2. PTA	528	32.2
11. $5	77	4.7
12. $10	6	0.4
13. $15	2	0.1
14. $20	14	0.9
15. $25	89	5.3
16. $50	106	6.4
20. $100	129	7.8
21. $200	41	2.5
22. $300	33	2.0
23. $400	1	0.1
24. $500	75	4.6
25. $1000 (501-1000)	169	10.3
30. $2000 (1001-2500)	36	2.2
31. $5000 (2501-5000)	19	1.2
32. $10,000 (5001-10,000)	8	0.5
33. over $10,000	3	0.2
39. OK, other	55	3.4
	1640	100.0%

low of $5 to over $10,000, but that most are clustered at $5, $25, $50, $100, $500, and $1,000. Most of the bonds of $50 and under were posted in cash, while the larger ones were surety bonds posted by a bondsman. The $5 and $10 bonds are frequently not intended to assure appearance, and in fact are used in certain types of minor offenses to encourage people not to appear in court, at which time the prosecutor will close the case by asking the judge to call for a bond forfeiture, ordering no further action. This device is familiar to anyone who has received a traffic ticket. It is also often used in minor gambling cases and an occasional "sex" case as a way of allowing people to pay "fines" in a convenient manner.

Pretrial Release: Process

The Role of the Police   Although most students of the pretrial process focus on judicial bail setting at arraignment, their observations may often miss the mark, since in many jurisdictions—including New Haven—the bulk of the pretrial release decisions is made by other people before the accused is ever presented in court.[11] In New Haven it is not the judge or the bail commissioner who dominates the release process, but rather the police. They are responsible not only for arresting and charging suspects, but also for releasing them before a trial. A number of observers have commented that Connecticut in general, and New Haven in particular, has liberal policies on pretrial release. They attribute these to the multi-layered system of decision and review, and the existence of bail commissioners. But in fact one cannot attribute these practices directly to this elaborate system. In fact, they probably have more to do with the intuitive judgments of the initial decision makers, the police.

Unless a suspect is released on a field citation at the site of an arrest, the arresting officer takes him to the central booking facility. After the booking, the officer is required by departmental order to complete a detailed bail interview form which seeks information about the arrestee's ties to the community and other factors on which the release decision is to be based. The form also provides a space for reasons if the arrestee should not be released. Rarely is there anything that might be characterized as an "interview." Only occasionally is the bail interview form completed in detail, and whatever information it does record is likely to have been filled in *after* a release decision has already been made. While different officers have different practices, most of them require little more than the accused's name, address, and the charges being pressed before making a decision to release on PTA or a small bond.

If the charges are more serious, or if the arrestee has a prior record of arrests or failure to appear (and well over 50 percent do), then the officer may insist on a bond. In setting its amount, he often consults a "bail schedule." This document, prepared by the Judicial Department and adopted by a resolution of all Circuit Court judges in 1967, specifies a monetary amount for each type of charge, and provides for "discounts," depending upon the accused's ties to the community.[12]

Although officers setting the conditions of release must complete a section of the bail interview form which calls for a statement of reasons if an arrestee is not released immediately, this section is rarely filled out. In my review of over 100 bail interview forms for people who were *not* immediately released, only a handful—15 or so—had this section completed. Only occasionally did they specify that the arrestee was a "poor risk" because he had no local address, or because he had a record of failures to appear. Most of the reasons related instead to the police officer's perception of the arrestee's condition, which was often characterized as "abusive," "threatening," or "wants to return to the incident," reasons which encouraged them to favor immediate situational justice or specific deterrence.

These officers are often in a dilemma. They are agents of the community, expected to enforce the law and make arrests. But then they must immediately turn around and release those very people whom they have just apprehended and arrested. It is not surprising that the tensions produced by these conflicting roles place a strain in the formal rules these people are charged with applying, and that they have taken advantage of the lax enforcement of the law to pursue their own conceptions of rough justice. Occasionally they use this detention power arbitrarily to administer their own system of punishment. Often they fear that an arrestee will return to a fight if he is released, so that they purposefully set bail beyond the arrestee's means in order to detain him until they think he has calmed down. The statutes on release make no provision for this latter concern, and the police can pursue it only by ignoring the literal letter of the law. But in bending the law in this "reasonable" direction, the door is opened for justifications to bend it for other, less benign reasons. Police may impose situational sanctions on arrestees whom they think deserve to "sit in jail for a time" because the courts will just "let them out."

Many argue it is altogether unreasonable to expect those responsible for arresting and charging to also administer a liberal release policy, and Connecticut statutes seem to reflect this skepticism. They require that a bail commissioner "immediately" review all cases in which arrestees have not been released by the police, to act as a disinterested "backup" decision maker. In practice, however, the bail commissioners are inactive and all but invisible.

The Role of the Bail Commissioner   The court has two bail commissioners: a "day man" assigned to advise judges on conditions of release and to keep track of and issue warnings to those who fail to appear; and a "night man" who is supposed to be available in the evenings for immediate review of police releasing decisions. The night man during my study rarely came to the lockup. At times he dropped in around 10 P.M. for half an hour, but even then he did little more than sit around talking to the desk officers. During one several-week period of observation, this bail commissioner completed only two of several dozen interview forms, and I never actually saw him interviewing an arrestee, despite the fact that a great number of people could not meet the conditions of release established by the police. The "day man" followed his example. Typically, he arrived at the lockup just moments before court was to convene, picked up the bail interview forms which had been filled out by the police during the previous night, and routinely signed his name to them below the name of the police officer who had filled them out the night before, without so much as looking at those who had not received their release. Upon very rare occasions, the bail commissioner went back to the lockup to ask a detainee a question or two in order to complete the form, but never was he seen "interviewing" an arrestee. Rather he gave the impression of having interviewed the arrestee by signing the interview form which had been completed by the police officer *after* he had already set the conditions for release.

While court is in session the judge must set bail, and he frequently seeks the advice of the bail commissioner. The bail commissioner in turn usually relies on the amount established by the police the night before. Or he may recommend an amount suggested to him by the prosecutor just moments before. Occasionally he is not in court even for these functions, and on at least one occasion a bail bondsman signed the bail commissioner's name on the form so that a release could be effected.

The Courtroom Decision   Usually, neither the prosecutor nor the defense attorney has had an opportunity to give the case file anything more than a fleeting glance. Despite this, the conditions of release are usually subject to brief negotiation. The prosecutor proposes the bail established by the police and reiterated by the bail commissioner. The defense attorney or even the defendant himself may counter that he cannot post this much money but might be able to produce a smaller amount, or that he can only gain his freedom if released PTA. If the charges are serious, especially if there was a gun involved, the judge may agree with the prosecutor's recommendation, justifying his decision by pointing out that it is a "serious charge" or that the accused has a record of arrests involving violence. At times he may reduce the recommended bond, especially if the defense attorney can convince him that the arrestee can post it (for example, "Your honor, my client has indicated to me that if you set bond at no more than five hundred dollars he can make it.") or that he may lose his job if he is not released quickly. Usually, however, the judge splits the difference in a process which takes twenty seconds or less. When judges do pause to justify a decision for setting a bond, their reasons resemble those given by the police officers in the lockup or those they give when imposing sentence. Typically they emphasize the gravity of the charges or the seriousness of the arrestee's record; only occasionally do they mention community ties.

Despite these liberties with the law of pretrial release, there have been *no* sustained efforts to appeal the judges' bail rulings. When I posed this possibility to attorneys who had reputations as vigorous advocates, their uniform response was that such an effort would ultimately hurt their clients' interests. One attorney argued that it is easy for a judge to come up with a reasonable sounding excuse for establishing bail so that little real change would occur, and all argued that such a challenge would result in an even harder line from the prosecutors. Even if they won on the bail issue, most agreed that their clients would suffer for it at sentencing if they were convicted. The problem, they agreed, was that abstract principles must always give way to the immediate interests of their clients.

But despite this skepticism among defense attorneys about the desirability of trying to litigate bail reform, they are not all passive, and there are significant differences in the ways they argue bail hearings. When scheduling a second appearance after arraignment, the LAA attorney and many private attorneys ask for two- or three-day continuances for clients in pretrial detention, while the PDs routinely ask that *all* their cases be continued for one week. This suggests that the former group of attorneys are especially concerned about their clients who cannot make bail, and want to get them back before the court for a bail rehearing as soon as possible. But the PD appearing with the arrestee at arraignment is *not* necessarily the PD who will eventually be assigned to handle these cases. He is simply the person assigned to cover the arraignments of all PD clients in "the pit" that day. It can be several days later before these new cases are assigned to a specific attorney, which may be the reason for the longer period between appearances. An assigned PD may not know about his client's continued detention until they meet for the first time at the scheduled second appearance.

The Bondsman's Role   In chapter four I described the or-
 organization of the bonding business in New Haven. One of the
features I pointed out was the lack of real competition among
the bondsmen. For instance, they rarely respond to night-time
calls from freshly arrested potential clients, preferring instead to
make a first contact at their convenience in court. Bondsmen
justify this by claiming that most defendants cannot raise the
necessary money until business hours, and that the small fee
produced by most bonds is not worth the effort of weekend and
night work. Despite their right to immediate release, then, arrestees for whom a bond has been set are at the bondsmen's
mercy.

Bondsmen are businessmen; they release for a fee. The
bondsman's maximum commission, established by law, varies
according to the type (professional or insurance company) and
the amount of the bond. For professional bonds up to $300 the
maximum fee permitted is $20. Over that amount the maxi-
mum fee is 7 percent of the face value of the bond. Insurance
bondsmen charge a flat 10 percent of the value of the bond
(which is split 30/70 between the insurance company and its
bondsman-agent), and since one of the partners in the dominant two-man business wrote both "professional" and "insurance" bonds, this team frequently wrote the type of bond which
gave them the highest return.[13]

There are no requirements as to whom a bondsman must
take out,[14] and they are free to use their own discretion and
criteria. While the arrestee's financial condition is obviously
their central concern, bondsmen have differing standards, and
the difference between release and detention or between immediate and delayed release may simply be a matter of which
bondsman is contacted first. Smaller bondsmen are fiscal conservatives who insist on solid collateral or restrict themselves to
"good risks" with low bonds.[15] Bondsmen who do a large volume of business are more flexible. Their greater resources not
only allow them to take more risks and absorb more losses, but

they also provide the means to cope with recalcitrant clients. They can mobilize a sizable network of community contacts to "put the word out" or retain a police officer to track down a reluctant client. If these efforts fail they are in a good position to arrange continuances in the absence of a client or to negotiate advantageous "compromises" in the event of a continued nonappearance.

At the time of this study women were at a special disadvantage in obtaining bail. After arraignment, they were not taken to the city jail, as were male detainees, but transferred to the state's correctional facility for women, fifty miles away and far from friends, family, and bondsmen. Even if they could afford it, they were not likely to be able to post bond until their next scheduled court appearance, when it was convenient for the bondsmen to do business with them.

Recent Pretrial Release Reforms In New Haven as elsewhere in recent years, there have been programs established to mitigate the harshness of money bail. One was a jail-based program sponsored by the Department of Correction, a "Redirection Center" to counsel pretrial inmates and help them secure release.[16] Perhaps because it was a child of the Department of Correction, during its four years of existence most of its efforts were directed at making life in jail more tolerable rather than securing pretrial releases. Although the Center did help a number of low-bond detainees secure release, this service usually involved little more than giving them access to a telephone. The Center also had more ambitious plans to develop a supervised release program for "marginal risks." After floundering about trying to round up volunteers to serve as supervisors, the Center finally instituted a modest supervised release program during its last full year of operation, but by all counts it was a failure. It was able to effect only a handful of releases, and moreover it appears that in its absence these supervisees would have been released under less stringent conditions on PTA.

Securing an Attorney

A person accused of a criminal offense must decide whether or not to obtain an attorney. This seemingly simple choice in fact involves a complex set of decisions: whether or not to get a lawyer; and who to get, a public defender or a private attorney; if a private attorney, then which one? The decision is confusing and costly in terms of both time and money.

Private Counsel Unless an arrestee has had prior experience with a particular lawyer and has been satisfied, he is confused about what to do, whom to call, if anyone, how much it will cost him, and whether the amount is reasonable. He is overly suspicious and afraid of being taken advantage of. Some arrestees will call an attorney with whose name he or his friends are familiar. Others may turn to other inmates or their captors —the police—for advice, or perhaps to a bondsman.[17] Still others, fearful of the expense, decide to do without representation.

If the arrestee telephones an attorney from the lockup, the attorney is likely to ask him a few questions about the charges, then ask to speak to the police officer in charge or contact a bail commissioner in an effort to get the bond lowered to an amount the arrestee can make. After this he may contact a bondsman. If the arrestee secures his release before arraignment, the case is scheduled for a week or two later, and in the interim the attorney will arrange an appointment with his caller. If the arrestee is not released, the attorney will try to meet his prospective client just before arraignment in order to argue for bail reduction and afterward hold a brief conference to discuss financial terms and the case.

It is important that an attorney assess his would-be client's ability to pay early on; once he has begun to represent a defendant, he is bound by the canon of ethics to continue his representation until disposition. While it is possible to withdraw later from the case, it can be awkward and embarrassing. Most attorneys can relate instances of being "taken" by clients, and the result is a rather hardnosed approach to fees, even among the more liberal "client-oriented" attorneys who are frequently young, not well-established, and in particular need of the income.

Fees and billing practices vary widely from attorney to attorney and from case to case. Most private attorneys expect an initial retainer based on their own assessment of the "worth of the case." As one private attorney observed:

I want to get enough at the outset, so that if I don't get any more out of the case, I won't get burned. This amount varies. For instance, I told a guy it would cost a minimum of five hundred to take his case—it was a messy child-molesting thing—and perhaps more, but that I wanted five hundred dollars to begin with. He later called and said he could come up with three hundred, and I said I would take it. So now, even if he can't pay, I won't get burned too badly. . . . I suppose as I pick up business, I'll have to get tougher on this, but now I need the business and will take the chances. On a routine breach [of peace], or disorderly [conduct], I might very well take fifty dollars.

Although most attorneys bill clients based on the amount of time they spend—or say they spend—on a case (and all things being equal, they feel that the type of charge provides a rough indication of this), they also adjust this amount according to their assessment of their client's ability to pay. Some attorneys are critical of such billing practices, but those who use them claim that they allow the better-off to subsidize the less fortunate.

Some attorneys have experimented with a flat fee for a case, which in one small firm is $300 for a case in the lower court and $1,000 for a case in upper court. But this means that those people whose cases are disposed of quickly after only one or two court appearances pay an extremely high per hour or per appearance cost, while those whose cases require considerable research, investigation, court appearances, or a trial get a real bargain.

Still other attorneys assess a fixed fee for each court appearance. Rates vary considerably; private attorneys assigned as "special public defenders" receive a fee of $35 per court appearance, while the County Bar Association's Schedule of Minimum Fees for 1962 specifies a fee of $125 per appearance.[18] The Schedule states:

Minimum fees are interpreted to mean the lowest amount which the attorney shall consider is reasonable for the services rendered.

and

The Committee suggests that *violation* by members of the New Haven County Bar of the Minimum Fee Schedule (except where charitableness to a particular client in some particular case demands otherwise) should be discouraged since it can only result in undesirable competition on a fee basis.

Although the Minimum Fee Schedule is not binding, it is difficult to view it meaningfully for still another reason. Attorneys frequently handle several cases on a single visit to court, and theoretically could easily double, triple, or even quadruple the bill for each visit, a practice which few if any follow. The rule of thumb is, as one attorney observed, "to charge what the traffic will bear." Whatever the charge, the practice of billing for each court appearance provides attorneys with an incentive to boost the number of court appearances, which may account for the fact that on the average, private attorneys make more appearances per case than public defenders.

Attorneys do not always have an easy time collecting payment. Most defendants who can afford private counsel at all can just barely afford it, and making full payment is often a substantial burden. Furthermore, a bout with the criminal courts is rarely a satisfying experience; even people who "win their case" often experience disappointment and may be reluctant to pay promptly. Some of this problem is overcome by insisting on a retainer, but attorneys must often rely on installment payments which are not always paid promptly. A standard "lawyer story," more apocryphal than real, is that unpaid attorneys will appear before the bench ready for what should be the last appearance and request a continuance in order to locate a last crucial witness, "Mr. Green" (meaning their fee), and that the judge will grant the requested delay. Prosecutors I queried on this tactic could identify only one defense attorney in the city whom they said occasionally used this ploy, although as one close associate of a judge observed: "Judges and prosecutors remember those lean days when they began practicing law and are sympathetic to lawyers who want continuances as leverages to collect fees."

Although it is far from an accurate guide, the minimum fee schedule provides a basis for estimating the cost of a private attorney's services. Taking the figure of $125 per court appearance as a basic charge, the average cost per privately represented case would be $587.50 (4.7 x $125). In contrast, a private attorney appointed to a case as a "special public defender" is compensated at the rate of $35 per court appearance. This would yield a fee of $164.50 for the average case. Private attorneys who take these cases complain that they receive only about half their normal fee, about $300 to $350, an amount that a number of attorneys volunteered when I asked them to estimate their fees in an "average" case.

Public Defenders In order to obtain a public defender a person must be poor. There are rather rigid guidelines for eligibility, but they are not strictly adhered to, and in fact most arrestees who apply for a PD routinely obtain one. There are several reasons for this. Perhaps most important is the prevailing belief among prosecutors, public defenders, and most judges that the formal guidelines are overly restrictive, and that by denying a person *free* counsel they are in effect denying him *any* counsel. As a consequence they may overlook an income ceiling or an obvious undervaluing of personal assets. Although some judges occasionally suggest it, few in fact seriously expect an applicant to sell his five-year-old automobile in order to raise an attorney's fee.

A second reason is the drive for administrative efficiency. The application form requires detailed information about the applicant's financial condition, and to verify all of it would require more effort than the PD is willing to extend in most cases. The PD's staff finds it far easier to take the partial information at face value and recommend assignment of a PD knowing that errors will be made. They justified this by arguing that it might permit a few more people to have a PD than deserve one, but at least it does not exclude those who do. In addition, PDs are reluctant to question or challenge ambiguous or inconsistent answers about income and assets, feeling that to do so would create an atmosphere of suspicion and hostility, and undercut their ability to gain the full confidence of their clients.

But it can still be difficult to obtain an attorney. In court, the prosecutor's first question to an unrepresented defendant is: "Do you want to get your own attorney, apply for a public defender, or get your case over with today?" The very way the question is phrased encourages people *not* to seek counsel, and suggests preferential treatment if they plead guilty immediately. If someone asks for a PD, then he is shunted off for an interview to determine his eligibility, and the interview itself can become a humiliating experience.

Back before the bench, the accused may have to face a barrage of rhetorical but nevertheless humiliating questions from the judge. More than any other court official, judges lose sight of the fact that they are dealing with different individuals, that each case is new and distinct. Their tendency to stereotype becomes most obvious in the rhetorical questions they pose to confused defendants as they are applying for a public defender. After appointing a PD to the last six cases in a row, a judge might become frustrated and ask a startled defendant, "Why do all you people want a PD? They're already so overworked!" Or in a borderline application, a judge might skeptically question the defendant about why he hasn't sold his car for funds to obtain a private attorney. Despite these occasional outbursts—which usually come toward the end of a particularly hectic day when everyone is tired and short-tempered—the judge will invariably approve the application, although he might trail the announcement with a gratuitous comment expressing displeasure that the state has to pay for attorneys in such petty cases.[19] Although the services of a PD are free, the path to the appointment is frequently strewn with small indignities.

Students of the criminal process frequently observe that public defenders are second-rate attorneys, who because of their meager talents and large caseloads are not very vigorous or effective in serving the interests of their clients. Both of these observations are true for PDs in New Haven's Court of Common Pleas, but only in part. The reputations of the PDs are not as good as those of most private attorneys, and they have a poorer image among defendants.[20] In fact, many defendants do not even realize that public defenders are full-fledged lawyers, thinking they are apprentice attorneys or paraprofessionals.[21] These opinions may be an inevitable product of the very structure and name of the organization. An LAA criminal attorney, who was by a near consensus of the prosecutors and the defense bar one of the best criminal lawyers in the city, noted that clients occasionally compliment him by telling him that he is as good as any "real lawyer." They urge him to stop being a "legal aid" and become a "real lawyer." PDs may suffer a similar fate, reinforced by the fact that their offices are located in the courthouse, next door to the prosecutor.

PDs are frequently accused of not caring about their cases, of dealing in stereotypes and routinely processing their cases as fast as they can.[22] There is some considerable measure of truth in this, as witnessed by the way PDs handle continuances. But PDs often have to do battle with their clients in a way that other defense attorneys do not. Many defendants are anxious to reduce their contact with the criminal process to a minimum, and

look to PDs *not* for careful analyses and vigorous representation, but rather for reassurance that nothing too bad is going to
happen to them. Defendants whose applications for a PD have
just been approved often approach a PD asking for and expecting an instant opinion, something that the PDs are loathe to
express. Invariably the PDs firmly and politely tell them to
make an appointment so that they can review the case in detail.
While most defendants accede to these suggestions, many of
them continue to press the PD, emphasizing that they want to
get their case "over with today," and become irritated when the
PDs refuse. This results in tension between PDs and many of
their clients, a tension that contradicts popular opinion. For it is
the defendant, anxious to get his case over with, who wants the
quick advice, and it is the PD, anxious to preserve a sense of
professionalism, who wants to extend the case and review it
more carefully. Although precise figures were impossible to
come by, this type of problem is at least as pervasive as the
problems of too much work and too little concern by the PD.

In light of the consistently lenient sentences and the casual
way in which so many cases linger on, it is understandable why
many defendants do not obtain attorneys—public or private—
at all, and when they do, why so many of them desire little more
than a quick and perfunctory meeting with their attorneys.

Continuances

Although defendants usually want to get their cases over with
as quickly as possible, they are not always successful. The court
has its own pace, which is often at odds with the defendant's
self-interest. Defense attorneys and prosecutors usually turn (or
return) their attentions to a case on the morning it is scheduled
on the calendar, and if they are not able to resolve any differences before the calendar call, they will agree to a (or another)
continuance. Problems which impede the resolution of a case

can vary considerably, and a great many continuations stem from confusion and carelessness. A defense attorney may have overcommitted himself on that day, or in a more difficult case be unwilling to spend a few additional moments to track down a full-time prosecutor. Occasionally a defendant may appear in court only to find that his case is not on the calendar. Or the defense attorney may forget to show up. A court-ordered report such as a laboratory report on drugs may not have been completed, or a defendant's file may simply be lost. Whatever the reasons for delay, it may be two or three hours after the defendant has first taken his seat in the gallery before he is informed that his case will be continued. Rarely is this decision made in consultation with him or even with an appreciation of the problems it might involve for him. Unable to comprehend the details of court operations, most defendants are overwhelmed by the details of the processes. Rarely can they distinguish reasonable from unreasonable, careful from careless decisions, and they are left with generalized discontent and haunting suspicions.

But delay is not always the result of bumbling, and it is often a highly effective defense strategy. As one attorney observed:

We can make life difficult for the prosecutors by filing a lot of motions. . . . So when I push a legalistic line I am not expecting to have a complicated legal discourse; rather it's part of my ammunition to secure my objectives. They know I'm serious and that I'll spend a lot of time to pursue it. I'll wear them down that way.

Motions may be filed one at a time, so that a case may be strung out over a long period. Strategic delay can also be secured by pleading not guilty and asking for a trial by jury. This request automatically provides a several-week (and at times a several-month) continuance, during which period the complainant may calm down or restitution can be arranged.

Because delay can be and often is an effective defense strategy, it can also be used successfully by a defense attorney to justify his own carelessness or actions performed for the sake of convenience. While public defenders may use it to cope with a pressing caseload, private attorneys may use it to boost their own fees or insure payment. In any case, all but the most knowledgeable of defendants will be unable to identify the *real* reasons for delay.

Failure to Appear

The Causes of Nonappearance For many arrestees the central question is not how to maneuver to reduce the chances of conviction, a harsh sentence, or the number of court appearances, but whether to show up in court at all. This consideration is not restricted to a small handful of "absconders" or would-be absconders; it concerns large numbers of arrestees. Roughly one-third of those in my sample missed one or more of their scheduled court appearances, and a substantial number (one person in five) never did return to court even after they received repeated letters of warning. While a number of these people had their cases terminated by a court action which called for a "bond forfeiture with no further action," about one in every eight or nine cases was never formally resolved by the court in any way, and are filed as outstanding, closed only if and when the accused is arrested on other unrelated charges. Most of those who fail to appear (FTA) are charged with minor misdemeanors, but the problem is by no means restricted to them. A third of the FTAs were charged with the most serious class of misdemeanors, and fully 20 percent of them were charged with felonies. Both in terms of absolute numbers and the seriousness of the charges, failures to appear present a serious and continuing problem for the court.

Table 7.5 summarizes various FTA rates according to type of release.[23] Two features of this table stand out: the relatively large number of defendants who fail to appear, and the relatively high proportion of FTAs among the presumably better risks (i.e., those released on the least restrictive conditions of

TABLE 7.5

Percent of Failure to Appear by Type of Release

	Yes	No
Letter of warning sent to those released on *citation and PTA*	34.5% (279)	65.5 (530)
Warrants issued for rearrest of those out on *citation and PTA*	18.4% (149)	81.6 (660)
Warrants issued for rearrest of those out on *bond*	06.9% (35)	93.1 (473)

citation or PTA). Many people, especially bondsmen, have made much of such findings, arguing that the first set of figures points to a major problem for the court, and the second to a possible solution to this problem. They suggest that increased reliance on money bond would be a way to reduce the rate of failure to appear at little if any cost to the state.

While there is some truth to this argument, there is another much more important explanation for the lower FTA rate among defendants out on bond. These people are not corralled into appearance by their bondsmen; rather the court's record-keeping system is adjusted to overlook their failures to appear. Bondsmen are relatively passive in supervising most of their lower court clients, preferring to pursue those few who fail to appear in court and spending little time overseeing the appearances of all those who would show up anyway. But this strategy depends upon a cooperative court; if a bondsman's client does not appear in court, then he must be able to convince the court temporarily to pass over the case or grant him a continuance in his client's absence. In contrast, a person released without a surety bond or on a cash bond is not likely to have someone intervene on his behalf, and his nonappearance will usually result in an automatic warrant. In short, variations in FTA rates by *types of release* are probably due more to differences in the presence or absence of someone to intervene on the accused's behalf than to actual differences in the two types of release programs.

This casual attitude toward FTAs is shared by a great many defendants as well. Despite a high nonappearance rate, few of those who fail to appear do so because they are fleeing the court's jurisdiction. Many simply do not want to appear. They make no effort to hide from the court; they simply ignore it, hoping perhaps that the problem it represents will go away. This strategy usually pays off. The Police Department makes no serious effort to serve the FTA warrants and those who choose to ignore the court are not likely to be bothered unless or until they are rearrested on other, unrelated charges. But the result is a type of self-fulfilling prophecy. The court's permissive attitude toward nonappearance encourages the practice so that the problem mushrooms.

There is another set of reasons which foster nonappearance and have more to do with the characteristics of the court itself than with characteristics of the defendants. An appearance in court is a bewildering experience, and many arrestees leave their arraignments thinking that after a night in the lockup and the few moments before the bench their cases are over when in fact they have only begun. Others remember that they have been told to return to court, but have forgotten the date, and do not bother to try to find out when it is. While much of this inability to hear or remember is attributable to selective perception, the problem is fostered by the rapid pace of the proceedings, the telegraphic code in which the court regulars communicate with each other, and the casualness with which the accused is treated.

People fail to appear for still other reasons. All defendants are told to appear in court at ten o'clock in the morning, although many of their cases will not be called until after the lunch break. By tradition, the cases of those not represented by counsel are called last, which usually means that they have a several-hour wait. And during this long wait many of those who were present at the outset drift off. Some get tired or bored and leave after an hour or two. A few think that court is over when it recesses for lunch, and depart thinking that their case was not on the day's calendar. Others step out to a restroom or for a cigarette, miss their call, and are classified as a nonappearance. Even if a person returns to court shortly after this has happened, the prosecutor will not always have the order withdrawn. If it is late in the afternoon or the prosecutor is harried and tired, he may simply tell the defendant to reappear on another day, and keep the finding of FTA in effect, an action which creates a *record* of failure to appear, something that may come back to haunt the defendant if he is rearrested.

Realizing that they have contributed to many of these FTAs, and that there may be mistakes because of confusion or concern with speed, prosecutors and judges have a relatively tolerant attitude toward them. It is easier to ignore or overlook the problem than make the effort to sort out reasonable from unreasonable excuses. This attitude explains why none of the 234 people in the sample charged with FTA was convicted on this charge. Once the defendant is returned, usually voluntarily or as a result of a new arrest, the court nolles the FTA charges. This policy, which is rational for individual prosecutors and judges, is irrational for the court as a whole. In any given situation the casual treatment of FTAs may save time, but in the aggregate such behavior fosters failures to appear and enlarges the problem. By failing to sanction those who do not appear in court, the deterrent effect of the FTA charge is squandered, and nonappearance is in effect encouraged. Leniency in the name of individual efficiency, then, produces collective inefficiency.

Some arrestees are encouraged *not* to appear in court. These people are usually charged with minor offenses and have been released on bonds as low as five or ten dollars. Prosecutors are actually happy when these people fail to appear. In these cases, rather than requesting the standard warrant for rearrest the prosecutor will recommend that the bonds be forfeited and the case terminated. Over 16 percent of all the cases in my sample had dispositions of this sort. Many involved Puerto Ricans charged with gaming, a minor misdemeanor. (Since I collected my data, this action has been decriminalized.) While gaming was still a criminal act, police periodically raided Puerto Rican "social clubs," storefront centers in which men gather to drink beer, socialize, and play cards, and arrested those who were gambling or illegally dispensing liquor. With an almost ritual regularity, these arrestees were released on low bonds—often set according to the amount of money in their pockets, but rarely over ten or fifteen dollars—but would not bother to appear in court, preferring instead to have the court order a bond forfeiture with no further action.

At one point during my investigation, this equilibrium was almost destroyed when the arresting officers began releasing these arrestees on field citations. Officers manning the lockup resented the amount of paperwork these "Mickey Mouse" cases involved and successfully prevailed upon the patrol officers to issue citations in the field, a form of release which bypassed the lockup altogether. While the arresting officers accommodated themselves to their colleagues' request, the Chief Prosecutor was furious because it caused an administrative crisis in his office. Without a bond, the charges for this group of arrestees could no longer be conveniently disposed of by a bond forfeiture, so that the prosecutor's backlog of outstanding cases rose dramatically. Cases that were once routinely terminated had to remain open and unresolved, a problem that could only grow worse, since no one had any incentive to actually serve the warrants. After threats first and then polite supplications, the Chief Prosecutor was able to prevail upon the police to revert to their old practices, and the crisis passed.

Dispositions by bond forfeitures are by no means restricted to petty gambling offenses. Occasionally someone from out-of-town will indicate his reluctance to return to the city, and a cash bond forfeiture arrangement will be suggested by the officer at the lockup, or perhaps even negotiated by telephone with a prosecutor. Some use this device to escape the embarrassment of a court appearance, especially in cases involving charges of homosexual solicitation or other socially disapproved actions, for which the arrestee wishes to avoid public exposure and humiliation and the prosecutors are willing to be cooperative. At such times an arrangement may even be negotiated by an attorney for the defendant, and one prosecutor recalled a few instances in which arrestees originally released on their own recognizance later requested that bail be set. That way they could have a bond to forfeit so that the case could be closed without their having to make an appearance. In these rare cases, everyone views himself as coming out ahead. The accused is neither exposed to public humiliation nor forced to make an admission of guilt. The prosecutor views this action as appropriate in situations in which someone has already "suffered enough," and regards nonappearance and bond forfeiture as equivalent to an admission of guilt and a fine.

Predicting Failures to Appear   Within the past two decades there has been an increased effort to rationalize pretrial release by basing the decision on an evaluation of the likelihood the arrestee will appear.[24] The factors used in this evaluation include ties to the local community such as length of residency in the area, number of dependents, family status, and employment status; those who are long-term residents, living with their family, and employed are considered the best risks.

In the early 1960s the Vera Institute of Justice in New York City instituted a pilot program which developed a community ties "point system" for making release decisions. If an accused's total "community ties" score was high enough, then the Vera interviewers would recommend that he be released on his own recognizance. The Connecticut Bail Commission was heavily influenced by the Vera experiment, and the state's Bail Reform Act of 1967 explicitly tied the conditions of release to the types of factors with which Vera had been experimenting.[25]

This interest has prompted a host of research reports seeking to test and improve the predictive capacities of these efforts. They have correlated a host of different factors about the accused—marital status, employment, purchasing habits, prior record, type of charge, etc.—with appearance/nonappearance in an effort to refine the original model and make more accurate predictions. On the whole these efforts have been dismal failures. None of these factors taken individually or in combination seems to be a good predictor of appearance. In one study of Philadelphia, researchers found that the single most consistent factor in their multivariate analysis was whether the accused had paid a utility bill within the past three months.[26] In New York other researchers concluded that another single factor—whether the accused could be reached by telephone at his primary residence—was the best predictor of appearance. It was at least as or more reliable than the long list of factors about family, community ties, and employment status, which the bail agency had traditionally relied upon to make its release recommendations.[27] In both cases, however, the ability to predict appearance remained dismally low.[28]

I made a similar effort for a subset of my New Haven cases and the results were again disheartening.[29] I included seventeen separate independent variables in a multiple regression analysis; one group of factors consisted of community ties such as marital status, residency, length of time in the community, employment status and number of dependents, and seriousness of the charges. A second group consisted of "extralegal" factors such as the accused's race, age, sex, whether he was represented by an attorney, and several other factors about police reaction to the arrest, and type of initial release.

Table 7.6 summarizes the results of this effort. In a word they are dismaying. Regardless of the order in which they were introduced into the equations, none of the factors proved to be important (e.g., none of them was even statistically significant at the 5 percent level), and in the aggregate they accounted for only a little more than 2 percent of the total variance of the

TABLE 7.6

Regression Results for Attempt to Account for Failures to Appear

Variable Description	Coefficient	Standard Error of Coefficient	Standardized Coefficient	Unique Variance
Race*	−0.06	0.04	−0.09	.008
D. had counsel*	−0.00	0.00	−0.08	.006

Multiple Correlation (R) = 0.13
Multiple Correlation Squared (R^2) = 0.02

Partial Correlations with Dependent Variable (FTA) for Variables Not Entered in Multiple Regress (none of them increased R^2 by more than 0.010)

Variable Description	Partial Correlation
Original Charge	0.024
Original Charge	−0.027
Original Charge	−0.034
Prior Convictions	−0.038
Original Charge	−0.074
Marital Status	0.046
Dependent	0.030
New Haven Address	0.049
Length of Time in Area	0.007
Employed at Present	0.023
Reasons for Release Given	0.043
Reasons for Release Given	−0.006
Reasons for Release Given	−0.021
Sex	−0.016
Age	0.052

*Statistically insignificant at the .05 level.

dependent variable. Furthermore, those two variables which stood out as most important—in a group in which nothing was even statistically significant—were the accused's race and whether he was represented by counsel. These factors are probably marginally more important because bondsmen probably do not have as good a network of contacts in the Black community as they do in the white community, and because those repre-

THE PROCESS IS THE PUNISHMENT

sented by counsel are more likely to be reminded of their obligations than those without attorneys.

Like other efforts, mine to identify predictors of appearance/ nonappearance focused on characteristics of *individual* defendants. Yet the discussion above suggests that the label FTA itself is problematic because it depends in part on whether a bondsman is present in court to secure a continuance and whether a prosecutor is willing to make accommodations for those who step out of the courtroom momentarily. Furthermore, by focusing on the *personal* characteristics of the defendant we overlook the importance of *organizational features* in the court which may encourage nonappearance. People without attorneys may *show up* in court with the same frequency as those with attorneys, but because their cases are not called until late in the day some of them give up and go home, either because they are bored and irritated or because they think a recess is an adjournment. My observations of the court lead me to believe that nonappearance is more likely to be accounted for in terms of how well defendants understand the operations of the court (for example, are they in the correct courtroom?), how much respect they have for the court, how seriously they take the proceedings, how aware they are of their scheduled court appearances, and what they believe the consequences will be if they fail to appear. In other words, the *interaction between the court organization and the accused* is likely to provide the best explanation for appearance or nonappearance.

Pretrial Diversion

One way for an accused person to reduce the chances of conviction and postconviction penalty is to make an advance effort to "rehabilitate" himself. There are a variety of ways in which the accused can demonstrate this effort to the court, some of which were described in chapter six. One way is the Pretrial Diversion Program sponsored by the New Haven Pretrial Services Council. Representatives of this program approach new arrestees who meet its initial eligibility criteria, and offer them an opportunity to participate in its in-house group counseling program or to take advantage of its job placement services. If those who are accepted faithfully participate in these activities for a period of ninety days, then the program will recommend to the prosecutor that the charges be nolled.

Despite the seeming benefits which flow from this program, very few of the eligible arrestees take advantage of it. Estimates constructed from my sample indicated that over three-quarters of all arrestees met the program's *initial* eligibility requirements, but of the 800 eligibles for whom data were available, only 19, or 2.3 percent of them, actually participated in the diversion program.[30] Officials of the diversion program attempt to account for these low numbers by pointing to the prosecutor's discretion to veto prospective participants who are otherwise eligible and interested. While these factors certainly limit the program's size, there is another much more important reason for its limited effectiveness: arrestees consider participation in the program itself a penalty that is much more severe than the one they think they will receive if they do *not* participate.

One evaluation of the program attempted to estimate what might have happened to the program's participants if they had not been "diverted."[31] Identifying a control group and tracing its path through the court, the researchers found that one-fifth to one-third of the "control group" obtained nolles or dismissals; most of them pleaded guilty and received a small fine of $10 to $20. *None* of them went to jail. In short, they concluded tentatively, those people who are eligible but decline to enter the diversion program are not likely to be treated harshly by the court.

In contrast, people who do participate in the program must agree to participate in regularly scheduled meetings for a three-month period with no definite assurances that their cases will be nolled afterward. It is not surprising, then, that so many people pass up the diversion program.

Proponents of pretrial diversion programs justify their support for three different reasons.[32] First, they argue, diversion offers a *beneficial alternative* to the harsh formal process of adjudication. Second, it is designed to *reduce social control* over those accused of minor offenses which many do not even regard as "criminal." Third, adherents claim that these programs contribute to the *efficiency* of the courts by freeing time for the fewer more serious cases.

In practice, however, the New Haven pretrial diversion program increases rather than decreases the harshness of the criminal process, expands rather than contracts the scope of social control over arrestees, and increases rather than decreases the workload of the court. The relative harshness of the programs is manifested in the fact that most of those arrested are not interested in them, and prefer to follow the standard path of adjudication. The case outcomes of the "control" group described above reinforce this conclusion. The alternative to a lengthy and cumbersome program is at worst a small fine, not jail, and often it is an immediate rather than a delayed nolle.

Second, diversion represents a net expansion of social control when in comparison with the alternative of standard adjudication. Roughly one-fifth to one-third of those whose cases are nolled *after* participation in the diversion program would probably have had their cases nolled outright had they *not* participated. As for the other participants, none of them would have received a harsh sentence and almost all of them would have had their cases disposed of and been removed entirely from the criminal justice system much sooner had they *not* been "diverted."

Third, diversion programs do not seem to free prosecutors' and judges' time to concentrate on other more serious problems. Like all institutions the court has developed informal routines to handle business rapidly and efficiently. By introducing one more option—one which is used infrequently and requires *special* considerations and consultations—the standard routine is disrupted and the process is slowed down because a disproportionate amount of time is spent on them. And since it is likely that there will always be very few of them, they will continue to take up time. Furthermore, if the staff of the diversion program is itself considered part of the "court system," then diversion is not cost-effective either, since the per case costs are much higher than the court's.[33]

The Imbalance Ratio

However lenient decisions in the pretrial stage appear to be, they often fall more harshly and on more people than do sanctions imposed after adjudication, and as a consequence they shape events at later stages. In a concise and overwhelmingly persuasive essay, Daniel Freed discusses one of the anomalies of the criminal process.

Of the many paradoxes which beset the criminal justice system, few surpass the picture of judges and jailers imprisoning more accused offenders before their trials than after conviction.[34]

In order to demonstrate this paradox he developed a simple index, the "imbalance ratio," by which he could compare the size of a jail's pretrial population with its sentenced population.[35] If the ratio is close to zero, he argued, "this would indicate that comparatively few people who are jailed prior to trial are later released upon conviction. If on the other hand, a significant proportion of pretrial detainees were released prior to trial or sentencing, the ratio would be a high fraction . . ."[36] Applying this test to two available sets of gross figures on jail population in Connecticut, he found that the "imbalance ratio" hovered around .70, indicating that many more people were detained prior to trial than jailed after sentence, a fact which he concluded literally "turns justice upside down."[37]

This is a dramatic and convincing demonstration of the imbalance between pre- and posttrial costs, but the concept of imbalance can be extended to other areas and yield the same type of results. The pretrial process imposes a host of sanctions, and it is instructive to weigh them against conviction and post-conviction costs. The results are less dramatic than the figures on incarceration, but as the discussion below shows, the imbalance is skewed in the same direction.

Pretrial Detention   Out of 1,640 cases, 146 persons were held in detention until their cases came up. While this group was more likely to be convicted than those who were released (70 percent to 51 percent), few of them were sentenced to substantial jail terms. Roughly four times as many people were incarcerated before disposition than *after* disposition, producing an imbalance ratio—according to Freed's formula—of .73, a figure which understates the imbalance, since some of those sentenced to jail terms were free before trial.

Conditions of Release   While roughly 50 percent of the arrestees in my sample were released without having to post bond, the other half did have to purchase freedom.[38] *Excluding* those who paid their "fines" by forfeiting low cash bonds, the average bond was over $1,000, which means that the average bondsman's commission was $76. While this commission may not appear to be severe, it is significant in contrast to the sanctions imposed at sentencing.

Table 7.7 compares the cost of securing pretrial release with fines. Obviously a strict comparison is not possible, but comparing the money collected for bondsmen's fees with court fines and bond forfeitures is instructive. In the aggregate the criminally accused lose *three times* as much money to bondsmen in the form of commissions than the convicted or assumed offenders do in fines and bond forfeitures. This difference is not entirely because bond fees are spread out among all arrestees and fines are concentrated on only a few. The average fine is $28.44, about one-third the amount of the average bondsman's

TABLE 7.7

A Comparison of the Costs of Bonds, Fines, and Bond Forfeitures

Bonds and Fines (in $)	Bonds			Fines and Bond Forfeitures		
	Estimated Bondsmen's Commission*	No. of Bonds	Est. of $ to Bondsmen	No. of Fines	No. of Forfeits	Est. of $ to Court
$ 5	–	(77)	–	23	65	$ 440
10	–	(6)	–	50	4	540
15	–	(2)	–	46	3	735
20	–	(14)	–	37	4	820
25	–	(89)	–	130	24	3,850
50	–	(106)	–	52	18	3,500
100	20	129	2,580	11	5	1,600
150	20	0	–	2	5	1,050
200	20	41	820	4	2	1,200
300	20	33	660	–	–	–
400	28	1	28	–	–	–
500	35	75	2,625	–	–	–
1,000	70	169	11,830	–	–	–
2,000	140	36	5,040	–	–	–
5,000	350	19	6,650	–	–	–
10,000 or more	700	11	7,700	–	–	–
Totals		514 ($100 or Over)	$37,903	355	130	$13,735

Estimated Average Bondsmen's Commission = $73.74
Average Fine = $28.44
Average Bond Forfeiture = $28.00

*This estimate is based on the lower of the two commission rates, the independent rather than the insurance bondsmen's rate. The figures may be conservative.

commission. Furthermore, the minimum bond fee is $20, equal to or greater than fully one-third of all the fines (232 or 48 percent of all the 485 fines or bond forfeitures were $20 or less). At the upper limits, while only seventeen people, or less than 5 percent of those who were convicted, paid $100 or more in fines, another twelve who were *not* convicted forfeited bonds of this amount, and a total of sixty-six people paid bondsmen's commissions of $100 or more. However one looks at it, the bond commission exacts more of a penalty from more people than the fines which they might pay upon conviction, or even the bond they would have to forfeit for a nonappearance.

Many observers of the pretrial process argue that many people plead guilty simply because they are poor and want to escape prolonged detention. These data suggest an additional reason. Even those who *can afford* to retain a bondsman may wish to plead guilty in order to avoid paying the commission. If bond is set at $1,000, the commission would be $70 or perhaps $100, while in all probability the accused if convicted would receive a suspended sentence, unrestrictive probation, or at worst a small fine. If the stigma of conviction does not greatly bother the arrestee, then it makes little sense for him to pay a bondsman's commission and face the continuing possibility of a fine as well, when he can pay a small fine at the outset and quickly extract himself entirely from the process.

Obtaining an Attorney   To retain a private attorney, a defendant must spend more money during the pretrial process than the court would collect in fines. The average fee for a private attorney is about $350, whereas the average fine is less than 10 percent of this amount. Few private attorneys accept cases of any type for less than $100, yet few fines exceed this amount. I estimate that in the aggregate more than $50,000 was paid to attorneys by clients in my sample, while only a small fraction of this amount was paid in fines.

Many defendants unwittingly endure delays and complications imposed on them by their attorneys. Even when counsel is provided without cost, many resent the conferences on which the PDs insist. While the PDs are frustrated by this attitude, it is not completely irrational. If in the end it makes little difference in terms of sentencing whether the defense attorney mounts a casual or a vigorous defense, the defendant may prefer the former since it reduces his pretrial costs.

This suggests that standard comparisons between the performance of public and private attorneys in lower courts may be misleading if not meaningless. The conceptions and expectations about their functions may be quite different for their respective clients. In the minds of many defendants, the PD is little more than a free expert from whom to obtain *quick* advice. But *all* those who go to the expense of retaining a private attorney are likely to have intense feelings and want and expect more from their attorneys. If someone with an income above the PD eligibility limits only wants quick, perfunctory advice, then he may be unwilling to invest in a private attorney and prefer to do without counsel instead.[39]

Continuances While delays often benefit defendants, they are purchased at a price which can quickly come to outweigh the benefits. First, an appearance in court is likely to involve a substantial portion of the defendant's day. Court convenes at 10 A.M., two to three hours after the working day has begun. Two or three hours is too short a period for most people to show up for work, but long enough a period to cause problems. Once a defendant is in court, it is impossible for him to get an accurate estimate as to when the case will be called. Only defendants with private attorneys are likely to have been told that they will probably be through before noon, although in fact most of the PDs' clients are finished for the day by this hour. Those without attorneys often have to wait until after the lunch recess before they are called.

Each appearance in court usually involves a minimum of half a day, which often translates into half a day's docked wages. Again, to *illustrate* the imbalance of costs in the pretrial process

—in this instance the costs of continuances—and the postconviction sanctions, we can compare an estimate of the aggregate value of lost wages with the aggregate value of the collected fines. The average number of court appearances for *all* defendants in my sample was 3.3. Estimating that each court appearance causes a wage earner to miss four hours of work, and figuring lost income at $2.31 per hour (the prevailing minimum wage at the time of my study), the *average* case costs the accused $30.49 in lost income. Of course, defendants without attorneys averaged only 2.14 appearances per case, while those with private attorneys averaged 4.70, translating into lost income per case of $19.77 and $43.43, respectively. In contrast, the average fine was less than $28.00.

Still using this method of estimation, the total income lost as a result of court appearances for *all* defendants in the sample was a little over $50,000, an amount approximately *five times as great as the amount the court collected in fines.* This figure is misleading unless we realize that these two costs are spread out differently. Only some of those who have been convicted pay fines, while all the defendants—innocent and guilty, fined and jailed—are subject to loss of income because they must make court appearances. While this undercuts the dramatic impact of this five to one ratio, remembering that the cost is spread among and absorbed by those who are not convicted tends to reinforce that impact.

Failures to Appear   The figures on lost wages are little more than educated guesses and must be interpreted with extreme caution, but they are based on conservative projections and go a long way toward explaining why so many people do not want even a court-appointed attorney to represent them, and indeed why so many people never show up in court at all. This behavior—often characterized as irrational or irresponsible by frustrated court officials—seems both rational and reasonable given the circumstances I have identified. It is a reasonable way to cope with and reduce the primary penalties of the lower court process, penalties exacted in the pretrial process. The court intuitively understands this. Roughly 25 percent of the money it takes in as "fines" is in fact bond money which has been forfeited because of nonappearance.

Conclusion: The Aggregated Effects of the Pretrial Process

The figures on pretrial costs presented in the preceding discussion are rough estimates and should not be interpreted as facts. Because they suggest comparisons between groups and costs which are themselves quite different, they must also be interpreted with caution. Still, these figures point to the inescapable conclusion that the costs of lower court—the tangible, direct, and immediate penalties extracted from those accused of minor criminal offenses—are not those factors which have received the greatest attention from legal scholars, social scientists, or indeed court officials. Liberal legal theory directs attention to formal outcomes, to the conditions giving rise to the application of the criminal sanction at adjudication and sentence. Much social science research has followed this lead, searching for the causes of sanctioning at these stages. But this emphasis produces a distorted vision of the process and the sanctions it dispenses. The real punishment for many people is the pretrial process itself; that is why criminally accused invoke so few of the adversarial options available to them.

This inverted system of justice dramatizes the dilemma of lower courts. Expanded procedures designed to improve the criminal process are not invoked because they might be counterproductive. Efforts to slow the process down and make it truly deliberative might lead to still harsher treatment of defendants and still more time loss for complainants and victims. Devices designed to control official discretion do not perform their expected functions (the failure to litigate bail is a clear case-in-point). And whereas rapid and perfunctory practices foster error and caprice, they do reduce pretrial costs and in the aggregate may render rough justice.

In light of the pretrial costs and the actual penalties meted out in the lower court, one is tempted to scoff at the formal theory which so ineffectively governs official behavior in the lower court and to dismiss it as unworkable and overly elegant —as proceduralism run amok—for the types of petty problems presented to the court. Would not simple summary justice with a minimum of procedures provide a more appropriate and workable set of standards? Perhaps the police court magistrate meting out immediate kadi-like justice without reliance on defense counsel—but also without the need for bail, repeated court appearances, and the like—might be more satisfactory. Or perhaps community-based courts might be more adept at ferreting out the underlying causes of conflict and providing ameliorating responses.

In a great many cases these alternatives might work more effectively; yet the impulse for formality, even with its manifest shortcomings, cannot be so quickly dismissed. While lower courts sentence very few people to terms in jail, in theory almost all of those appearing before them face a slim possibility of incarceration. While creating a record of petty criminal offenses may not significantly affect the future of most people who find themselves before the bench, it can have a long-lasting and unpredictable impact on some. Citizenship can be placed in jeopardy, careers destroyed, aspirations dampened, delinquent propensities reinforced. Such problems may be few in number, but they do occur. And it is impossible to tell in advance which cases may precipitate these more serious consequences, since the specific impact of a record may not make itself felt until much later in life.

As long as conviction for petty criminal offenses carries the possibility of a jail sentence or of jeopardizing one's future, the ideal of a formal, adversarial process will remain strong and attractive even to those who acknowledge that the process itself is the punishment for most people. However, there may be some alternatives which both facilitate the rapid handling of petty cases and protect the interests of the accused. The causes of rapid case handling, the failure of the adjudicative ideal, and alternatives to adjudication will be examined in the next two chapters.

CHAPTER 8

The Myth of Heavy Caseloads:

An Exploration and Rejection

of an Alternative Explanation

Introduction: The Caseload Hypotheses

Chapters five and six portrayed a process that bears little resemblance to the popular image of the American criminal courts. Rather than hard-fought trials ending with harsh sentences for the guilty and vindication of the innocent, there are hardly any trials at all. Instead, there is a variety of informal dispositional practices, lenient sentences, and a general spirit of cooperation among supposedly adversarial agents. Moreover, the evidence shows that these practices have parallels in a great many other criminal courts.[1] In the preceding chapter I focused on the importance of the pretrial costs, arguing that often the process itself is the primary punishment, and that it leads arrestees and the court to ignore the opportunities available under formal adversarial proceedings.

This is not the conventional explanation for perfunctory

processing of criminal cases. The pervasive and seemingly persuasive explanation places responsibility for these practices on the impact of heavy caseloads. Responding to some of my preliminary findings, one prosecutor in New Haven summarized this position as follows:

> Your findings on the way cases are handled in lower courts confirm our beliefs. The burgeoning crime rate of the past few years has put an impossible strain on the courts, and in reaction a number of devices have grown up which allow courts to cope with this staggering workload. Among them are the decline in the use of trials, reliance on plea bargaining, and the adoption of a cooperative—as opposed to combative—strategy between counsel.

Other court officials echoed this theory, and the argument has come to represent the orthodox explanation for the shortcomings of criminal courts in general.[2] Both the most vociferous critics of the "twilight of the adversary process" and the many, although usually reluctant, defenders agree that the assembly-line processing of defendants is in large part a consequence of the system's inability to manage its heavy workload.[3]

It is surprising that this cause-and-effect argument has not itself been the object of careful scrutiny.[4] Observers have noted growing calendars in the nation's larger cities, along with understaffing, poor facilities, and mechanical justice, all of which provide a sharp contrast to the standard idealized version of the adversary process which pervades law school training, legal ideals, and popular notions of justice. The causal connection between heavy caseloads and perfunctory processing appears obvious.

This chapter subjects this orthodox explanation to closer scrutiny. It breaks down the argument into its separate components, each of which needs careful examination, and then subjects each to an attempt at "disproof." It examines the consequences of varying caseloads by comparing low- with high-volume courts, explores the logic of the argument and the assumptions implicit in it, and considers the relationship between caseload and the court's operating procedures and decision-making processes.

The major claims of the heavy caseload-cursory disposition argument may be separated and stated as follows:

• The lack of adversarial practices in lower criminal courts is a result of the heavy volume of business before the courts, a workload that allows virtually no one—defense attorneys, prosecutors, or judges—adequate time to prepare fully for cases. The adversarial relationship is compromised because no one has time to engage in it. The clearest indication of this is the lack of trials in the lower criminal courts.

• The pressure caused by heavy caseloads affects not only the rate of trials, but also the *quality* of the proceedings at all other stages of the process. Other forms of short-circuiting the process include the reluctance to file formal motions, the defense waiver of other pretrial rights, and the casual yet rapid treatment of defendants before the bench.

• Pressure for ways to circumvent the complication of an elaborate adversarial process goes still farther and leads to the adoption of "work crimes," shortcuts designed to save time and effort. These devices are usually implemented at the expense of the defendant, ironically the only central person in the process who is *not* a regular participant in the ongoing and interdependent system. This shortcut is most often and most visibly institutionalized in the form of plea bargaining, the exchange of a plea of guilty for a consideration of leniency by the prosecutor. This practice is constitutional but dubious, since it may facilitate improper or inappropriate convictions and is governed by few standards.

• Caseload pressure leads not only to the "abandonment" of certain types of proceedings, but also has a dramatic effect on the substantive outcome of cases. Defendants who find themselves in a system pressed with a crushing workload are treated arbitrarily and harshly. Heavy caseloads affect not only the final determination of guilt or innocence and the sentence; they also have an impact on the earlier stages of the process as well, most particularly the conditions for pretrial release. The court's inability to make careful assessments of defendants' backgrounds results in harsher release conditions.

• The high volume of cases requires a high-speed mass production of justice. Defendants in high-volume courts are shuffled through as quickly as possible without ever comprehending what is happening to them and without anyone caring about their confusion. Not only is justice itself denied, but also the *appearance* of justice is denied.

All of these arguments cut two ways. That is, each of them implies an opposite; in the absence of heavy caseloads there will be more trials, less reliance on plea bargaining, an increase in motions, and different types of outcomes. This chapter will examine the arguments by contrasting the high-volume, heavy-caseload court in New Haven with a low-volume, lighter-caseload court in a neighboring community. If the traditional assertions about caseload are true, then there should be some differences in the ways cases are handled in the two courts. If there are no substantial differences, then we can question the importance of caseload and begin to look elsewhere for explanations.

Since the heavy caseload argument includes a strong historical dimension (for example, observers speak of the "decline" of the trial, the "rise" of plea bargaining, and the "twilight" of the adversary system), we will try to establish an historical context and analyze trends during a period in which caseloads increased. We will compare caseload and trial rates in Connecticut criminal courts during the past seventy-five years, looking at other earlier studies of urban courts, and reviewing contemporary assessments of the effects of increased court personnel.

Selecting a Comparison Court

Although the New Haven court was not originally selected with these caseload hypotheses in mind, it turned out to be an ideal choice for this purpose. Among the eighteen lower courts in Connecticut, it is one of the busiest. With an annual caseload of over 7,000 criminal cases, it has the second largest volume of business in the state. I then had to determine how this busy court stacked up against the others in the state so that I could select a second, low-caseload court for comparison.

Several considerations went into the selection process. First, I decided to confine the choice of a second site to a court within the state of Connecticut in order to control for state-imposed jurisdictional variations.[5] Next I had to formulate a *precise* definition of caseload. Almost all discussions of caseload refer to the absolute numbers of cases, so that courts in New York, Los Angeles, Chicago, and other major cities are sometimes cited as having the heaviest caseloads. But numbers alone are an inadequate indication of the actual concern that underlies most of the discussions of caseload. The load should be measured in terms of both absolute number of cases *and* the size of the staff handling them.

Rather than identifying and ranking Connecticut courts solely by their volume of business, I devised a measure of per capita workload (cases/size of court-related personnel). Two indicators were eventually selected; one was cases/judge days in the court and the other was cases/prosecutors. The New Haven court remained high on both these and other caseload measures. Of the eighteen lower courts in the state, it ranked second highest in cases per judge day (21.7) and fifth in average annual prosecutor caseload (1,753). A court at the opposite end of this spectrum was located in a neighboring town and had jurisdiction of the suburban communities of West Haven, East Haven, Branford, North Branford, and Guilford. While this court did not process the fewest number of cases in the state, it had the lowest daily case/judge ratio (6.1) and was among the lowest (fourteen of eighteen) in average annual prosecutor caseloads (898).[6] The New Haven judges, then, handled roughly three times as many cases per judge as the comparison court, and its prosecutors handled about twice as many cases as their counterparts.

The study of the two courts did not fit a perfect experimental design because the courts differed on factors other than caseload. Overall the types of offenses charged in the two circuits were similar, but there were some important differences. There were more offenses against property charged in the New Haven court than in the comparison court (37 percent to 19 percent) and fewer offenses against public order (29 percent to 43 percent). There were also differences between the defendant populations in the comparison and New Haven courts: The comparison court had many fewer Blacks and Hispanics (10 percent to 61 percent), more males (89 percent to 80 percent), more young defendants (42 percent to 28 percent under 22 years of age), fewer with prior arrest records (35 percent to 50 percent), and fewer with prior records of time served in jail (6 percent to 23 percent). In addition, defendants in the comparison court were more likely to have attorneys (67 percent to 50 percent). Finally, defendants in the New Haven court were more likely to have their cases nolled (46 percent to 25 percent).

While these differences posed some problems in testing the caseload argument, they were minimal. As was seen in the previous chapters, most of these factors were not significantly related to case outcomes *within* the court. The one factor that was most strongly and consistently related to case outcome—presence of an attorney, particularly a private attorney—leads one to expect that the court with the greater proportion of attorneys would be likely to have more deliberative and adversarial practices, but this was not the case.

A total sample of 270 cases was obtained for the comparison court. Procedures for obtaining these data were similar to those used in New Haven.[7]

The Caseload Hypotheses Explored

The heavy-caseload–cursory-disposition argument focuses on the degree of adversary activity in the system. In general, this position argues that criminal cases should be resolved through combat between the two parties, and that the state should prove beyond a reasonable doubt to the judge or jury that the defendant did commit the particular offense with which he was charged. The defendant is presumed to be innocent and should be able to invoke available procedures to protect himself.

An examination of this position poses serious problems for any researcher. At the outset it raises important conceptual questions: What precisely is an adversarial relationship? What is the minimum that the criminal process requires? To what extent can adversary activity be characterized as a zero-sum game in which one player's victory is another's loss, or a mixed strategy game in which both players can lose something but both can also gain?

Neither critics nor defenders of the general lack of trials or other combative features available in the criminal process have developed an explicit yardstick against which to judge actual practices. Available standards are very general and discussions tend to proceed by assuming that the claims they make are obvious.[8] For instance, Blumberg is one of the most outspoken critics of the "decline" of the adversary process, but he never spells out precisely what an adversary system entails or what the minimum standards should be. Certainly a perusal of the various discussions of the problems of administering criminal justice does not lead to a clear consensus as to the precise nature of an "acceptable" or "typical" adversarial relationship.[9] Whereas some suggest that anything less than a full-fledged jury trial is a departure from the ideal resolution of criminal charges, others who adopt an implicit civil law analogy view the very inability to resolve cases by a negotiated settlement or through informal motion practices as unprofessional.[10] But my purpose here is not to construct a complete theory of the criminal adversary process. Rather it is to go beyond trial as the sole indicator of an adversarial process and identify several other practices associated with a combative process in order to determine how they too may be affected by variation in caseload.

Trials and Motions

The Connecticut data do not support the central argument that there is a relationship between heavy caseloads and lack of trials. In fact, none of the cases in the samples of the two courts was decided either by jury or court trial. This pattern represents the typical pattern in these two—and in the other sixteen —lower courts in Connecticut. A separate check of the annual reports of the state's Judicial Department indicated a paucity of trials in any of the Connecticut courts.[11] For example, in 1972 there were only three jury trials in the New Haven court and none in the comparison court. Not only is there a lack of trials in the busier courts, there is also a corresponding lack in the smaller, lower-caseload courts as well.

But trials are only one of several possible indicators of an adversary relationship. Another is use of formal motions by the defense. Motions can test the prosecution's case against the defendant and require him to take the defense effort seriously. A defense attorney can use these as a way of forcing prosecutors to demonstrate the strength of their evidence and to consider reducing charges or abandoning prosecution altogether. Motions serve many of the same functions as trials, including the central one of making the prosecution "prove" its case.

There is a variety of motions available to the defense. Pleas in abatement, motions to dismiss, motions to suppress illegally seized evidence, and probable cause hearings all attack the sufficiency of evidence and the grounds for arrest. Motions of discovery and bills of particulars help the defense learn more about the charges and circumstances of the arrest. Mental competency exams may produce mitigating factors as well. A successful motion to have the court handle charges under the state's youthful offender statute protects the defendant, if convicted, from having a public record of conviction. Again, one would expect that smaller caseload courts would have a higher rate of motions, but again a comparison between the two courts revealed no substantial differences. In the comparison court, 90 percent of the cases were resolved without filing motions.[12] In 9 percent more of the cases one motion was filed, and in only 1 percent of the cases were two or more filed. These figures were almost identical with those for New Haven. In 92 percent of the cases no motions were filed, in another 7 percent one was filed, and in only 1 percent of the cases were two or more filed. By this indicator as well, then, there were no significant differences between the degree of adversariness in the two courts.

Plea Bargains

Plea bargaining occupies a central place in discussions of heavy caseloads. The standard argument is that plea negotiations are a necessary evil reluctantly accepted by an overworked court, and by implication a reduction of caseload will result in less or perhaps no plea bargaining. This argument is extremely difficult either to support or to refute because it is usually not stated with much precision, and the logic of decision making in response to the press of a heavy caseload is not clear. This lack of precision may stem from the ambiguity surrounding the central concept. Are *all* pleas of guilty *prima facie* evidence of plea bargaining? Are all nolles? Would critics of plea bargaining expect to resolve *all* cases by trial? It is difficult to imagine anyone taking such a position, although there may be some support for it.[13] The absence of trials need *not* be taken as an indicator of plea bargaining if bargaining implies actual give-and-take and acknowledged agreement to compromise by both parties before a final decision.[14]

Identifying plea bargaining is complicated for still another reason, as we can see by drawing an analogy to a market economy. While a market is characterized by a bargaining process—consumers shopping around for the best price—individual consumers may rarely be involved in any *direct* bargaining. Rather they pay the "going price," frequently affixed by a stamp to the goods purchased. Is this purchase then part of the bargaining process characterizing a competitive marketplace? The answer is both yes and no. While the exchange may not be reached through the kind of haggling characteristic of a Middle Eastern bazaar or the classic plea bargaining session—"you give on this, I'll give on that"—the system may be competitive in another way. Bargaining and competition may be tacit, indirect, and meaningful only in the aggregate; it may take the form of substitution, shifting purchases, and comparison shopping. Likewise, plea bargaining can be understood in at least two ways; it can be considered the product of joint haggling and higgling, or it can be seen as a process which establishes a "going rate." One's assessment of the nature and scope of plea bargaining obviously depends on how it is viewed.

One measure often used to examine the magnitude of plea bargaining is the frequency with which the most serious charge(s) are reduced. While defendants may plead guilty for a variety of reasons, pleas to *reduced* charges are much more likely to result from an explicit agreement between the defense and prosecution, and to represent a significant concession by both parties. They are more likely to be meaningful indicators of plea bargaining than the rate of guilty pleas or the rate of cases with other types of charge reductions. Even more important are cases in which original felony charges are disposed of by pleas of guilty to misdemeanors. From the defendant's perspective, escaping a felony record is extremely desirable, but prosecutors are reluctant to reduce felony charges to misdemeanors. In these reductions, then, both the prosecution and the defendant have a great deal to gain or lose.[15]

On the first measure, the percentage of *total* charge reductions, the two courts differ significantly. Thirty percent of all guilty pleas in New Haven involve a plea to a lesser (or substituted) charge, while this is the case for only 11 percent of the guilty pleas in the low-volume court. In the low-volume court it seems there is less need or pressure to settle cases by reducing charges.

TABLE 8.1

Charges at Conviction*

	Court	
Convicted on	New Haven (high)	Comparison (low)
Reduced or Substituted Charges	30.2%	11.1%
Original Charges	69.8	88.9
	100.0%	100.0%
	(764)	(180)

*Includes those cases where the court ordered bond forfeiture and no further action.

There were even more startling differences when we considered only felony charges which eventually led to misdemeanor convictions. Eighteen percent of the original class D felony charges in the comparison court were reduced to less serious charges, while in the New Haven court the figure was 70 percent. On this one crucial indicator it appears that caseload is strongly related at least to charge reductions. The heavier caseload court appears much more willing to reduce charges than does the court with the lighter workload.

Sentences

Sentence practices, like reductions in charges, are an important indicator of the nature of adversary relationships. In fact, the sentence is perhaps the central concern in any vigorously negotiated settlement. It was therefore of interest to see if sentence practices varied in the two courts and to examine the expectation that more lenient sentences were more likely to be handed down in the heavier-caseload setting which presumably had to "give away" the most in order to keep treading water.

The profile of sentences indicated no major differences between the two courts, and roughly the same proportions of defendants received each of the three types of sentences. In both

TABLE 8.2

Distribution of Sentences

Sentence	Court	
	New Haven (high)	Comparison (low)
Conditioned Discharge, Suspended Sentence, or Probation	29.7%	30.6%
Fine*	65.1	63.8
Jail Term	5.2	5.6
	100.0%	100.0%
	(737)	(160)

*Includes those cases in which the court ordered bond forfeited and no further action.

of them, only slightly over 5 percent of the convicted defendants were sentenced to jail. In short, there was little evidence for linking caseload with sentencing practices; sentencing practices in the two courts were remarkably similar, even controlling for seriousness of charge and prior record.

Pretrial Processing

One complaint about high-volume systems is that officials are unable to cope with the large number of defendants and the overwhelming amount of information that must be compiled on each case. This inability often means that important early decisions must be made on the basis of incomplete and inadequate information. Again, the heavy-caseload courts are more likely to have incomplete information and therefore more likely to have conservative and in this case "restrictive" pretrial releasing policies.

Looking at release practices in the two courts, however, this proposition is *not* borne out. Table 8.3 indicates that both in terms of total numbers released and in terms of numbers released without money bail, the high-volume court fares slightly

255

TABLE 8.3

Pretrial Release Status

	Court	
Status	New Haven (high)	Comparison (low)
Released on Cite or PTA	52.4%	47.2%
Out on Bond	36.8	39.7
Detained	10.8	13.1
	100.0%	100.0%
	(1541)	(267)

better than the low-volume court. Over 89 percent of those in the former are released prior to trial, while only 86.9 percent of those in the low-volume circuit are released. Furthermore, of those released, the high-volume New Haven court is more likely to release the accused on his own recognizance (52.4 percent to 47.2 percent).

The same pattern is true for the actual amount of money bond. Overall the New Haven court sets lower bonds than the comparison court. Not only is the court in New Haven slightly more willing to release arrestees, it also tends to set lower bonds. Of those who had money bonds set in New Haven, 18.5 percent had a bond of $50 or less, as opposed to only 2.7 percent for the comparison court. This same pattern appears throughout Table 8.4.

Of course, New Haven defendants may have been charged with less severe offenses, but even when controls for seriousness of offense were introduced, there were still no significant differences, and defendants in the high-volume court were still more likely to receive more liberal releases.

Another important aspect of the pretrial process is the length of time an arrestee is held in pretrial custody. One might expect that the court with the heavier caseload would take longer to process and release arrestees, but again, the data *do not* support

TABLE 8.4

Initial Bond Amounts

Bond Amount	New Haven (high)	Comparison (low)
Cite/PTA	49.1%	45.8%
$50 or under	18.5	2.7
$51-$100	8.1	15.9
$101-$500	9.5	18.6
$501-$2500	12.9	9.8
Over $2500	1.9	7.2
	100.0%	100.0%
	(1585)	(264)

the claim. Table 8.5 indicates that the heavy-caseload court had a larger percentage of arrestees released within three hours (60.4 percent to 49.7 percent), although the picture looks mixed if one considers the remainder of the table. In both

TABLE 8.5

| | Court | |
Time	New Haven (high)	Comparison (low)
0-3 Hours	60.4%	49.7%
4-7 Hours	5.7	21.3
8-12 Hours	6.4	7.8
13-24 Hours	21.4	17.0
Two or More Days	6.1	3.6
	100.0%	100.0%
	(1436)	(141)

courts around two-thirds of all arrestees are eventually released within seven hours, and only a handful are held beyond twenty-four. In sum, despite variations in workload there are no major pretrial release differences between the two courts.

Courtroom Observations

A quantitative analysis of case flow can provide only a partial picture of a court's work and only a limited test of the importance of caseload, so that I used courtroom observations to supplement this analysis. I wanted to see how variation in workload affects the ways in which courts organize themselves and conduct their daily business. In particular, I tried to determine whether defendants' courtroom experience would be different in the two types of courts, and if so, how and why. The norms of the legal process require not only that justice be meted out, but also that the *appearance* of justice be conveyed. I was interested in differences in decorum, the ways in which charges against the defendant were presented by the prosecutor, the care with which his rights were explained by the judge, and the deliberateness with which inquiries and explanations were made with respect to setting release conditions, determining sentences, altering charges and nolleing cases.

On the surface there were some dramatic differences between the two courts. The comparison courthouse was a new, modern structure and the courtrooms all had comfortable benches, clean floors, bright paint, and adequate light, in sharp contrast to the main courtroom in New Haven. This structure was an antiquated Victorian building which appeared never to have undergone a major interior renovation in its seventy-five-year history.[16] The furnishings of the courtroom showed the wear of heavy use and the shabbiness of a dozen coats of paint. Rather than sitting on benches, spectators sat on uncomfortable (and noisy) metal folding chairs. Clerks, prosecutors, defense attorneys, bail commissioners, bail bondsmen, and police officers were all cramped together in a small area before the bench. The public defender arranged his case files on the railing of the unused jury box, and frequently interviewed his clients huddled behind this box.

These differences were reinforced by differences in the people occupying the courtrooms. At the beginning of the day's session the courtroom in New Haven was crowded and noisy. People were constantly coming and going, and there were whispered exchanges among friends, and among attorneys and clients. Most of the people were Black or Hispanic and poor. In sharp contrast the comparison courtroom never appeared to be bursting. Although it was frequently full, the gallery was never noisy and did not have the constant sense of agitation which characterized the gallery in New Haven. The people in the gallery—defendants and their families and friends—were almost all white, and were better dressed and neater than their counterparts in New Haven.

The busier New Haven courtroom had a more businesslike quality about it; the press of the long daily calendar seemed to impose an air of seriousness on the proceedings. But the solemnity was directed at managing a long schedule of cases rather than at individual defendants. The comparison court seemed to have a more relaxed atmosphere, but again the casualness related more to the style of moving through the calendar rather than to the way defendants were treated. For instance, one morning in this court an older male judge and his pretty young female clerk engaged in a running game over the timing of various decisions. She presented various motions and continuances and the judge routinely granted them. After the decision the clerk would announce the time of disposition to the nearest five minutes. The judge would gleefully correct her, giving the time of decision to the nearest minute or half-minute, whereupon she would give an exaggerated apology and correct herself. This flirtation was greatly appreciated by everyone in the courtroom. It is unlikely that such a sustained playful exchange would take place in the tense atmosphere of the New Haven court, although comic relief is occasionally provided by spontaneous sarcasm and slips of the tongue.

Voices are restrained and formal in the comparison court; in contrast, the New Haven court has a frantic air about it. Voices are louder and harsher; there is much more movement and seeming confusion before the bench, casting an air of uncertainty about the entire process and giving the impression that the wrong file could easily be applied to the wrong defendant. The less-crowded court seems to manage its in-court paperwork in a less obtrusive manner.

But appearances can deceive. Despite their many differences in facilities and demeanor, both courts tend to move through their business rapidly and mechanically. Although it processes cases in a smoother, less hurried manner, the comparison court disposes of its business with about the same speed, examines cases as carefully, and appears to give as much concern to each case as the New Haven court. Judges make no noticeably greater effort to explain constitutional rights to defendants or to inquire into the reasons for a plea of guilty, a request for a continuance, or a decision to nolle. In the comparison court as well as in the New Haven court the prosecutor hastily states the complaint and charges against the defendant, defense attorneys quickly present their various points, and judges spend only a moment spelling out their reasons for sentencing. The basic tasks of the two courts are handled in the same rapid and perfunctory manner.

There is, however, one crucial difference in scheduling practices between the two courts. Differences in the daily workloads tend to be offset by differences in the actual lengths of time these courts are in session. In New Haven the court is usually in session by 10:10 A.M. and continues without interruption until 11:30 A.M., at which time it recesses for about 20 minutes, reconvenes, and remains in session until the day's schedule of cases is completed, usually between 1:30 and 3:00 P.M. In contrast, the low-volume court convenes ten or fifteen minutes later, breaks for recess at 11:00 A.M., and does not reconvene until about 12:30 P.M. The day's business is usually completed by 1:00 P.M. These differences in scheduling have corresponding effects on the time court is actually in session and the courtroom time given to each case. Although the comparison court handles far fewer cases per day than the New Haven court, it also has much briefer sessions, so that *court time* per case turns out to be about the same for both.

But there are some differences between the two courts. The short morning session in the comparison court inconveniences defendants with private attorneys. Rather than appear in court at 10:30 A.M. or so and take the chance of having to wait through a long recess before their cases are called, private attorneys frequently skip this session and appear at 12:30 P.M. If their cases are called in the morning, nothing is lost. The clerk routinely passes them over at the request of the prosecutor and calls them again in the afternoon. While this saves attorneys considerable time and helps them arrange their day more efficiently, attorneys do not always inform their clients of this, so that many a defendant is quite confused to find his lawyer not present when his case is called. The defendant must then sit through the recess waiting for his case to be recalled, often not knowing that this is a standard practice and that his attorney will appear after the recess.

The comparison court's longer recess and informal practice of temporarily passing over cases can provide defendants with benefits as well. They give the public defender an opportunity to do more for his newly assigned client at the first appearance than can the PDs in New Haven. A defendant assigned to a public defender in the morning session has the opportunity to talk to him during the recess. Occasionally the public defender will reappear with his new client later that same day and make an argument for bail reduction or enter a plea. In contrast, the PDs in New Haven complain that the court is too inflexible and that they are too busy to accomplish very much for their newly appointed clients at first appearance. This greater flexibility in the comparison court may help account for the fact that on the average it disposes of cases with fewer appearances than does the New Haven court.[17]

Historical Review

Some observers of contemporary courts speak of a "decline" of the adversary system because of the press of cases, while others speak of the crisis of criminal justice.[18] However, while it is a rhetorical convenience to speak of greener pastures in a bygone era when there were smaller caseloads and greater deliberation in criminal courts, it is not at all clear that this is an accurate comparison. The records and descriptions of American courts fifty and seventy-five years ago describe a process readily familiar to contemporary students of criminal courts.

Like the 1960s and 1970s, the 1920s and 1930s were a period of heightened concern with inadequacies in the administration of criminal justice, and during this time major studies of the administration of justice were conducted in both Cleveland and Connecticut. The Cleveland study, directed by Roscoe Pound and Felix Frankfurter and reported in a volume they edited jointly, describes in detail the conditions and practices of the lower courts in that city. Their observations have a familiar ring.

—The present prosecutor estimates that more cases are . . . disposed of without prosecution than are placed upon the court dockets. A former member of the office estimates that a case, whether dropped or prosecuted, receives, on the average, three minutes' attention in the office. The estimate is liberal.
—From 150 to 300 cases a day are assigned to the two courtrooms, and the visitor is immediately struck with the lack of orderliness in handling the list. The lawyer who has only an occasional case, perhaps an ordinance violation, may wait with his clients and witnesses from nine o'clock until two, not knowing when his case will be reached. . . . In neither room did the proceedings reveal the necessary dignity of a court. The rooms were crowded with lawyers, defendants, witnesses, police, hangers-on, and sightseers, many chewing gum or tobacco, even when addressing the court. . . . In order to make themselves heard in this courtroom, lawyers and others have to lean over the bench to address the judge. This produces an impression of a confidential communication, which, al-

though false, lends color to the belief that certain lawyers have "pull with the judge."

—[A table] gives the average time between arrest and disposition. It is to be noticed that it takes the least time to find a defendant guilty, a longer time to discharge him, and the longest time to "nolle" or dismiss his case.[19]

A 1920s Connecticut study also contains similar findings and observations that with slight modifications could easily be drawn from descriptions of the state's courts in the 1970s.[20]

Not only were conditions and practices in 1920s Cleveland and Connecticut similar to those which currently prevail in many urban courts, including the Connecticut lower courts, but heavy caseloads in the 1920s was also regarded as a serious obstacle to justice. While changes in procedure and differences in jurisdictions make any strict comparison impossible, it is nevertheless of interest to note differences in caseloads between 1920s Cleveland and 1970s Connecticut. The average annual *caseload per judge* in Cleveland was over 11,999, while it is currently about 7,300 in New Haven and 4,500 in the low-volume court.

Samuel Dash's study of criminal courts in Chicago provides another useful comparison. Writing in 1951, Dash sought to determine how the administration of justice in Chicago's lower criminal courts had changed in the twenty years after the Illinois Crime Survey had undertaken a major study which documented the poor conditions in the courts and made sweeping recommendations for reform. This survey had been greeted with publicity and widespread support. Quoting extensively from the 1928 report, Dash went on to document identical conditions in his twenty year update, and concluded that:

One of the most discouraging findings . . . is the similarity between most of the poor conditions existing today in the Municipal Court with those reported in the Illinois Crime Survey of 1928. After so intensive a study as the one made then by the Illinois Association of Criminal Justice and after 23 years of opportunity to improve, that there should be no improvement is indeed shocking. One of these unchanged conditions is the non-judicial atmosphere of the criminal proceedings and of the court itself, which is an important element in impressing spectators and defendants alike with a sense of unfairness and corruption.[21]

The original survey was conducted in 1928 and Dash's study in 1951. Recent descriptions of criminal courts in Chicago provide no reason to believe that most of Dash's assessments do not hold for the 1970s as well.

A look at the Connecticut courts during this century reinforces these patterns. A survey of Connecticut legal practices published in 1937, based on data collected from the records of cases handled a few years earlier, points to the infrequency of trials (fewer than 10 percent in New Haven Superior Court), frequent but variable reliance on nolles (a quarter of all cases in New Haven, but about one-half in Waterbury), and the practice of entering pleas of guilty after a reduction of the charges, all practices generally regarded as symptomatic of "problems." Like the Cleveland study, the 1930s Connecticut report also noted the considerable variation in the length of time it took for cases to be disposed of and the fact that nolles were frequently granted many months after the initial charges were presented, indicating that they were used for purposes other than screening out initially weak cases.

The official state records during the first quarter of this century also present a picture that is more or less consistent with current practices.[22] During this period trials were far from the typical form of disposition. From 1907 to 1927, only about 3 percent of all cases handled in the state's busiest court in Hartford were resolved through trial. In New Haven Superior Court —the next largest court in the state—trials accounted for roughly 7 to 8 percent of all cases, although the rate varied considerably from year to year, with a low of 3.5 percent and a high of over 16 percent. Corresponding figures for criminal cases in the lower Court of Common Pleas are not available for both cities, although figures for New Haven indicate an average trial rate of about 20 percent.

In a recent study of the trial rates in Connecticut, Milton Heumann collected detailed information on courts with the highest and lowest volumes over a seventy-five-year period.[23] He found considerable variation in rates of trials, and overall found a slight decline in the frequency of trials during the period from 1880 to 1954. However, when he compared the high- and low-volume courts, he saw no substantial differences between them, asserting that:

I think it fair to conclude, especially from 1910 and on, that despite the large difference in actual case pressure which was used to dichotomize the groupings, trial rate between them varied minimally, and indeed often the low volume courts tried proportionately fewer cases.[24]

In another part of his study Heumann again found no corresponding rise in the frequency of trials in Superior (felony) Courts after a change in jurisdiction, which substantially reduced the courts' caseloads while maintaining staffing at the same level.

Finally, we can consider the experience of New York City in increasing its criminal court facilities and staff. As perhaps nowhere else in the United States, New York has felt increased citizen pressure for more and better institutions to handle criminal problems. In the early 1970s, as one part of a stepped-up effort to deal with felony charges, the New York Criminal Court added fifty-one judges and felony trial parts. This meant more prosecutors, public defenders, and support staff as well. At the time this increase was expected to reduce the pressure to plea bargain, and to increase the number of trials. But a survey by the staff of the New York State Division of Criminal Justice Services concluded that this expectation did not materialize.

In a December 1974 document, the Commissioner of the Criminal Justice Services concluded that the findings of the survey:

. . . indicate that although 51 new felony trial parts have been added since September, 1972, and the number of defendants indicted has decreased substantially, the number of defendants awaiting trial has declined only slightly. . . . In addition, the proportion of defendants whose cases are disposed of by guilty plea has declined, while the proportions of those disposed of by dismissal and trial, respectively, have increased. Finally, the statistics concerning sentencing and delay indicate that only a relatively small percentage of defendants convicted in the Supreme Court are sentenced to "felony time," and that there are substantial median time delays from indictment to disposition.

The data indicate clearly that the expenditure of substantial sums for additional trial parts has not solved the problem of delay and backlog.[25]

While he was at a loss to explain precisely how this additional manpower was absorbed, the Commissioner was confident in concluding that the increase in personnel had not produced the predicted consequences. He concluded that "even if large additional sums could be found during the current difficult period, prudence would still dictate a cooperative effort to find better ways to organize felony case processing."

In summary, additional historical evidence for Connecticut and comparative materials drawn from other states all reinforce the findings for the two Connecticut courts. Obviously, strict comparison between the periods and courts is not possible because of a host of intervening and confounding conditions. The explosive changes in criminal procedure affect comparison in major and indeterminable ways, as do changes in the definitions and understanding of offenses and offenders. Nevertheless, similarities in the findings of these various courts and periods offer considerable support for the position that there has not been any particularly noticeable "decline" in or "twilight" of the adversary system. Rather, it seems that it has remained at a more or less constant level despite changes and variations in the magnitude of workload. Although some of the evidence dealt with felony cases, most referred exclusively to misdemeanor and "minor" felonies. These conclusions about the limited impact of caseload are most applicable to the lower courts. Of course, this caseload argument is limited by the conditions in the courts under study; greater extremes in either direction might produce more noticeable differences. But keeping these caveats in mind, it is interesting to ask why there has been such little actual change and why so many commentators have singled out spiraling caseloads to account for so many of the *observed* problems of the courts. In addition, we must still ask what accounts for perfunctory processing in the lower courts.

Why Caseload Is Considered So Important

The Implications of Due Process

Underlying the heavy caseload position is a pervasive but implicit assumption that is so ingrained in the thinking and ideology of American criminal justice that it frequently goes undetected and unexamined. This assumption is that each case brought into the criminal courts would "naturally" be resolved by means of heavy combat in the adversary arena. According to this understanding of the ideal, the sophisticated procedures and techniques for truth detection and rights preservation are not only available if desired, but should be used in every case. While this view is reinforced by popular presentations of the operation of criminal courts, historically there is no strong tradition or legal presumption that these devices are to be used in each and every case or in any substantial proportion of them. Rather, the *full-fledged* adversary process is only one of *several alternatives* available to participants. Other more expeditious alternatives also enjoy a well-institutionalized position in the criminal law. For instance, the right to plead guilty has never been seriously challenged, and although the United States Supreme Court has been somewhat squeamish about putting its formal stamp of approval on plea bargaining, through its traditional inaction and more lately through its explicit rulings, plea bargaining has been gaining a legally acceptable and honorable position in the administration of criminal justice.[26]

Much of the literature examining the nature and function of lower criminal courts and commenting on the infrequency of trials, then, is based on a premise that at best can be characterized as myth; it assumes that a full-fledged adversarial relationship is the most obvious, desirable, and "natural" way of proceeding. This means that observed processes are frequently measured against an unarticulated ideal of complete combat that has no firm basis in legal theory.[27] Moreover, these is no coherent theory, nor even a set of ideals implicit in criminal procedure that can lead one to expect that the "natural" or ideal function of the criminal justice system is to march into full combat in every case. It is therefore of dubious value to proceed with empirical analysis using deviation from this ideal—or for that matter degree of congruence to it—as a criterion of analysis.[28]

The Making of a Social Problem

"Crises" and "social problems" are often the consequence of increased concern over a particular process rather than of any dramatic change in behavior.[29] Frequently these concerns are cyclical, produced by an especially dramatic event followed by a media campaign for reform. For example, prostitution in Times Square is a target for periodic and cyclical concern, reform effort, quiescence, and renewed concern.

The "crisis of the courts" follows much the same pattern; there are periods of increased concern with a continuing phenomenon rather than new problems precipitated by increased caseloads.

Perhaps the major cause of recent concern is a series of important Supreme Court decisions over the past several decades.[30] These landmark cases have extended the right to counsel for indigents who commit virtually any offense that may receive a jail sentence. During this same period, the Court handed down decisions which limited the way in which evidence could be gathered and presented, limited police interrogation of suspects, and expanded the role of defense counsel beyond the courtroom to the station house.

By bringing the lower criminal courts under constitutional authority, these decisions have established a much higher set of standards for evaluating the administration of justice and have generated higher expectations about the ways cases should be handled. These in turn have produced increased public awareness about the operations of criminal courts. Academicians and the media have focused on the gap between ideal and actual practices; numerous commissions, committees, and organizations have investigated the courts in order to propose ways to implement these new standards; and others have sought to determine if they are being met. Clearly, there has been a dramatic increase in the expectations and standards for evaluating the ongoing process of criminal justice. And this upgrading of the *ideal* rather than an increase in caseloads probably accounts for the widening "gap" between the "ideal" and the "actual" practice perceived over the past decade.

Nonreactive "Causes"

Whenever there is discontent there is usually a search for someone to blame. Social organizations are not immune to this phenomenon, and indeed can function only because they are successful in assigning specific duties to designated individuals who can then be held accountable for their performance. Countering this, there is also a tendency for those with such responsibilities to develop techniques to protect themselves, devices which allow them to accept credit for success but disavow responsibility for failure. In large complex organizations these practices can be refined to a high art. Specialization, minute division of labor, and the corresponding inability of any one person to see "the whole picture" make it difficult to trace the ultimate impact of a particular action, and hence facilitate the diffusion and transfer of responsibility.

Transferring responsibility is not, however, an easy task. There is a tendency for those in whose arms blame is cast to reject or pass on the unwanted burden. Also, blaming someone else creates the possibility that the allegation can be returned at some later date. This is a risky business at best. An alternative is to find a more reliable culprit, a *non*reactive agency on whom blame can be placed without fear of reciprocity—to blame a *process* rather than a person. Pointing to factors beyond *anyone's* control avoids not only personal responsibility but also the possibility of retaliation and recrimination engendered by pointing to someone else. Furthermore, it is difficult to counter accusations against processes.

In the administration of criminal justice, three types of nonreactive factors have emerged as "the cause" of many problems confronting the system. Heavy caseloads, understaffing, and inadequate funding are all "enemies" which everyone can safely point to as causes for poor performance. As Peter Drucker noted, since these factors are universally claimed as the "causes" of poor performance, their importance is almost always overstressed.[31]

But if not heavy caseloads, then what does explain this ubiquitous practice of rapid and perfunctory processing of cases? Let us look at three interrelated sets of factors that have a bearing on the organization of the court system. The first focuses on the peculiar way the court's workload is distributed; the second is a consequence of the mutually advantageous practices inherent in a system of justice in which the stakes are not very high in comparison to the costs of going through the system; and the third deals with the problems of professionals in relationship with their clients.

Alternative Explanations

The Organization of the Court's Business

The working hours in a lower court are scheduled in a distinctive if not unique way. Participants are interested in getting through the calendar as quickly as possible so that they can leave the courtroom for the day, either to go home or back to an office and other work. Prosecutors have to prepare the following day's cases. Defense attorneys have other clients to meet, cases to prepare, and records to file, and clerks have the day's work to record and file.

Concomitant with this desire to press through the work is general irritation at any of a variety of events that can disrupt the usually smooth and steady routine and extend the length of time court is in session. The slow pace of a new attorney unfamiliar with the court's workings is viewed as a minor irritant by the regulars. A defense attorney who raises more than perfunctory arguments on behalf of his client may be interrupted and prodded by the judge to rush through his statement. At times a judge may indicate displeasure at even having to listen to such additional arguments and will make a ruling before the attorney completes his argument. While some disruptions of routine may provoke considerable interest from everyone in the courtroom—they usually involve a particularly vehement outburst by the defense attorney or a heated and sarcastic exchange between the prosecutor and defense attorney or between the defendant and the judge—and provide entertainment for most of the observers, nonroutine and slower procedures are usually viewed as irritating interruptions in an otherwise efficient operation. There is a set of half-conscious norms about what one can and cannot do, and any violation of them meets with disapproval.

This disapproval is not reserved wholly for uncooperative defense attorneys. Defense attorneys and prosecutors may grumble when a judge new to a court conducts business at a much more leisurely pace than his predecessor. But although a judge may begin his rotation taking his time, carefully warning defendants of their rights, explaining procedures to them, and inquiring into any deals arranged with the prosecutor, within a short time he will behave like everyone else and run through the docket as quickly as possible.

Clearly, the common interest in processing defendants rapidly is far more than an attempt on the part of various actors to keep their heads above the rising waters in an overburdened court. Stated more bluntly, regardless of caseload, there will always be *too many cases* for many of the participants in the system, since most of them have a strong interest in being some place other than in court. Court personnel and others in the extended court organization have a distinctive if not unique work arrangement. They need not be at their jobs from nine to five, nor do they get paid by the piece (except for private defense attorneys); if they did there would be an incentive to move cases rapidly, but there would also be one to work longer hours. Instead, lawyers have a predetermined total daily workload, and when it is completed many of them can leave. While a court with a heavier load may adjourn for the day at 4:00 P.M. and take only brief recesses and the smaller court may adjourn at 12:30 P.M., the incentive for rapid processing remains. This simple feature helps explain why there will always be a strong incentive to move cases through at a rapid pace, regardless of caseload.

Substantive Justice and Mutual Advantages

Another more fundamental feature of court life plays a prominent role in cutting down on trials and other time-consuming and costly adversarial proceedings: the belief that disputes settled through negotiation and/or pleas of guilty provide mutual benefits for *all* involved parties.

The savings in time and effort they provide for the prosecutor and defense attorney are obvious. The prosecutor does not have to present a formal case against the defendant with all anticipated procedural and substantive holes plugged. Nor does he have to rustle up all the witnesses and spend time interviewing and preparing them for testimony. Even in the most open and shut case this activity is time-consuming, and unless testimony is carefully prepared it can be lost on a variety of technical grounds. In contrast, the defense attorney need not mount a defense, and can avoid interviewing and preparing witnesses, carefully scrutinizing the prosecutor's case against his client, and grasping at the host of procedural opportunities he can use as roadblocks in the case against his client.

The normative stance that facilitates this "short circuiting" is a consensus by nearly everyone involved in most every case that the defendant is in fact responsible for *some* wrongdoing connected with the charges. The prosecutor and defense attorney do not puzzle over whether the defendant is innocent or guilty of the offenses charged; rather, they ask, "What is this case worth?" "How should we dispose of it?" and "What should we settle for?" They engage in a *joint* enterprise rather than a war and plan to reach a consensus on the "verdict" concerning the actions which precipitated the arrest. A noncooperative attitude would not only indicate a serious rupture in the long-standing goodwill among parties who must continue to work with each other day in and day out, but it is also almost inconceivable since there is a pervasive belief in the defendant's wrongdoing.

Prosecutors and defense attorneys have institutionalized incentives which arise through regular and continuous interaction with the court, but defendants come and go, and their interests vary considerably. Although a great many of them are familiar with the workings of the court, few have a sophisticated notion of all the alternatives—and expected consequences—available for their defense. According to defense attorneys, most defendants do not seriously profess innocence, but few have enough knowledge of criminal procedure to press their attorneys to investigate thoroughly the circumstances of their arrests, the quality of the prosecutor's evidence, statements by the arresting officers, and the like. Aside from an occasional question about arrest procedures in cases involving a charge of narcotics possession, defense attorneys rarely subject the arrest procedures or evidence collection to very close scrutiny, and instead emphasize an "equitable" disposition for the case. If the defendant is charged unfairly or overcharged according to the prevailing norms of the courthouse, then the defense counsel finds it more productive to "work with" the prosecutor to obtain an appropriate reduction in the charges or to argue quietly for a lenient sentence recommendation than to fight openly in court. Most defense attorneys argue that this practice benefits defendants both as a group and in individual cases. By dispensing with the trappings of formal procedure, they argue, they can provide equitable "substantive" justice in an efficient manner.

The findings for the two courts seem to bear these contentions out. First, there is a high rate of nolles for both courts. In New Haven almost one-half of all cases before the court were terminated by the prosecutor's decision not to press the matter. In the comparison court this figure was smaller, a little over 25 percent, but it still represented a sizable number of cases. Although it is impossible to know if these figures would rise if a more adversarial stance were taken, certainly defense attorneys and prosecutors *believe* that many defendants who now have their charges nolled are guilty *and* could have been convicted. These nolles, they believe, are "equitable" resolutions of cases in which a *finding* of guilt or a sentence would have no meaning or positive benefit for anyone. For instance, some prosecutors and judges believe that arrest, loss of money for bail, and the requirement to appear in court are themselves significant sanctions, and "additional" formal penalties would be overly harsh or even counterproductive. Cooperation and the wider range of alternatives it provides, they claim, offer solutions more beneficial to the accused and to society than would a more formalized, less discretionary system of criminal justice.

The Impact of Professionalism

To a great many people, the jury trial represents criminal court action at its best, a forceful prosecution countered by a careful defense, and an evaluation by a jury of one's peers. The jury also symbolizes the importance of amateurs in the criminal process, since juries are almost invariably composed of lay persons not skilled in the criminal law. Although jury trials have never been used with great frequency, their use has probably declined over the past 100 years. The decline in the importance of amateurs in this role has been accompanied by a decline in the role of amateurs in other positions in the criminal process. The past 100 years, and particularly the past 50 years, have seen a dramatic shift in the staffing of the criminal courts. Full-time specialists have replaced part-time personnel as policemen, prosecutors, defense attorneys, and judges. In the criminal justice field the demise of part-time nonspecialists was probably hastened by such technological developments as ballistic tests, fingerprints, blood tests, and by increasingly complicated rules of evidence and procedure. Problems that might once have engaged skilled amateurs in thoughtful deliberation and debate are now the objects of "expert" inquiry by trained specialists who rely not only on common sense and conjecture, but also upon professional competence. This has reduced the need for adversarial deliberations before a jury.[32] Public deliberation, debate, and judgment have been replaced by technical determination.

Modern society is characterized by a high degree of specialization and division of labor, and has increasingly come to rely on professionals to make decisions once made by amateurs. Although defendants and victims alike view the reduction in trials as an abandonment of their interests, the change may rather be a by-product of increased professionalism, impersonal judgment, and rapid agreement according to established criteria. Some of the increase in suspicion and confusion generated by the practices of courts in recent years must be attributed to the displacement of amateurs by professionals and to the frustrations of lay persons confronting "experts." The Anglo-American adversary system was originally designed to be operated by amateurs, and as the criminal courts have come to be dominated by full-time professionals some of the institutions designed for amateurs have fallen into disuse. Although we have traditionally equated professionalism in lawyers with their skills in trial practice, the primary measure of skills for attorneys is their ability to assess complicated materials accurately and efficiently *according to established criteria and accepted standards.* If a lawyer does his job well, he is more likely to encourage consensus than disagreement, and as the process of decision making has increasingly come into the hands of "experts" and the criteria for judgment have become increasingly refined, it is perhaps no small wonder that the number of trials has fallen off.

The distance between the lay person and the professional— the client and his lawyer—is reinforced by the norms of professionalism. Professionalism breeds impatience with naivete, intolerance with ignorance, a desire for efficiency, and reliance on its own technical language, all of which alienate the professional from his client.[33] Not only are defendants and victims alike suspicious of court processes they do not understand, patients are frustrated by the brusqueness of their doctors, students by their teachers, and motorists by auto mechanics. Dependence on "experts" and the suspicion it generates are endemic to modern life.

Conclusion: The Process as Punishment

A great many writers have characterized the criminal defendant as a dupe, a mark in a con game with an attorney who is willing to sell him down the river in order to obtain a rapid disposition for a case. Although it is clear that defendants rarely ever "manage" their cases or are even fully apprised of all the legal alternatives open to them, it is not at all clear that they are unwitting dupes who would much prefer to have their attorney go into full battle for them. Interviews with the attorney, corralling favorable witnesses, and repeated court appearances all take their toll on the defendant as well as the prosecutor and defense counsel.

The defendant in a minor criminal case is much like a party in a civil suit; frequently the most rational course of action for him is to forego principle and settle in order to minimize the costs of pursuing a decision by means of a formal process which entails expenses that can quickly come to outweigh the magnitude of the sentence itself. Although the defendant who retains his own counsel must pay for this service, in most instances the costs of having to make repeated court appearances and visit the attorney during regular working hours in order to participate in the construction of the defense more than overshadow the magnitude of the eventual sentence. As was shown in chapter seven, losing just one day's wages is likely to be more of a hardship than the typical fine imposed by the court.

Ironically, the cost of *invoking* one's rights is frequently greater than the loss of the rights themselves, which is why so many defendants accept a guilty plea without a battle.[34] This situation is true for defendants who are or consider themselves innocent as well as for those who readily acknowledge their guilt.

This situation poses serious questions about the efficacy of the adversary process and the value of elaborate procedures as institutions for protecting individual rights and assuring justice in lower criminal courts. When the costs of invoking the safeguards of the process are likely to be greater than the eventual criminal sentence, there is little incentive to engage fully in the process in an effort to vindicate oneself or minimize the sanction. The pat solution to the problems of adjudication—to expand "due process" in the adversary system—might produce negligible results or even be counterproductive. Expanding due process might give the illusion of improvement even if there were none, and also contribute to a set of standards and controls so remote from the existing system that they would be inapplicable and meaningless in all but occasional cases.

CHAPTER 9

The Criminal Process and

the Adjudicative Ideal

Introduction

In the opening chapter I argued that courts are not what they appear to be. They are not organizations structured to pursue clear-cut goals; they are aggregates of people pursuing different and often antagonistic interests who at best have established a tentative equilibrium with each other. Court officials do not necessarily share a common sense of justice embodied in or derived from fidelity to formal law; instead they have different senses of justice which often emphasize substance over procedure. The system of sanctioning in the lower courts is not lodged exclusively or even primarily in the formal institutions of adjudication and sentencing; instead sanctions are dispersed throughout the entire criminal process, and many of the most significant emerge as by-products of the pretrial process. In order to understand the nature and function of the Court of Common Pleas, it was necessary to consider each of these separate factors. For this I had to view the court on several different levels, approach it from diverse perspectives, and examine its less visible institutions.

In this effort I tried to avoid the pitfall of providing an over-determined explanation. The three themes which guided my investigation provided explanatory frameworks which complemented rather than competed with each other. The systems framework established the context for decision making in the Court of Common Pleas. It considered the fragile interrelationships among the separate components of the system and how they adjust to each other until they reach a tentative equilibrium. It pointed out the permeability of this system, showing how it is in part a reflection of the larger environment. It showed how as an institution the court generates its own concerns and interests, adapting the formalities of the criminal process to its own interests and conditions. But by itself the systems perspective cannot *explain* decisions; it can only establish the *context* of decisions. Decision making in the criminal process is purposive and presumably principled. In order to come to grips with these factors, it was necessary to consider the values, incentives, and concerns of the individuals who compose the court. This examination revealed two inescapable facts. Superimposed on the formal theory of adjudication and firmly ensconced in the informal system of the court is an acute concern with substantive justice and a sharp realization that "due process" itself is costly. These concerns are present in any system of justice but loom particularly large in those courts which deal almost exclusively with what the law labels as "petty" offenses. In the lower courts they have the capacity drastically to reshape the content and meaning of adjudication.

Many of the continuing problems in the criminal courts stem from these three factors: organizational structure; concern for substantive justice; and the importance of the pretrial costs. They all come together to frustrate many of the ideals of the criminal process. I have written elsewhere that because there is no hierarchy and no effective system for enforcing compliance, and because of excessive decentralization and fragmentation in the criminal court system, "there is no particular reason to expect an individual's behavior to coincide with the behavior prescribed by the formal goals of the system."[1] Yet there is a continuing drive to secure greater congruence between them, to impose the ideal upon reality and to judge the reality by it. This has often led to efforts to increase the formalism in lower courts.

But if my analysis is correct, such efforts are not likely to achieve their desired results, and many of them may in fact be counterproductive. There are no simple solutions to what so many observers have posed as the problems of the lower courts. These courts may always act with a considerable degree of casualness. While reforms in structure and organization can no doubt curb many flagrant abuses of authority, the pressures to adapt to organizational goals, the deeply felt impulses to render quick substantive justice, and the reality of the costs of the process will continue to assert themselves. The effort to impose formal uniform procedures will continue to be frustrated as long as it is imposed on situations which few view as seriously criminal. Efforts to increase the care and deliberateness with which decisions are made will also meet with fierce resistance and subtle subversion as long as they have the effect of further increasing sanctions against the accused. It is these tensions, tensions which have increased rather than decreased with the expansion of the notion of due process, which I wish to explore in this concluding chapter.

The Criminal Court System and the Adjudicative Ideal

Criminal procedure provides precise standards for conducting court proceedings, introducing evidence, presenting proofs, and determining guilt, and the theory of the adversary process provides for an elaborate division of labor for performing these tasks. In many respects the American criminal process can be regarded as a full expression of Max Weber's notion of formal rational organization. Yet practices in the criminal courts do not correspond to these principles. In practice at every stage the adjudicative ideal is warped almost beyond recognition. Modern students of organization have come to accept such divergences as natural, pointing out that all organizations have to be responsive to their larger environments and must devote considerable energy to adapting formal goals to the concerns of their own members The criminal court system is no exception to this pattern, and indeed is particularly susceptible to it. It is not organized hierarchically, has no formal monitoring system, and must rely on the expensive and essentially passive mechanism of appeal as a means for inducing compliance.

The criminal court then is a system rather than a formal organization, created and held together by the formalities of the criminal law, whose actions are shaped to a considerable extent by its relationship to the larger environment and its own members' sense of professionalism and private interests. These factors contribute to the tensions between the adjudicative ideal and the actual operations of the court, tensions which are inevitable in any organization, but which are writ large in the lower criminal court.

As an *open* system, the criminal court reflects and responds to its environment. For the court considered in this book, this means that the criminal process is inextricably intertwined with the political process. The courthouse is populated with officials recruited from the political arena who are adept at and comfortable with compromise and informality, features of decision making which emphasize pragmatism over principle and substance over procedure. This close connection with the political process not only fosters a concern with substantive rather than formal justice but also affects the particular nature of this substantive justice. Many of the positions in the court are filled by "ethnics" who are themselves not far removed from the insecurities of lower-middle-class existence. Although they are usually of a different race than those who appear before the bench, these officials are, in the words of one insightful defense attorney, "generally sympathetic to the impoverished conditions which are part of the lives of so many defendants."

Politics affect the court in other ways as well. Courthouse officials usually obtain their positions through the patronage system, and their security in those positions depends more on maintaining the goodwill of their political sponsors than on the quality of their performance within the court. Most try merely to cope, to survive, and have little incentive to excel or innovate. Their minimal fidelity to the task fosters casualness and breeds error. Reflective people within the court recognize these problems but usually dismiss or downgrade their significance. Casualness and error, they argue, are inevitable by-products of rapid rough justice, a system of which they approve. Whether these practices are pathological or normal, detrimental or beneficial to the accused, they run counter to the adjudicative ideal.

The internal organization of the court places further strains on this ideal. Noise in the courtroom helps to speed case processing, but it destroys the sense of decorum in the court. The rapid pace at which cases are handled minimizes the amount of time a defendant must spend in court, but it also fosters caprice and mistake. Other factors that facilitate the efficient operation of the court cannot even be justified in terms of promoting substantive justice. The symbolic nature of plea bargaining is largely a device used by defense attorneys to control their clients. Splitting differences in multiple charge cases and exchanging pleas across cases foster rapid disposition, but clearly operate at the expense of individual defendants. Prosecutor control of the calendar and the subtle threat of more severe sanctions after trial all function to keep time-consuming defense tactics to a minimum, but they also frighten defendants out of exercising their rights.

Many of the problems identified here are readily acknowledged by participants in the process, but they usually point to the press of heavy caseloads as the source of the problems. As we have seen, the press of a heavy caseload is at best a marginal factor in creating these problems. They are firmly rooted in the court personnel's own concerns with speed and efficiency. Officials do not abandon this concern with justice, but rather they create a sense of justice which is compatible with their concern for speed and efficiency. The court accepts this sense of justice not only because it is efficient, but also because it is considered fair as well.

Substantive Justice and the Adjudicative Ideal

The process of adjudication, particularly the portion that involves adversary interaction, is designed to narrow the zone of controversy, to focus intensely on precise issues of fact and law in order to arrive at a resolution of a dispute. It limits the elements of controversy in time, place, and scope. The function of formal adjudication is to narrow the focus of relevant concern. But the tendency of the court is to expand the focus of relevancy.

This way of looking at cases makes even the presumption of guilt largely irrelevant. Such a presumption implies that someone believes the charges could withstand challenge and are beyond rebutability. But rarely is a case considered in this way. Court officials rarely do focus precisely on formal distinctions between guilt and innocence or factual versus legal guilt. Rather, they tend to respond directly to the incident and the defendant; they feel their primary task is not to prove or disprove specific assertions, but rather to come to an understanding about the defendant's involvement in a troublesome situation in order to arrive at an appropriate disposition. Although the strength of the evidence is often considered an issue, it is but one of a number of factors that may determine the worth of the case. The process takes for granted that the defendant was involved in the trouble, and immediately tries to determine the magnitude of the trouble and the nature of his responsibility as a prerequisite for disposing of the case.

In many respects the decision-making process in the Court of Common Pleas is strongly related to the practices and theory of juvenile courts. The modern theory of juvenile justice argues for individualized justice tailored to treat a wide range of factors as relevant and to respond to the "whole" person. It deemphasizes the strictly "legal" proceedings, and purposefully expands its inquiry beyond and away from the provoking incident in order to determine the root of the child's trouble and consider appropriate alternative responses. It adopts a type of philosophical positivism that supports a reduced view of individual responsibility and culminates in the doctrine of *parens patriae*. Ideally, juvenile court's primary function is not to punish but to rehabilitate or "straighten out" the child. It attempts to provide what limited help it can in strengthening the child's ties with the more traditional institutions of social control.

Practices that in juvenile courts are fanned by a formal philosophy have grown up untended in the Court of Common Pleas through flexibility, selective use of discretion, and an over-determined system of rules. Some of the nurturing practices operate informally; others have been institutionalized. As we have seen, decisions to prosecute are based on a host of considerations other than the strength of evidence and applicable law: assessments of the "real" trouble; the defendant's prior history with the police and court; the assessment of his potential for future trouble; and the availability of supportive alternatives. Such "rehabilitative" alternatives as pretrial diversion, "prosecutor's probation," conditional nolles, restitution, family counseling, and drug counseling are frequently urged upon the defendant in lieu of prosecution. The court is sympathetic to "excuses" that diminish responsibility for the defendant. One private defense attorney who regularly practices in the court and is also known for his ability as a trial lawyer in Superior

Court declared, "I don't practice law, I'm a social worker. My job is to try to pull my client back together so that the prosecutor and judge will look favorably on him."

Although some of the acts of substantive justice are vindictive, a great many—perhaps the overwhelming majority—flow from a genuine concern with doing the "right" thing. But these decisions are suspect because they are based upon variable and ill-defined factors. By its very nature individualized justice makes the distinctive and unusual terribly important, which in turn makes the process appear arbitrary. For although "relevant" factors should be taken into consideration, there is really no way of knowing what they may or should be in any given situation. While it has been possible to identify categories of factors that regularly figure in the considerations of officials, various combinations of them provide for a nearly limitless number of possibilities, and there is no way for anyone to predict precisely how they will affect any single decision.

And of course "facts" do not speak for themselves. They must be mobilized, and within limits they are malleable and subject to manipulation and manufacture. Even if there are no clear-cut errors, recognizing the possibility of error breeds cynicism and a sense of injustice. In short, *all* outcomes are suspect. One could always argue that a more vigorous or slightly altered presentation of relevant facts or the addition or "manufacture" of others might have produced a more favorable outcome, or that an already favorable outcome was the result of luck or of manipulation or exaggeration. In either instance, the process seems fragile, uncertain, and inconsistent. The adjudicative ideal extols the virtues of a self-contained, "autonomous" legal system which is impervious to external pressures. This broad spectrum of appeals challenges that ideal; it violates the sense of closure that an "autonomous" institution must have.[2]

The same tensions long recognized as a serious problem within the system of juvenile justice seem to exist in much the same form in the lower criminal courts as well.[3] If I am correct, the central problem of the court is rooted in neither the poor quality of the personnel nor the tendency to avoid responsibility; it is entrenched in the officials' aspirations to do good, in the impulse for flexibility and substantive justice which gives rise to competing conceptions of justice. The freedom to pick and choose among these conceptions undercuts the morality of all of them, and ironically the impulse to provide justice seems to foster a sense of injustice.

This tension between formal and substantive justice is perhaps inherent in all systems of law, but because of the great variety of petty offenses they handle, it is especially important in lower criminal courts. Max Weber pointed out this dilemma when he made a classic distinction between irrational and rational justice. The former is characterized by a lack of concern for general rules and guided by reaction to the circumstances of the individual case, while the latter is characterized by a concern for general rules. In Weber's view the drift of modern societies has been away from irrational justice toward a system of rational justice, and there is little doubt that the *ideal* of modern American courts conforms to Weber's concept of formal, rational justice. Indeed the process of adjudication is understood largely in terms of procedure and concern with form. As Lon Fuller has written:

One is tempted to discern the essence of the judicial function in a requirement that the decision reached be *informed* and *impartial*. This will not do, however. The expectation that judgments should be informed and impartial applies to many social roles: that of supervisor toward those under their direction, of teachers toward pupils, of parents toward children, and so forth. The essence of the judicial function lies not in the substance of the conclusion reached, but in the procedures by which that substance is guaranteed. One does not become a judge by acting intelligently and fairly, but by accepting procedural restraints designed to insure—so far as human nature permits—an impartial and informed outcome of the process of decision.[4]

This understanding of the judicial function can go a long way toward understanding the essence of the ideal of the prosecution and defense function as well, for by their very nature the constraints placed on the judge impose definitions of the roles of the prosecution and defense as well. Fuller's statement might easily be paraphrased: "One does not become a good prosecutor or defense attorney by intelligent and fair arguments alone, but by making arguments that are persuasive within the procedural restraints designed to insure an impartial and informed outcome." Like the judge who is constrained by the arguments he can consider, the prosecutor and defense are limited and constrained by the appeals they can make. No one of these actors can successfully step outside these constraints or successfully abandon his role without endangering the integrity of the other participants in the process. They are all part of an interrelated system that must stand or fall as a whole.

Concern with procedure and the formal application of rules has an especially strong tradition in criminal law, which has long sought a corrective balance in the natural inequality of power and position between the state and the accused. The ideal of decisions based only on the application of rules and on the elimination of discretion runs strongly and deeply in the criminal justice system.

Joseph Goldstein identified this desire for the ideal and applied it to police practices, but his observations seem equally applicable for prosecutors, judges, and all decision makers in the criminal process.

The mandate of *full enforcement*, under circumstances which compel selective enforcement, has placed the municipal police in an intolerable position. As a result, nonenforcement programs have developed undercover, in a hit-or-miss fashion, and without regard to impact on the overall administration of justice or the basic objectives of the criminal law.

The ultimate answer is that the police should not be delegated discretion not to invoke the criminal law. It cannot be completely eliminated where human beings are involved. The frailties of human language and human perception will always admit of borderline cases. . . . But nonetheless, outside this margin of ambiguity, the police should operate in an atmosphere which exhorts and commands them to invoke impartially all criminal laws within the bounds of full enforcement.[5]

Herbert Packer expressed this same sentiment in his classic examination of American criminal law:

The basic trouble with discretion is simply that it is *lawless*, in the literal sense of that term. If police or prosecutors find themselves free (or compelled) to pick and choose among known or knowable instances of criminal conduct, they are making a judgment which in a society based on law should be made only by those to whom the making of law is entrusted.[6]

The police officer's decision as to whether or not to arrest has its analogues in decisions made by other officials in the criminal process. Plea bargaining, nolleing, casual continuances of cases, and wide latitude in sentencing—all decisions pursued without benefit of explicit principles—raise these same basic questions about the "rule of law versus discretion" or more bluntly, about "lawfulness" versus "lawlessness." Lon Fuller has reflected on this dilemma in a quite different context, but his observations are quite relevant to the problem at hand. He saw important differences between the roles of mediator and arbitrator and warned of severe consequences if one were abandoned midstream or if they were mixed together within the same forum:

Mediation and arbitration have distinct purposes and hence distinct moralities. The morality of mediation lies in optimum settlement, a settlement in which each party gives up what he values less, in return for what he values more. The morality of arbitration lies in a decision according to the law of the contract. The procedures appropriate for mediation are those most likely to uncover that pattern of adjustment which will most nearly meet the interests of both parties. The procedures appropriate for arbitration are those which most securely guarantee each of the parties a meaningful chance to present arguments and proofs for a decision in his favor. . . . Not only are the appropriate procedures different in the two cases, but the facts sought by those procedures are different. There is no way to define "the essential facts" of a situation except by reference to some objective. Since the objective of reaching an optimum settlement [mediation] is different from that of rendering an award according to the contract [adjudication], the facts relevant in the same two cases are different, or, when the same, are viewed in different aspects. If a person who has mediated unsuccessfully attempts to assume the role of arbitrator, he must endeavor to view the facts of the case in a completely new light, as if he had previously known nothing about them. This is a difficult thing to do.[7]

He then goes on to examine the dilemmas and pitfalls which appear when an arbitrator acts like a mediator. Slipping from one role to another and then back again, he suggests, destroys the integrity of the adjudication process. The arbitrator who sees value in trying to get the opposing parties together again to settle their differences in a mutually satisfactory way may work out a good solution in a particular case but weaken the institution of adjudication as a whole. He points out that the arbitrator does not reach an improper, an unreasonable, or a "bad" decision when he abandons his role to mediate a settlement; that he does not shed his adjudicative role simply to save himself time and effort at the expense of the parties in the dispute. Indeed, everyone involved may view an outcome as the best of all possible decisions and greatly appreciate the wisdom of the arbitrator. But there are implications for the action *beyond* the particular case. Abandoning the role of impartial rule-applier undermines the very *institution* of adjudication over the long run. Others come to see it as a sometime thing and then expect the judge or prosecutor to listen to their "extralegal" considerations or abandon procedure when it is convenient for them. It calls the *process* into disrepute, not necessarily particular outcomes.

Our examination of practices in the Court of Common Pleas showed that its official participants can assume alternative roles. A judge who applies formal, precise rules can turn around and cajole the complainant and defendant into reconciling their differences, or give paternalistic advice to a defendant. A defense attorney who may appear to be a lawyer's lawyer in one case may whisper in huddled conference with the prosecutor in the corridors on the next. A prosecutor who in one case claims that he has no discretion, that he *must* seek a conviction because the law was violated, will at other times nolle a case because "a conviction will serve no useful purpose." In short, each official has several conceptions of justice, each requiring different roles and a different set of relevant considerations. By shifting roles within the same forum, no role can maintain legitimacy, and the morality of the entire process is undermined. Ironically, the impulse to do justice contributes to the feeling that justice is not being done. Such tensions are inevitable in any complex system of law, but they are particularly prominent in the lower criminal courts where the stakes are usually low and the desire for swift justice is high.

Pretrial Costs and the Adjudicative Ideal

Although the *theory* of due process has been fueled by the ideal of perfectibility and has been developed in large part without regard to cost, in fact the process itself is costly. Participants—even defendants who have the benefit of court-appointed counsel—are well aware of this and adjust their sights accordingly.[8] The comparison of posttrial with pretrial costs in chapter seven helps, I think, to account for the rise of substantive justice and for the use of rapid and perfunctory procedures in the lower criminal courts.

In theory, bringing lower court procedures under the Constitution should provide a finely tuned and carefully calibrated instrument capable of rendering fair decisions. But this expansion has altered the capacity of the courts, and may even have reduced it. Because of the costs of invoking many of these options, these new-found rights and opportunities may function largely as hollow symbols of fairness or at best as luxuries or reserves to be called upon only in big, intense, or particularly difficult cases. The findings in this study suggest they are not useful guides for the great majority of criminal cases. Appeals are all but unheard of, trials are virtually nonexistent, and formal pretrial motions are extremely rare.

Clearly, one of the functions of the adjudicative ideal is to insure that decisions are fair, both in fact and in appearance, and that they are based on universal rather than particular criteria. But if invoking rights becomes problematic, what criteria does one use to make decisions? We found that the sense of substantive justice filled the vacuum created by the absence of formal proceedings; decision makers do not abandon concern with fairness, but they do abandon the formalities of the adjudicative ideal, creating inevitable tension within the court system itself.

This distortion of the ideal is further twisted, if not inverted, when one considers the informal as well as formal sanctioning processes at work in the court. The adjudicative ideal is concerned with the determination of guilt or innocence, and to a lesser extent with the sentence. Yet we found that the accused were not sanctioned most severely at, or primarily concerned with, these stages. Rather, the cumulative effect of several pretrial and by-product decisions imposed the most significant *tangible* sanctions upon the accused, sanctions which for the most part are not different for the innocent and the guilty.

Although court procedures could be streamlined and bail practices liberalized, for the most part these pretrial costs are inevitable. Processing costs are part and parcel of the externalized operating costs in any organization. Shoppers must wait in line in the grocery store, and welfare recipients must endure the intrusiveness of the caseworker.

But concern with these costs shapes the entire process in lower court and literally stands the criminal process on its head, distorting and frustrating the adjudicative ideal. Learned Hand stated the legalist's position well when he observed, "Thou shalt not ration justice." This admonition notwithstanding, the criminal process is rationed because it is costly, and there is an enduring tension created by the court's inability to fulfill ideals which are too costly to invoke.

A Concluding Note on Reform

The lower court is a complex, flexible institution that is able to absorb efforts to change it and adapt to new circumstances without abandoning old ways. Whatever new programs or directions are added to the court will be deflected, adapted, and absorbed in a variety of unpredictable ways.

Furthermore, changes will not be achieved without some corresponding losses. For instance, one distinctive feature of the court is its lack of fidelity to "The Law." This practice is fostered by political patronage in the selection process, so that one might reasonably conclude that patronage ought be reduced or eliminated, and indeed there has been a slow trend to do so over the years. But in fact, considerations of patronage will be replaced by other considerations. And fidelity to the formalities of the law might not yield better outcomes or fairer decisions. The impulse for reform often springs from a desire to minimize the harshness of the criminal process on the accused, but it is not at all clear that as a group defendants would be better off in a more "formal" court system. As Martin Levin's study of two courts has shown, greater reliance on formal legal criteria for decision can lead to harsher rather than more lenient treatment for defendants, so that such changes are of dubious value to the accused. Skepticism about the consequences of increased formalism is clearly one of the major reasons so many of the vigorous and liberal defense attorneys in New Haven are decidedly lukewarm and passive about the idea of substantial "reforms" in the lower court.

Indeed, there is a chance that increased formalism would *increase* the harshness of the criminal process for a great many defendants. At present large numbers of defendants fail to appear in court, and many could be considered poor risks for pretrial release. Taking this problem more seriously could mean imposing harsher conditions for pretrial release and increasing pretrial detention. Stricter formalism could mean that substantial numbers of cases would require prolonged court time to clarify facts, mount proofs, and counter with defenses. While these changes might result in a higher appearance rate in court and vindication of the innocent in some cases, and could conceivably lead to higher standards of police conduct, they could also lead to a tendency to invest a great many cases with a degree of seriousness that few people currently give to them, a tendency which would be resisted fiercely by all involved. In the lower courts a great many appearances are ritualistic terminations of problems that for all practical purposes were resolved with the arrest itself, an act which defused a potentially explosive situation. The adjudicative ideal not withstanding, there are intense feelings to maintain this view.

Other reform efforts respond to the harshness and rigidities of the formal criminal process by proposing informal alternatives to formal adjudication. But again it is unclear what the concrete consequences of such efforts would be. One program which was in full force in the New Haven court during my study was the pretrial diversion program. Like its counterparts in a great many other cities, this program was founded in the belief that a more humane and individualized program of counseling is preferable to the rigid, harsh methods of traditional adjudication. Yet this program, and diversion programs in general, attracted few participants because it subjected them to more rather than less social control.

The same problem applies to other efforts to increase informality in the criminal process. Neighborhood justice centers and community courts are currently gaining great favor in this country.[9] They try to substitute informality, understanding, and the perspective of local community opinion for the formal, rigid procedures of the courts. But their proponents fail to realize that lower courts do *not* operate according to rigid formalities; they operate with flexibility and the concern for substantive justice. Thus these new centers may end up doing in a time-consuming and cumbersome manner what the lower courts do more quickly and more effectively.

With these brief concluding remarks I want merely to suggest that reformers should reflect carefully on their concrete objectives as they contemplate change and replace the abstractions of theory with real situations. As I observed at the outset of this chapter, courts are often not what they appear to be, and reformers should bear this in mind as they contemplate plans for change.

These comments should not be taken to mean that I see no room for constructive change, rather, I mean to convey the idea that the informal practices of lower courts are more flexible and functional and the impact of change more complex than they seem at first. As a consequence I am skeptical of drives to make lower courts adhere more closely to the high standards of formality or to supplement or replace them with informal "dispute settlement" councils. The former are likely to be overly rigid, and the latter overly optimistic about the capacities of legal institutions to affect people's lives. And because both want to complicate the process and hence make it more costly, both fail to appreciate what this study has made so clear, that for a great many criminal defendants the process *is* the punishment.

There are still other alternatives to cope with the problems of lower courts. Many argue that the criminal law is overextended, that congestion in courts can be relieved by decriminalization which would keep many (usually petty) cases out of the courts. No doubt the criminal sanction is overextended and selective decriminalization is desirable, but it is not likely that such a move would increase the deliberativeness of the lower courts. It is even debatable if *formal* decriminalization would measurably reduce the business of the courts. Most offenses are decriminalized *de facto* long before they are erased from the statute books (for example, there were few cases involving possession

THE CRIMINAL PROCESS AND THE ADJUDICATIVE IDEAL

of marijuana in my sample and even then many of them got to
court because the police originally intervened for other, unrelated reasons). A review of the types of cases brought to court
(see Table 2.1), coupled with my observations in the court,
leads me to conclude that in the vast majority of cases there is a
substantial social interest for official intervention (as distinct
from questions of appropriateness of the arrest of the particular
person, the strength of the evidence, the applicability of the
precise charges, etc.). It is not unreasonable for society to have
its agents intervene to put an end to bothersome behavior. Arrest puts an end to an immediate problem and defuses hostility,
and appearance in court formally puts an end to the incident
which in a great many instances was resolved by the arrest
itself. It also subjects the accused and the police to some minimal degree of public accountability. To treat these incidents
with greater deliberation as the formalists would have it would
be to invest a great many of them with a seriousness that few
involved in the process are willing to grant them. Invoking thera-
peutic techniques to root out basic causes would run the risk of
trivializing therapy or intruding into citizens' lives.

Some of my colleagues have argued that I do not adequately
appreciate the serious implications of a criminal record, that in
fact petty criminal cases are more serious, and hence the pretrial costs less important than I have suggested. Ultimately there
may be no satisfactory answer to this question, for at the time
of arrest and adjudication there is no way of knowing precisely
how a record will affect someone's future. Whereas it is clear
that a great many people—including defendants—discount the
possibility of serious future consequences of conviction, it is
also clear that a record of a criminal conviction for even a petty
offense *can* and at times *does* lead to consequences far more
damaging than those meted out by the court. Other than not
arresting and convicting in the first place, there is no way of
eliminating the impact of such extralegal sanctions outside the
courtroom.

Still there are ways of minimizing the extralegal impact and

295

long-term consequences flowing from conviction on a petty offense while at the same time preserving the social interests served by arrest and conviction. One device is little more than a sleight-of-hand, but one that might yield great dividends. By reducing selected offenses from misdemeanors to violations, the significance of conviction for a *crime* would evaporate. Conviction for a traffic violation does not carry the social stigma that conviction for a crime does, although a great many traffic violations involve matters likely to be viewed as more serious than actions now labeled "crimes," and impose penalties harsher than those typically meted out in the lower courts. Downgrading the seriousness of selected offenses to "violations" or some other such term would not only preserve society's interests in intervening in minor but nevertheless bothersome problems, it would also reduce concern over elaborate procedures, for it is the seriousness of consequences that can flow from decisions that prompts such concern. Few people object to the rapid pace and truncated proceedings of traffic courts if they are managed even-handedly, and if those who want it have the opportunity to contest their arrest. The administrativelike proceedings and even the working "presumption of guilt" are in fact often appreciated by the accused who recognize that the rapid pace reduces their contact with the court.[10] Even if errors are made, and most certainly they are, they are often errors that people can live with, for they usually carry no long-lasting implications.

The analogy to traffic court can be extended. In chapter seven, I described how a handful of cases was disposed of with bond forfeitures. Rather than issue a warrant for arrest for those who do not appear in court, the court simply closed out the cases by ordering a forfeiture of the posted bond. The device is, of course, the standard way that a great many so-called traffic fines are paid in this country. A similar device is also institutionalized and widely employed in nontraffic offenses in Northern Europe.

In West Germany this device is known as *"strafbefehl,"*

which is commonly translated as "penal order." In Sweden it is known as *"strafförelaggande,"* translated literally as "punishment laid before" someone.[11] Both provide for the option of summary judgment and punishment in minor criminal offenses. After arrest and release—which can be effected at the scene of the arrest—a prosecutor reviews the arrest report, screens out insubstantial cases, and if appropriate, draws up a penal order for a judge's signature. This order describes the allegations against the accused, summarizes the evidence, cites the applicable provisions of the criminal code, and specifies a punishment, usually a fine. It is then sent to the accused, who has the option of accepting it and paying the fine or contesting it and asking for a judicial hearing. Not surprisingly, a great many people prefer the former. The penal order appears to work tolerably well for a substantial number of offenses, many of which are roughly equivalent to American misdemeanors. With this experience, what has emerged only informally and piecemeal in the United States through the use of traffic tickets and bond forfeitures might now be embraced more fully.

American law has a very real concern with the innocent and the inappropriately convicted, and guards against the possibility that they might suffer severe sanctions and endure unfair consequences. It has sought to curb this fear by fostering an ideal of perfectibility and a preoccupation with procedure. In the process it has created a system so complex and cumbersome that in the great bulk of minor criminal cases these protections and procedures serve limited functions at best.[12] Adopting administrativelike structures such as the penal order to deal with some criminal cases might at first glance appear to run counter to these concerns, but if these practices are coupled with the elimination of the possibility of long-lasting stigma, they might in fact go a long way toward fulfilling the ideals of the law. As long as the process is itself the punishment, the adjudicative ideal will continue to conflict with the substantive goals of the American criminal law.

NOTES

Introduction

1. For a thoughtful discussion of this problem in an entirely different but nevertheless relevant context, see A. O. Hirschman, "The Search for Paradigms as a Hindrance to Understanding," chapter 16 in his book *A Bias for Hope* (New Haven: Yale University Press, 1971), pp. 342–361.

2. I am deeply indebted to the writings of a large number of people, and list here only a few of those whose works have been especially useful to me: Abraham Blumberg, *Criminal Justice* (Chicago: Quadrangle, 1967); George Cole, "The Decision to Prosecute," *Law and Society Review* 4 (1970): 331–333; Martin Levin, *Urban Politics and the Criminal Courts* (Chicago: University of Chicago Press, 1977); James Q. Wilson, *Varieties of Police Behavior* (Cambridge: Harvard University Press, 1968); James Eisenstein and Herbert Jacob, *Felony Justice: An Organizational Analysis of Criminal Courts* (Boston: Little Brown, 1977); Herbert Packer, *The Limits of the Criminal Sanction* (Palo Alto: Stanford University Press, 1968); Robert Merton, *Social Theory and Social Structure* (Glencoe, Ill.: Free Press, 1957); Robert Dahl, *Who Governs?* (New Haven: Yale University Press, 1961); and Peter Blau, *Exchange and Power in Social Life* (New York: John Wiley, 1964).

3. For an interesting examination of this issue with respect to the police, see the introduction in David Bayley (ed.), *Police and Society* (Beverly Hills: Sage Publications, Inc., 1977). For implications for courts, see Martin Levin, *Urban Politics and the Criminal Courts.*

4. The foremost student of this is, of course, Max Weber. See his *The Theory of Social and Economic Organization*, A. M. Henderson and T. Parsons (trans.), T. Parsons (ed.), (New York: Free Press, 1947).

5. John Hogarth, *Sentencing as a Human Process* (Toronto: University of Toronto Press, 1971); Willard Gaylin, *Partial Justice* (New York: Vintage Books, 1975); Martin Levin, *Urban Politics and the Criminal Courts*; William K. Muir, *Police: Street Corner Politicians* (Chicago: University of Chicago Press, 1977); Philip Selznick, *Law, Society and Industrial Justice* (New York: Russell Sage Foundation, 1969); and Lon Fuller, "What Problems Can Be Solved by Some Form of Adjudication?" *Wisconsin Law Review* (1963): 1–30.

6. For examinations of these types of costs in other jurisdictions and other types of cases, see Ronald Goldfarb, *Ransom: A Critique of the American Bail System* (New York: John Wiley, 1965); Herbert Jacob and James Eisenstein, "Sentences and Other Sanctions in the Criminal

Courts of Baltimore, Chicago, and Detroit," *Political Science Quarterly* 90 (1975): 617–626; and Jonathan Casper, *American Criminal Justice: The Defendant's Perspective* (Englewood Cliffs, N.J.: Prentice-Hall, 1972). For a theoretical treatment of this problem by an economist, see William Landes, "An Economic Analysis of the Courts," *Journal of Law and Economics* 14 (1971): 61–107.

7. Robert Dahl, *Who Governs?* and Raymond Wolfinger, *The Politics of Progress* (Englewood Cliffs, N.J.: Prentice Hall, 1974).

8. Wolfinger, *The Politics of Progress*, p. 29.

9. Anthony Platt and Randi Pollock, "Channeling Lawyers: The Careers of Public Defenders," *Issues in Criminology* 9 (1974): 1–31.

Chapter 1

1. Roscoe Pound, *Criminal Justice in America* (New York: De Capo Press, 1975; first published 1924).

2. Pound, *Criminal Justice in America*, pp. 174*ff*.

3. Pound, *Criminal Justice in America*, pp. 190–191.

4. 407 U.S. 25 (1972).

5. Excerpts from a letter from John Hersey to members of The Forum, August 11, 1972, quoted with the kind permission of John Hersey. The courtroom described is no longer in use. The lower court has since moved to a newer building, but the scene still resembles the one depicted here.

6. For an examination of the "heavy caseload hypothesis," see chapter eight.

7. See chapter eight.

8. For arguments that suggest that bargaining has long been a standard practice in the criminal process, see Milton Heumann, "A Note on Plea Bargaining and Case Pressure," in *Law and Society Review* 9 (1975): 515–528; and Jay Wishingraed, "The Plea Bargain in Historical Perspective," *Buffalo Law Review* 23 (1974): 499–527.

9. There are several studies which have sought to characterize courts as self-serving bureaucratic organizations. In particular, see Abraham Blumberg, *Criminal Justice* (Chicago: Quadrangle, 1967).

10. Blumberg, *Criminal Justice*, pp. 39–72, 169–188.

11. For an interesting discussion of criminal courts by an organization theorist, see Lawrence Mohr, "Organizations, Decisions and Courts," *Law and Society Review* 10 (1978): 621.

12. For such an argument, see Austin Sarat, "Research on the Nature and Function of Trial Courts" (Conference on Social Science Research on the Courts, National Center for State Courts, Denver, January 20, 1977). For an opposing view, see James Eisenstein and Herbert Jacob, *Felony Justice: An Organizational Analysis of Trial Courts* (Boston: Little Brown, 1977). pp. 43–53. They argue that courts can usefully be considered as organizations, focusing on the "courtroom workgroup," most particularly the judges, prosecutors, and defense attorneys who regularly do business with each other in a specific courtroom. In doing so, they seek to account for variation in the way cases are handled and sanctions are administered in terms of the traits of these workgroups, i.e.,

how they structure authority and influence relationships, possess common goals, develop specialized roles, use a variety of work techniques, engage in a variety of tasks, and have different degrees of stability and familiarity, as well as how their members relate to their own sponsoring organizations and the larger environment. As they have characterized organization, one must agree with their argument. They present convincing evidence that the ways these workgroups are organized and institutionalized explain differences in the ways cases are handled both in different courts within the same city and in different cities.

13. I distingush my use of the term "system" from its popular usage, which seems to imply a well-integrated institution, smoothly operating according to predetermined norms. In this view, there is a criminal justice "nonsystem," as has been argued by Daniel J. Freed, "The Nonsystem of Criminal Justice," in *Report to the Task Force on Law and Law Enforcement* (Violence Commission, vol. 13, 1969), pp. 265–284. I use "system" as an analytic concept, to characterize a regular and recurring process. For a discussion of "system" from this perspective, see David Easton, *A Systems Analysis of Political Life* (New York: John Wiley, 1965), and Anatol Rapoport, "Some System Approaches to Political Theory," in David Easton (ed.), *Varieties of Political Theory* (New York: John Wiley, 1966), pp. 129–142.

14. For a dramatic illustration of this, see Martin Levin, *Urban Politics and the Criminal Courts* (Chicago: University of Chicago Press, 1977). Levin compares sentencing practices in two cities and accounts for them in terms of the differences in political culture and judicial recruitment process.

15. Eisenstein and Jacob, *Felony Justice*, pp. 19–39.

16. Eisenstein and Jacob, *Felony Justice*, pp. 43–53.

17. Philip Selznik, *Law, Society and Industrial Justice* (New York: Russell Sage Foundation, 1969), p. 17.

18. Lon Fuller, "Collective Bargaining and the Arbitrator," *Wisconsin Law Review* (1963): 17.

19. Max Gluckman, *Politics, Law, and Ritual in Tribal Society* (Oxford: Blackwell, 1965); Richard Abel, "A Comparative Theory of Dispute Institutions in Society," *Law and Society Review* 8 (1974): 217; and Martin Shapiro, "Courts," in Fred Greenstein and Nelson Polsby (eds.), *Handbook of Political Science: Governmental Institutions and Processes*, vol. 5 (Boston: Wadsworth, 1976), pp. 321–372.

20. For a recent work that juxtaposes the operations of juvenile court philosophy and practices against those of adult criminal court, see W. Vaughn Stapleton and Lee E. Teitelbaum, *In Defense of Youth* (New York: Russell Sage Foundation, 1972). See also David Matza, *Delinquency and Drift* (New York: John Wiley, 1964), and Robert Emerson, *Judging Delinquents: Context and Process in Juvenile Court* (Chicago: Aldine, 1969). For a statement of the "medical model," see Karl Menninger, *The Crime of Punishment* (New York: Viking, 1968).

21. See, for instance, Blumberg, *Criminal Justice*.

22. Herbert Packer, *The Limits of the Criminal Sanction* (Stanford: Stanford University Press, 1968), p. 163.

23. Two excellent studies which emphasize the importance of "facts" in the plea bargaining process are Arthur Rosett and Donald Cressey, *Justice by Consent* (Philadelphia: Lippincott, 1976), and *Felony Arrests:*

Their Prosecution and Disposition in New York City's Courts (New York: Vera Institute of Justice, 1977).

Chapter 2

1. Between 1960 and 1970 the population of New Haven declined by 9.4 percent, while Bridgeport's and Hartford's remained more or less constant. Source: U.S. Bureau of the Census, *Statistical Abstracts of the United States: 1974,* 95th edition (Washington, 1974), pp. 25–30.
2. Robert Dahl, *Who Governs?* (New Haven: Yale University Press, 1961).
3. Dahl, *Who Governs?* pp. 260–264.
4. Dahl, *Who Governs?* pp. 121–122.
5. In addition to Dahl, see Raymond Wolfinger, *The Politics of Progress* (Englewood Cliffs, N.J.: Prentice-Hall, 1973); Joseph Lieberman, *The Power Broker: A Biography of John M. Bailey* (Boston: Houghton Mifflin, 1966); and Douglas Yates, *Neighborhood Democracy* (Lexington: D. C. Heath, 1973).
6. Source: U.S. Bureau of the Census, *City-County Data Book,* 1973 (Washington, D.C., 1973), p. 161; and *U.S. Bureau of the Census Statistical Abstracts,* 1973 (Washington, D.C., 1973), p. 149. All figures are for 1970.
7. *City-County Data Book,* p. 149.
8. *City-County Data Book,* p. 149.
9. See Edwin Schur, *Our Criminal Society* (Englewood Cliffs, N.J.: Prentice-Hall, 1969), pp. 27–36, and David Seidman and Michael Couzens, "Getting the Crime Rate Down: Political Pressure and Crime Reporting," *Law and Society Review* 8 (1974): 457–494.
10. Figures on arrest rates are drawn from annual FBI reports and were supplied to me by Ned Wilson of the University of New Haven. Some of the figures are reported in his study, *Final Report: Juvenile Delinquency Planning Study* (Connecticut Planning Committee on Criminal Administration, May 1974).
11. Source: U.S. Bureau of the Census, *1970 General Social and Economic Characteristics, Final Report* (PC [1]-C8 Connecticut), Washington D.C.
12. The court's jurisdiction is broader than the boundaries of New Haven. A small number of cases is produced by arrests in two smaller suburban communities, Bethany and Woodbridge.
13. In this section I have drawn heavily on Dean Goodman, "The Politics of Police Promotion" (New Haven: Yale University, A Working Paper, Institution for Social and Policy Studies, January 12, 1972).
14. In 1976 the state legislature enacted a statute which provided for a fully unified court system by 1980. For a discussion of the history of this and other efforts to reform the court system in Connecticut, see pp. 49–53.
15. A review of the files of all those cases disposed of in Superior Court for 1972 indicated that only a handful originated in a "street ar-

rest," in which the defendant was first taken to the Court of Common Pleas for arraignment. These data were supported by my sample of lower court cases; only a few of them were bound over to Superior Court.

16. This is reported in Joseph Lieberman, *The Power Broker*, pp. 234–238.

17. Jon Newman, "Prosecutor and Defender Reform," *Connecticut Bar Journal* 44 (1970): 567–583.

18. In at least one city it has long been common knowledge that party organizations raise substantial sums of money by extracting "contributions" from those they support for judicial positions. According to one account, the going rate is from one to two years' salary. See Wallace Sayre and Herbert Kaufman, *Governing New York City* (New York: Russell Sage Foundation, 1960), pp. 542ff; Susan and Martin Tolchin, *To the Victor* (New York: Vintage Books, 1972); and Jack Newfield, *Cruel and Unusual Justice* (New York: Holt, Rinehart and Winston, 1974).

19. For a detailed description of this, see Raymond Wolfinger, *The Politics of Progress*, pp. 177–202; and Philip Singerman, "Political Competition in New Haven" (mimeo, paper on file in Department of Political Science, Yale University, 1975).

20. Singerman, "Political Competition," pp. 3–12.

21. Max Weber, "Rational and Irrational Administration of Justice," in Max Rheinstein (ed.), *Max Weber on Law in Economy and Society* (Cambridge: Harvard University Press, 1954), p. 350.

22. This is, of course, continuing evidence in support of Robert Merton's famous analysis of the functions of the political machine. See Robert Merton, "Manifest and Latent Functions," in his *Social Theory and Social Structure* (New York: Free Press, 1968), pp. 73–138.

23. 407 U.S. 25.

24. Martin Levin, *Urban Politics and the Criminal Courts* (Chicago: University of Chicago Press, 1977).

Chapter 3

1. For two accounts of judicial recruitment in Connecticut, see Mary-Lou Weisman, "Lords of the Bench," *Connecticut Magazine* 39 (May 1976): 19; and Donald Dale Jackson, *Judges* (New York: Atheneum, 1974).

2. Jackson, *Judges*, pp. 62–88. One of the judges I interviewed claimed that if he followed his inclinations and started appointing Special Public Defenders to alleviate the heavy caseloads of the regular PDs, he would soon find himself shipped off to the boondocks, or transferred to the motor vehicle courtroom.

3. See pp. 69–70 for a discussion of the problems and functions of noise in the courtroom.

4. In a survey of defense attorneys, *Connecticut Magazine* found that only one Common Pleas Court judge rated among the top ten judges in the state, while five of the bottom ten were Common Pleas Court judges. See Charles Walsh, "Judicial Report Card," *Connecticut Magazine* 39 (May 1976): 23.

5. Donald Matthews discussed the functions of formalistic language in Congress, and observed:

> The Senate of the United States exists to solve problems, to grapple with conflicts. Sooner or later, the hot, emotion-laden issues of our time come before it. Senators as a group are ambitious and egocentric men, chosen through an electoral battle in which a talent for invective, righteous indignation, "mud-slinging" and "engaging in personalities" are often assets. Under the circumstances one might reasonably expect a great deal of manifest conflict and competition in the Senate. Such conflict does exist, but its sharp edges are blunted by the felt need—expressed in the Senate folkways—for courtesy.
> . . . Courtesy, far from being a meaningless custom as some senators seem to think it is, permits competitors to cooperate.

Donald Matthews, *U.S. Senators and Their World* (New York: Random House, 1960), pp. 97, 99.

6. Jon Newman, "Prosecutor and Defender Reform," *Connecticut Bar Journal* 44 (1970): 567–572.

7. Philip Singerman, Ph.D. thesis in progress, Yale University, p. 29.

8. Robert Dahl, *Who Governs?* (New Haven: Yale University Press, 1961), p. 109.

9. Barry L. Master and Gregory C. Demakis, "The Public Defender, the Prosecutor, and the ABA Standards: The Good, the Bad, and the Ugly" (Yale Law School, 1974): 100–108.

10. The part-time prosecutors are assigned full-time duty every other week. Although they are only paid $7500 per year for this half-time work, the job is more attractive than it seems because they often do not arrive until 10 A.M., just minutes before court convenes, and are usually able to depart by 2 P.M. or 3 P.M., and often earlier, so that their "half-time" job can be squeezed into the middle of a regular working day.

11. A questionnaire was sent to thirty of the city's defense attorneys who most frequently handled cases in the Court of Common Pleas. They were asked to rate the prosecutors on three criteria: their willingness to engage in plea bargaining favorable to the defendant; their knowledge of the law; and their attitude toward defense attorneys. Not surprisingly, there was a high intercorrelation among the three scales, and the rankings of prosecutors on each of them remained stable. Seven of the eight prosecutors were consistently given high ratings; only one appeared to be disliked and out-of-step with the office norms and expectations. Prosecutors agreed with this characterization.

12. A count of the number of attorneys listed in the 1975–76 telephone directories of these cities showed that New Haven had 735 attorneys, Bridgeport 741, and Hartford 1,289. Adjusting for populations, New Haven is sandwiched between the other cities. The substantially higher number for Hartford is attributable to the large number of insurance companies which have national headquarters there.

13. For another look at such types of attorneys, see Anthony Platt and Randi Pollock, "Channeling Lawyers: The Careers of Public Defenders," *Issues in Criminology* 9 (1974): 1–31.

14. Abraham Blumberg, *Criminal Justice* (Chicago: Quadrangle Books, 1967), p. 104.

15. See pp. 90–93, which discuss the results of a survey of the city's criminal lawyers.
16. See pp. 82–86.
17. For a journalist's account of this well-publicized trial, see Donald Freed, *Agony in New Haven: The Trial of Bobby Seale, Ericka Huggins and the Black Panther Party* (New York: Simon and Schuster, 1973).
18. Other older attorneys recall the freewheeling negotiating sessions and their ability to "fix" minor cases by exploiting friendships and political connections. Years ago prosecutors' desks were covered with liquor bottles at Christmas time; now most defense attorneys do not bring such presents, and those few who do have them delivered to the prosecutor's home.
19. 372 U.S., 335 (1963).
20. For a brief treatment of the Connecticut courts in historical perspective, see Milton Heumann, "A Note on Plea Bargaining and Case Pressure," *Law and Society Review* 9 (1975): 515–528.
21. For an account of this effort, see Robert Dahl, *Who Governs?*; Raymond Wolfinger, *The Politics of Progress* (Englewood Cliffs, N.J.: Prentice-Hall, 1973); and Allan Talbot, *The Mayor's Game* (New York: Praeger, 1970), pp. 174–177.
22. Richard Cass and Stuart Beck, "An Evaluation of the Connecticut Circuit Court Public Defender System" (Yale Law School, 1971).
23. Master and Demakis, "The Public Defender," p. 119.
24. See pp. 115–122 for an examination of the recruitment of the court's auxiliary officials.
25. See Jonathan Casper, *American Criminal Justice: The Defendant's Perspective* (Englewood Cliffs, N.J.: Prentice-Hall, 1972).
26. See pp. 155–167, 216, 219–222 for a discussion of attorney-client relations.

Chapter 4

1. One notable exception is a fine article by Forrest Dill, "Discretion, Exchange and Social Control: Bail Bondsmen in Criminal Courts," *Law and Society Review* 9 (1975): 639–674.
2. Ronald Goldfarb, *Ransom: A Critique of the American Bail System* (New York: Harper & Row, 1965), p. 102. The classic study of bail bondsmen is Arthur L. Beeley, *The Bail System in Chicago* (Chicago: University of Chicago Press, 1966; first published 1927).
3. This discussion draws on several papers prepared by Yale students and on file in the Yale Law School library, and I wish to express my indebtedness to them. See David Hinden, "The Role of the Bail Bondsmen in the Connecticut System of Pretrial Release" (Yale Law School, 1971); Kurt Hallock, "Bail Bondsmen in the Lower Court" (Yale University, 1975); and Diane Pike, "Bail Bondsmen: Unofficial Court Officials" (Yale University, 1976). In addition, see Diane Pike, Malcolm M. Feeley, and Daniel J. Freed, "Evaluation of the Wider City Parish Bonding Program" (New Haven: Yale Law School and New Haven Foundation, 1976).

4. Hinden, "The Role of the Bail Bondsmen," p. 1.

5. Bondsmen cannot write bonds whose total face value exceeds 90 percent of their posted assets. Most of the aggressive bondsmen tend to remain at or near this level, and occasionally exceed it. Those who write both "professional" and "insurance" bonds simply switch to the latter type once they approach their capacity. See pp. 97–101 for a discussion of how this is maintained.

6. Connecticut General Statutes 29-151 (rev. 1958; rev. to 1968).

7. For a detailed examination of the Connecticut law governing the operations of bail bondsmen, see Paul R. Rice and Mary C. Gallagher, "An Alternative to Professional Bail Bonding: A 10 Percent Cash Deposit for Connecticut," *Connecticut Law Journal* 5 (1972): 143–203. See also Paul Rice, "Bail and the Administration of Bail in the State of Connecticut," *Connecticut Law Review* 4 (1971): 1–34.

8. Rice and Gallagher, "An Alternative to Professional Bail Bonding," pp. 160–163.

9. Rice and Gallagher, "An Alternative to Professional Bail Bonding," p. 161.

10. Hinden, "The Role of the Bail Bondsmen," p. 10.

11. Drawing on figures for 1970 supplied by the Commissioner of State Police, Rice and Gallagher found that statewide the bondsmen averaged 1.89 times their capacity, a figure substantially lower than what they might have done.

12. The average length of time between arrest and adjudication for those cases in Common Pleas court for which bail was set was between two and three months.

13. Rice and Gallagher, "An Alternative to Professional Bail Bonding," pp. 164–171.

14. For a discussion of bond forfeitures which are *not* followed by an order for rearrest, see pp. 227–229.

15. Rice and Gallagher, "An Alternative to Professional Bail Bonding," pp. 163–164.

16. Connecticut General Statutes 54-70.

17. Rice and Gallagher, "An Alternative to Professional Bail Bonding," p. 162.

18. Rice and Gallagher, "An Alternative to Professional Bail Bonding," pp. 166–171.

19. Connecticut General Statutes 54-63a through 54-63g.

20. The statute also permits the arresting officer to make and issue a written complaint and release the arrestee on his own recognizance at the site of the arrest. This is known as citation arrest and release in New Haven.

21. Connecticut General Statutes 54-63b(b).

22. Connecticut General Statutes 54-63b(a).

23. For a history of the Vera Institute's early efforts on pretrial release, see Charles Ares, Anne Rankin, and Herbert Sturz, "The Manhattan Bail Project: An Interim Report on the Use of Pretrial Parole," *New York University Law Review* 38 (1963): 67–95; see also Lee S. Friedman, "The Evolution of Bail Reform," *Policy Sciences* 7 (1976): 281–313.

24. In another Connecticut jurisdiction, a smaller town, the Court

Liaison Officer reportedly sits in regularly on plea bargaining sessions, and according to one observer, this significantly inhibits the prosecutor's ability to reduce charges and settle cases.

Chapter 5

1. Abraham Blumberg stresses this argument. See his "The Practice of Law as a Confidence Game," *Law and Society Review* 1 (1967): 15–39. Albert Alschuler also argues that plea bargaining imposes a serious and significant penalty on those who want to exercise their right to trial. See his three major articles, "The Prosecutor's Role in Plea Bargaining" *University of Chicago Law Review* 36 (1968): 5–112; "The Defense Attorney's Role in Plea Bargaining," *Yale Law Journal* 84 (1975): 1179–1314; and "The Trial Judge's Role in Plea Bargaining: Part I, *Columbia Law Review* 76 (1976): 1059–1154. Peter Nardulli has argued that Cook County courts impose significantly longer terms on defendants who have "disrupted" the process by filing motions, or insisting on a trial. But Eisenstein and Jacob, using the same data, come to quite a different conclusion. They claim that there is no substantial penalty imposed on those who refuse to plea bargain and insist on their right to go to trial. The differences between these authors appear to be due to the way they standardized their data on sentences. See Peter Nardulli, "Sentencing: An Organizational Perspective" (paper presented at the Annual Meeting of the American Political Science Association, Chicago, September 1–5, 1976); and James Eisenstein and Herbert Jacob, *Felony Justice: An Organizational Analysis of Criminal Courts* (Boston: Little Brown, 1977), pp. 270–282.

2. This seems to be the assumption underlying much of the recent "speedy trial" legislation (for which the 1974 Federal Speedy Trial Act is the prototype). For a view to the contrary, see Martin Levin, "Delay in Five Criminal Courts," *Journal of Legal Studies* 4 (1975): 83–131.

3. One of the first of a series of articles documenting this was Anne Rankin, "The Effect of Pretrial Detention," *New York University Law Review* 39 (1964): 641–655. Since this pioneering effort, there have been numerous other studies which point to the same general conclusions—that those detained prior to trial are treated more harshly at adjudication and sentencing than those free on bond—solely because they have been detained. See Eric W. Single's study reported in Plaintiff's Memorandum in *Bellamy* et al., v. *The Judges Authorized to Sit in the New York City Criminal Court and the New York State Supreme Court in New York County* (1973); and *Roballo* et al., v. *The Judges and Justices Authorized to Sit in the New York City Criminal Court and the New York State Supreme Court in New York County* (1974).

4. For a history of the use of nolle in Connecticut, as well as an interesting study of its use in the New Haven lower court, see William A. Davis, "Nolle Prosequi in the Sixth Circuit Court: Prosecutor Discretion to Dispense with Charge" (Paper on file at the Yale Law School Library, 1974).

5. During the period of my observations only occasionally would a

judge show any interest in the prosecutor's reasons for granting a nolle. On only one occasion did a judge "refuse" to accept a nolle. The judge chastized the prosecutor for "giving too much away," whereupon the prosecutor asked the judge to delay the matter until they could speak together in chambers. Later the prosecutor explained privately to the judge that the defendant was facing far more serious charges in the Superior Court and the nolle here was part of an arrangement with the prosecutor in Superior Court who was anxious to move forward on his case. After hearing this, the judge agreed to the original nolle-sentence recommendation.

6. At first glance it is easy to see how one can draw the inference that there is racial discrimination at adjudication. Whites are in fact treated more favorably than Blacks; 57 percent of the white defendants in my sample received nolles in contrast to only 47 percent of the Blacks and Hispanics. Even controlling for seriousness of charge, this gap remains. However, it disappears once additional factors—most notably prior record—are introduced.

7. See Stuart Nagel and Lennie Weizman, "Women as Litigants." *Hastings Law Review* 23 (1972): 171–198.

8. For a discussion of bail setting practices, see pp. 209–222.

9. Thomas Schelling, *The Strategy of Conflict* (Cambridge: Harvard University Press, 1960).

10. See pp. 205–206.

11. The results were confusing and difficult to interpret. Few of the two-way and virtually none of the three-way interactions were statistically significant, and those which were did not conform to any intuitively understandable model. Rather than clarifying the sentencing process and improving the explanatory power of the variables, the tests for interaction cast further doubt on the meaningfulness of these types of variables in accounting for the sentencing decision. Similarly discouraging results were obtained from each of the several techniques applied to the data. For instance, the analysis of variance correlation ratio for both the total direct and total interaction efforts for the various models tested ranged from .07 to .15, hardly an impressive figure. Testing for interactions by regression analysis and Goodman's log-linear analysis produced similarly discouraging results.

12. By statute the Court of Common Pleas cannot impose sentences longer than one year. However this limit applies to each charge, and in cases involving multiple charges, judges can and occasionally do impose consecutive sentences whose total exceeds one year.

13. This process is quite arbitrary, and there is no consensus on how to weight sentences. The weighting I used was influenced to some extent by the work of Beverly Blair Cook and research conducted by the Federal Judicial Center. For a discussion of the problems of sentence index construction, see Beverly Blair Cook, "Sentencing Behavior of Federal Judges: Draft Cases—1972," *University of Cincinnati Law Review* 42 (1973): 597–641.

14. See, for example, Nagel and Weizman, "Women as Litigants."

15. For a review of these studies, see John Hagan, "Extra Legal Attributes and Criminal Sentencing: An Assessment of a Sociological Viewpoint," *Law and Society Review* 8 (1974): 357–383.

16. See pp. 76–93 for a discussion of these differences.

17. See note 9.

18. Leo Goodman, "Analysis of Dichotomous Variables," *American Sociological Review* 37 (1972): 28–46.

19. Hagan, "Extra Legal Attributes and Criminal Sentencing," p. 379.

20. John Hogarth, *Sentencing as a Human Process* (Toronto: University of Toronto Press, 1971).

21. See Hogarth, *Sentencing as a Human Process*; Eisenstein and Jacob, *Felony Justice*; and Leslie Wilkins, et al., *Sentencing Guidelines: Structuring Judicial Discretion* (Report to the National Institute of Law Enforcement and Criminal Justice, Law Enforcement Assistance Administration, U.S. Department of Justice, 1976).

22. Hans Zeisel has reflected on this point at some length. See his thoughtful note, "Methodological Problems in Studies of Sentencing," *Law and Society Review* 3 (1969): 621–632.

Chapter 6

1. See p. 313, note 12, for a discussion of the use of the "bail schedule."

2. This tension between police practices which anticipate trouble and avoid it by arrest is nicely explored in Martha H. Field and H. F. Field, "Marital Violence and the Criminal Process: Neither Justice nor Peace," *Social Service Review* 47 (1973): 221–241.

3. As a result of this clamor, an additional "prostitution judge" was assigned to the New Haven court to handle the increase in arrests for prostitution. According to newspaper accounts, however, despite numerous arrests there were only nine convictions, and the special judge was assigned other duties.

4. The range was from 27 percent to 49 percent, with the prosecutor known for being tough having the lower percentage and the prosecutor known as the most reasonable having the higher rate. These figures probably exaggerate the *actual* differences between these two prosecutors. Because one is known as "tough," many attorneys may take their cases elsewhere, although in fact he might have nolled them. Conversely, the higher rate of nolles may be the consequence of a similar pattern; what may in fact be only marginal differences are turned by self-fulfilling prophecy into a twenty-two–point spread. The nolle rates for the other prosecutors hover around 38 percent.

5. There is a large literature on this. See Daniel J. Freed and Patricia Wald, *Bail in the United States: 1964* (Washington: U.S. Department of Justice and Vera Foundation, Inc., 1964); Anne Rankin, "The Effect of Pretrial Detention," *New York University Law Review* 39 (1965): 941–955; and Plaintiffs' Memorandum in *Roballo* et al. v. *Judges and Justices of New York City Criminal Court* et al. (1974). For an excellent summary of other research in this area, see *An Evaluation of Policy-Related Work on the Effectiveness of Pretrial Release Programs* (Denver: National Center for State Courts, Publication No. R0016, October, 1975).

6. Connecticut statutes provide that defendants can file motions re-

questing that the judge consider them for "accelerated rehabilitation." If those requests are granted, the case is in effect delayed for up to six months, during which the defendant is to make progress in rehabilitating himself. If after this period the court is satisfied that the defendant is not likely to repeat his (alleged) criminal activities, then the judge has the option to dismiss the charges. Various judges read this statute quite differently. Some view it as a provision by which to handle rare exceptions—the proverbial starving person who was caught stealing a loaf of bread—while others argue that it might be used broadly but does not apply to persons charged with drug-related offenses or persons with prior records. Still other judges are willing to hear a great variety of motions for accelerated rehabilitation, but feel free to consider each request on its own merits without having to articulate general standards.

On the whole, prosecutors do not like accelerated rehabilitation. If there is good cause for leniency, they reason that it can be handled through their office by means of a nolle after the defendant has successfully participated in a diversion, drug, alcohol, or family counseling program. To the extent that judges grant accelerated rehabilitation, this challenges prosecutorial control of pretrial rehabilitation. In fact, accelerated rehabilitation is requested so infrequently that many defense attorneys often have no idea how to go about making a convincing argument to the judge. Indeed, a great many private defense attorneys—and some judges, so I am told—are altogether unaware of the option.

7. I use the term "normal" in much the same way that David Sudnow does. See David Sudnow, "Normal Crimes: Sociological Features of the Penal Code in a Public Defender's Office," *Social Problems* 12 (1965): 255–276.

8. This is explored at greater length on pp. 227–229.

9. There were no trials in my sample of 1,640 lower court cases. A sample of cases for the higher court in New Haven yielded only a 5 percent trial rate. Blumberg reports a 2.5 percent rate in his study of one county in New York City, and my own perusal of data for all the New York City courts shows similar results. Even when there are more trials, one must be careful not to jump to premature conclusions about the adversarial process. Lynn Mather, for instance, notes that fully 30 percent of the cases in Los Angeles are disposed of through trial, but then goes on to note that the process is a trial in name only. Such trials, known as "slow plea bargains" among court officials, take only about thirty seconds to two minutes, and are simply another form of plea bargaining. See Lynn Mather, "Some Determinants of the Method of Case Disposition: Decison-Making by Public Defenders in Los Angeles," *Law and Society Review* 8 (1973): 187–216.

10. A state-of-nature fallacy pervades much of this reasoning; it is unclear whether in fact there ever were better days with less plea bargaining and more trials. See pp. 262–267, and see also Milton Heumann, "A Note on Plea Bargaining and Case Pressure," *Law and Society Review* 9 (1975): 515–528, and Jay Wishingrad, "The Plea Bargain in Historical Perspective," *Buffalo Law Review* 23 (1974): 499–527.

11. In fact, private attorneys probably have a heavier workload than the PDs. Most private attorneys are engaged in a general law practice, handling both civil and criminal matters, and the frequency of their ap-

pearance in criminal court is not at all an accurate indicator of their total workload. Although many discussions of public defenders imply that the press of heavy caseloads causes them to be overly cooperative, this argument implies that the private attorneys' lighter caseloads allow them to be more combative. This assumption about differential workloads is not only wrong; it is probably just the reverse of the truth. Most of the private attorneys I talked to put in long working hours, handled a great variety of legal work, and also felt extremely pressed for time.

The PDs' workload only *appears* to be heavier because it is concentrated in one highly visible location—the courtroom—and is compressed into a four-hour period, between 10 A.M. and 3 P.M., with an hour out for lunch. Many of the PDs leave by 4 P.M. and rarely take work home with them or spend much time outside the courthouse interviewing clients or witnesses.

12. The rise of plea bargaining has coincided with the refinement—and expansion—of the criminal codes. While once crimes were crudely classified into only a handful of broad categories, now there are a host of classifications and categories which finely distinguish one type and one degree of offense from another. Available historical evidence suggests that the vast majority of convictions have always been secured by pleas of guilty. (See Wishingrad, "The Plea Bargain in Historical Perspective," and Heumann, "A Note on Plea Bargaining and Case Pressure.") If this is true, then the importance of plea bargaining in securing convictions may be grossly overrated, and the relationship between increased caseloads and increased plea negotiations may be spurious. The relatively recent practice of reducing charges in exchange for a plea of guilty may have more to do with the increased flexibility of the charging process brought about by the expanded classification system than with the increase in caseloads. If this hypothesis is correct, then one would expect to find a high rate of guilty pleas even in jurisdictions which do not permit plea bargaining. There is indeed some evidence to suggest this. See Thomas Church, "Plea Bargains, Concessions and the Courts: Analysis of a Quasi-Experiment," *Law and Society Review* 10 (1976): 377–402.

13. In contrast, George Cole found that Seattle prosecutors and defense attorneys regularly and frequently traded cases off each other in a systematic pattern of exchange. See his "The Decision to Prosecute," *Law and Society Review* 4 (1970): 331–343.

Chapter 7

1. Over half the arrestees in my sample had a record of prior arrests by the New Haven police, and a large proportion of them had records of conviction. These figures are probably drastically low, however, since local authorities do not systematically obtain records from other jurisdictions, either within or outside the state.

2. Discussions of arrest and conviction frequently assume that arrestees have a great fear of the stigma of a conviction and will go to great lengths to avoid being formally labeled as criminals. But my observations are

consistent with the findings of many criminologists who have studied juvenile delinquency and concluded that the disproportionate rate of criminal conduct by young lower-class males stems from a subculture which promotes such activity as a social mechanism for becoming a male adult. Rather than being a brand of inferiority for many lower- and working-class youths, arrest and conviction often reinforce the values of their subculture and can even enhance their status among their peers. This has been noted time and again in the literature on juvenile courts, but altogether overlooked and ignored in "adult" courts. See Walter B. Miller, "Lower Class Culture as a Generating Milieu of Gang Delinquency," *Journal of Social Issues* 14 (1958): 5–19, and Albert K. Cohen, *Delinquent Boys: The Culture of the Gang* (New York: Free Press, 1955). Also see Edwin H. Sutherland and Donald Cressey, *Principles of Criminology*, 7th ed. (Philadelphia: J. B. Lippincott, 1966), pp. 183–199, and Richard Quinney, *The Social Reality of Crime* (Boston: Little Brown, 1970), pp. 207–276.

3. See Edward Banfield, *The Unheavenly City* (Boston: Little Brown, 1971), pp. 45–56; and Edward Banfield and James Q. Wilson, "Public Regardingness as a Value Premise in Voting Behavior," *American Political Science Review* 58 (1964): 876–887.

4. Only arrestees who commit capital offenses cannot be released on bail under Connecticut law. All other cases can be, and the conditions set for release shall be the minimum necessary to assure the arrestee's appearance in court.

5. Connecticut General Statute 54-63(c)(a).

6. Toward the end of this study the pretrial detention facility moved from the rear of the old courthouse to larger facilities in the new headquarters of the Department of Police Services. The old lockup was probably large enough to hold all the arrestees not normally released, but occasionally space was a problem because the cells were divided into three sections, one each for whites, Blacks, and Hispanics. Police found that if they did not segregate arrestees, interracial conflict would erupt.

7. There are numerous studies attesting to this. An early and important one is Anne Rankin, "The Effect of Pretrial Detention," *New York University Law Review* 39 (1964): 941–965. Other more recent and sophisticated studies bear out this same point. See, for example, Eric Single, "The Bellamy Memorandum," *The Criminal Law Bulletin* 8 (1972): 459–506. For an overview of the great volume of literature on this point, see *An Evaluation of Policy-Related Research on the Effectiveness of Pretrial Release Programs* (Denver: National Center for State Courts, Publication No. R0016, October, 1975).

8. Daniel J. Freed, "The Imbalance Ratio," *Beyond Time* 1 (1973): 25–34.

9. Actually the percentage of the sample released on bond is probably several points higher. I was unable to obtain complete pretrial release data for 3 percent of my sample, most of whom had multiple arrests and a complicated history of release on both PTA and bond on different occasions.

10. A quiet tension between the races is always present in the courtroom; and, as suggested here, there is some evidence to support charges of racial discrimination. On the whole, however, no strong evidence dem-

onstrates any significant or even measurable amount of racial discrimination in outcomes. The fast pace and standardized routines of the court probably minimize the importance of race. But offhand racial slurs by court personnel are occasionally overheard in courtroom and corridors; and it is these remarks, coupled with the disproportionately high numbers of Black defendants in an otherwise "white" courtroom, that give the impression of *pervasive* racial discrimination by the court. This belief is widespread among Blacks and many whites. Here court personnel are more guilty of fostering the *appearance* of discrimination than of fostering its actual practice.

11. See, for example, Frederic Suffet, "Bail Setting: A Study of Courtroom Interaction," *Crime and Delinquency* 12 (October 1966): 318–331.

12. The resolution contains a section entitled "Bail Schedule," and orders police departments to take community ties into consideration when setting bail, then identifies a dollar amount for each charge. This original amount is followed by two lesser amounts to be applied to those individuals whose ties to the community are strong. A portion of this nine-page schedule is reproduced below:

	Group I	Group II	Group III
Disorderly Conduct	$ 50	$ 250	$ 500
Breaking and Entering, daytime	400	2000	4000
Breach of Peace, small likelihood of recurrence	1000	1500	2000
Larceny – shoplifting between $15 and $250	50	250	500
Carrying Dangerous Weapon	300	1500	3000

Group I   = Strong ties to all of the following: family, employment, community, special conditions (e.g., student, pregnant, rich, etc.).
Group II = Strong ties on only *some* of the above factors.
Group III = Strong ties on only one or two of the above factors.

Source: *Resolution of the Judges of December 19, 1967* (no date on document).

13. This ambiguity causes numerous complaints of overcharging. Arrestees who are unaware of the two types of bonding systems and fee schedules often feel cheated when they later learn that someone else may have obtained release for less money than they did. In most instances this is not because of illegal overcharging, but rather because the bondsman takes them out on an "insurance bond" which permits him to charge the higher rate.

14. This freedom has recently been challenged. In an interesting case the Supreme Court of Kentucky upheld the state legislature decision to abolish the bonding business, ruling that such action fell within the state's police powers. See *Stephens* v. *Bonding Association of Kentucky*, Kentucky File No. 76–504.

15. I am indebted to two of my students whose papers on New Haven bondsmen were extremely useful to me. They are Kurt Hallock, "Bail Bondsmen in the Lower Court" (Yale University, August 1975), and Diane Pike, "Bail Bondsmen: Unofficial Court Officials" (Yale University, 1976). In addition this section draws on an unpublished study by Diane

Pike, Malcolm M. Feeley, and Daniel J. Freed, "Evaluation of the Wider City Parish Bonding Program" (New Haven: Yale Law School and New Haven Foundation, 1976).

16. This discussion draws on material in a case study of the history of the Redirection Center by Malcolm M. Feeley, "Innovation and Implementation in Public Agencies: The New Haven Redirection Center," in Richard Nelson and Douglas Yates (eds.), *Innovation and Implementation in Public Agencies* (Lexington, Mass.: Lexington Books, 1977), pp. 39–68.

17. It is rumored that at least one area bondsman has an arrangement with some attorneys to direct business their way. Another is the brother of a prominent criminal lawyer. In other areas of the state it is said that police officers and bail commissioners have fee-splitting arrangements with bondsmen and attorneys.

18. This was the last year the Association distributed its annual schedule of minimum fees. During the 1960s and 1970s such schedules came under increasing attack by consumer groups, the Justice Department, and many attorneys. This unrest culminated in the Supreme Court's decision in *Goldfarb* v. *Virginia State Bar Association*, 95 S. Ct., 2004 (1975), which held that the minimum fee schedule of a county bar association in Virginia violated the federal antitrust laws because it restricted competition. Nevertheless, it is safe to conclude that some rules of thumb about billing continue to be publicized by local attorneys' associations.

19. Despite their occasional grumbling, judges are often willing to approve applications for public assistance of counsel. However this has not always been the case in New Haven. During its heyday and before the growth of the PD's office, LAA attorneys came under constant criticism for allegedly accepting clients who were ineligible for their services, a charge which was no doubt frequently true, for the same reasons that now apply to the PDs' cases. The attack was vocal and vigorous, carried on by local private practitioners in bar association meetings and judges from the bench, who at times refused to make appointments and used the opportunity to criticize LAA. With the institutionalization of the PD system and the demise of the size and radical image of LAA, this criticism subsided, although some private attorneys still complain that the PDs are taking some clients who really could afford to retain private counsel.

20. The most detailed study of PDs from their clients' perspective is Jonathan Casper, *American Criminal Justice: The Defendant's Perspective* (Englewood Cliffs, N.J.: Prentice-Hall, 1972).

21. This may account for an oft-quoted exchange used by Casper as the title of an article: "Did You Have a Lawyer When You Went to Court?—No, I Had a Public Defender," *Yale Review of Law and Social Action* 1 (1971): 4–9.

22. See David Sudnow, "Normal Crimes: Sociological Features of the Penal Code in a Public Defender's Office," *Social Problems* 12 (1965): 255–276. But for a criticism of Sudnow and an effort to compare PDs to private attorneys, see Jerome Skolnick, "Social Control in the Adversary System," *Journal of Conflict Resolution* 11 (1967): 52–70. See also Jackson Battle, "Comparison of Public Defenders' and Private Attorneys' Relationships with the Prosecution in the City of Denver," *Denver Law Journal* 50 (1973): 101–136; and Abraham Blumberg, "The Practice

of Law as a Confidence Game," *Law and Society Review* 1 (1967), 15–39.

23. There is no simple uniform practice for recording FTAs, so all figures are at best rough estimates. If people who are released on PTA or through a citation fail to appear for a first time they are usually sent a letter of warning which states that they are in violation of the law by not appearing and informs them of a date for their appearance. If they fail to appear after this, then the court usually issues a warrant for rearrest. If a person out on bond fails to appear, he is not likely to receive the letter or warning, and instead the court is likely to issue a warrant for rearrest and order the bond forfeited. There are frequent exceptions to this general practice. At times the court issues warrants for rearrest without first sending a letter to those out on PTA, and occasionally letters of warning are sent to those out on bond, although they are not entitled to this type of warning. The problem is made even more complex by virtue of the fact that judges occasionally continue cases in the absence of the defendant.

24. The first major effort to examine this problem systematically is Daniel J. Freed and Patricia Wald, *Bail in the United States: 1964* (Washington: U.S. Department of Justice and Vera Foundation, Inc., 1964). The results of the first early experiment to explicitly tie conditions of release to such factors is reported in Charles Ares, Anne Rankin, and Herbert Sturz, "The Manhattan Bail Project: An Interim Report on the Use of Pretrial Parole," *New York University Law Review* 38 (1963): 67–95. Since this first effort there have been numerous other studies along similar lines. For an excellent summary and assessment of this work see *An Evaluation of Policy Related Research on the Effectiveness of Pretrial Release Programs* (Denver: National Center for State Courts, Publication No. R0016, October 1975).

25. For discussions of the Connecticut Bail Commission and the administration of bail in Connecticut, see Thomas O'Rourke and Robert Carter, "The Connecticut Bail Commission," *Yale Law Journal* 79 (1970): 513–527; and Malcolm M. Feeley and John McNaughton, "The Pretrial Process in the Sixth Circuit Court: A Quantitative and Legal Analysis" (Paper on file at the Yale Law School Library, 1974).

26. See Robert A. Wilson, "A (Practical) Procedure for Developing and Updating Release on Recognizance Criteria" (mimeo, University of Delaware, Division of Urban Affairs, March 1975).

27. Paul Lazarsfeld, "An Evaluation of the Pretrial Services Agency of the Vera Institute of Justice: Final Report" (mimeo, December 16, 1974).

28. Even though these factors are marginally related to failure to appear, basing decisions on them would engender a large number of Type I and Type II errors. That is, many people who have the FTA-prone characteristics but who would nevertheless appear if released, will be held on bond, and many people who do not possess these characteristics will be released on low bond or PTA, and will subsequently fail to appear. The problems of basing policy on weak predictors are explored in Note, "Preventive Detention: An Empirical Analysis," *Harvard Civil Rights and Liberties Law Review* 6 (1971): 291–396.

29. I excluded those FTAs in which the court ordered cash bonds to be forfeited in order to close out the case.

30. An extended discussion of eligibility and participation is found in Feeley and McNaughton, "The Pretrial Process in the Sixth Circuit Court," pp. 44–49.
31. Daniel J. Freed, Edward J. de Grazia, and Wallace D. Loh, *The New Haven Pretrial Diversion Program—A Preliminary Evaluation (May 16, 1972–May 1, 1973)* (New Haven: Report to the New Haven Pretrial Services Council, June 1973, revised September 4, 1973).
32. For a useful history and assessment of pretrial diversion programs, see Raymond T. Ninmer, *Diversion: The Search for Alternative Forms of Prosecution* (Chicago: American Bar Foundation, 1974).
33. Freed, de Grazia, and Loh estimated the average cost per participant to be $691, several times more than the cost of the average community-based supervision for misdemeanants (which the President's Commission on Law Enforcement estimated at $142). See Freed, de Grazia and Loh, *The New Haven Pretrial Diversion Program*, pp. 68–69.
34. Freed, *The Imbalance Ratio*, p. 25.
35. The ratio is expressed as $[(A-B)/A]$, where A is the accused population in jail and B is the sentenced population in jail.
36. Freed, *The Imbalance Ratio*, p. 28.
37. Freed, *The Imbalance Ratio*, p. 25.
38. Recall also that a number of people were released on PTA only after they had spent several days in jail unable to raise money for bond. There were, in addition, some reported instances in which detainees could not secure their release simply because they were not permitted to go to a bank to withdraw money from their accounts in order to post the cash bond or pay the bondsman's commission, a Catch-22 which the criminal justice system occasionally imposes on its "clients."
39. I want to emphasize that this observation is drawn primarily from my experience with lower courts and its logic may not extend to cases in which the stakes at sentence are much higher. Furthermore, I do not wish to suggest that all PDs always treat cases casually because their clients only want perfunctory service. There are many diligent PDs, and there are many PD clients who want to "take their cases to the Supreme Court." In addition, there are many PDs who because of carelessness, overwork, or both misperceive the desires of their clients, mistaking the inarticulate for the unconcerned. The point I wish to make here is that a substantial portion of the PDs' clients turn to them seeking quick or perfunctory advice and little more, and that neither private attorneys nor the LAA attorneys are as likely to have this type of client.

Chapter 8

1. See, for example, Dallin Oaks and Warren Lehman, *A Criminal Justice System and the Indigent* (Chicago: University of Chicago Press, 1968), and the collection of articles reprinted in John Robertson (ed.), *Rough Justice* (Boston: Little Brown, 1974).
2. See, for example, Abraham Blumberg, *Criminal Justice* (Chicago: Quadrangle, 1967); George Cole, *Politics and the Administration of Jus-*

tice (Beverly Hills: Sage Publications, 1973); The President's Commission on Law Enforcement and Administration of Justice, *The Challenge of Crime in a Free Society* (1967); and the Commission's *Task Force Report: The Courts* (1967).

3. Leonard Downie, *Justice Denied* (New York: Praeger, 1971); Howard James, *Crisis in the Courts* (New York: David McKay, 1968).

4. Some recent studies have begun to consider this problem more fully. See Milton Heumann, "A Note on Plea Bargaining and Case Pressure," *Law and Society Review* 9 (1975): 518–527; James Eisenstein and Herbert Jacob, *Felony Justice: An Organizational Analysis of Criminal Courts* (Boston: Little Brown, 1977); and Arthur Rosett and Donald R. Cressey, *Justice by Consent* (Philadelphia: J. B. Lippincott, 1976).

5. Many comparative studies of courts and police may not adequately control for variation caused by state-imposed legal requirements rather than the particular local conditions on which they focus. This may be a problem in Martin Levin's otherwise outstanding study of judicial behavior in Minneapolis and Pittsburgh, *Urban Politics and the Criminal Courts* (Chicago: University of Chicago Press, 1977).

6. These figures and rankings of all eighteen lower courts are drawn from 1973 data supplied by the Office of the Chief State's Attorney, Waterford, Connecticut.

7. During the period in which data were collected in the comparison court, there was a Connecticut Supreme Court decision which altered the scope of the lower courts' felony jurisdiction. These cases constitute such a small portion of the total caseload that the change does not appreciably alter the overall pattern of this court's business. See *Szarwak* v. *Warden, Connecticut Law Journal* 34 (1974): 1.

8. For an extended criticism of the failure to develop explicit and specifiable standards in evaluative studies, see Malcolm M. Feeley, "Two Models of the Criminal Justice System: An Organizational Perspective," *Law and Society Review* 7 (1973): 407–426, and John Griffiths, "The Limits of Criminal Law Scholarship," *Yale Law Journal* 79 (1970): 1388–1474.

9. See, for example, Blumberg, *Criminal Justice.*

10. This position is held by many practicing defense attorneys, prosecutors, and judges, including most of those active in New Haven.

11. The annual reports of the Judicial Department during the past few years indicate that there are very few trials in any of the lower courts. See *The Annual Report of the Judicial Council of Connecticut.*

12. Motions of application for the appointment of a public defender were not considered in calculating these figures.

13. This would, in essence, eliminate the right to plead guilty.

14. It is difficult to imagine the elimination of the possibility for plea negotiations in the absence of such an extreme measure. But reliance on trials is no assurance that plea bargaining will not still take place. See Lynn Mather's description of court trials as "slow pleas" in "Some Determinants of the Method of Case Disposition: Decision-Making by Public Defenders in Los Angeles," *Law and Society Review* 8 (1974): 187–216.

15. Although criminal offenses in this jurisdiction are classified on a seven-point scale (three grades of misdemeanors and four felonies)

coupled with a steadily increasing maximum sentence, there seems to be a quantum leap between misdemeanors and felonies. Despite the gradations, judges, prosecutors, defense attorneys, and defendants tend to reduce these distinctions to those with no record, those with only a misdemeanor record, and those with a previous record of felony conviction. The distinction between felony and misdemeanor is an important clue to the seriousness of the defendants' prior trouble.

16. Since my observations in the summer of 1974, the lower court in New Haven has moved into newer and more spacious facilities, the old New Haven Superior Courthouse.

17. Fifty-six percent of all cases in the low-caseload court were disposed of at first appearance, in sharp contrast to only 27 percent in New Haven. Correspondingly, only 4 percent of the cases in the former court required five or more appearances, again in sharp contrast to the 22 percent in New Haven. But it is difficult to interpret these figures since there are a number of conflicting motives for seeking or avoiding continuances. On one hand the flexibility of the low-volume court allowed public defenders to accomplish more for their clients at the first appearance. On the other, continuances are a standard device used by the defendant and his attorney to stall in order to wear down the prosecutor's case, so at times continuances may be in the defendant's interests and at other times not. Whatever the precise set of reasons, it is clear that the heavier-volume court does not process cases out of a system as efficiently as the low-volume court.

18. See note 4.

19. Roscoe Pound and Felix Frankfurter (eds.), *Criminal Justice in Cleveland* (Cleveland: The Cleveland Foundation, 1922), pp. 136, 279–280, 283.

20. Charles E. Clark and Harry Shulman, *A Study of Law Administration in Connecticut* (New Haven: Yale University Press, 1923).

21. Samuel Dash, "Cracks in the Foundations of Justice," *Illinois Law Review* 46 (1951): 385–406.

22. The figures are drawn from the annual volumes, *Public Documents of the State of Connecticut.*

23. Milton Heumann, "Plea Bargaining Systems and Plea Bargaining Styles" (paper presented at the annual meeting of the American Political Science Association, Chicago, 1974. Some of this interesting discussion also appears in "A Note on Plea Bargaining and Case Pressure," *Law and Society Review* 9 (1975): 515–528).

24. Heumann, "Plea Bargaining Systems and Plea Bargaining Styles." p. 10.

25. Personal communication with Bruce Eichner of the New York State Division of Criminal Justice Services. The quotation is from a memo from Archibald Murray, Commissioner of the New York State Division of Criminal Justice Services, December 16, 1974.

26. The most important decision is *Santobello* v. *New York,* 92 *S. Ct.* 495 (1971).

27. For an interesting examination of the history of bargaining in the criminal law see Jay Wishingrad, "The Plea Bargain in Historical Perspective," *Buffalo Law Review* 23 (1974): 499–527.

28. For a discussion of this problem as it applies to the study of legal

phenomena, see my "The Concept of Laws in Social Science: A Critique and Notes on an Expanded View," *Law and Society Review* 10 (1976): 497–524.

29. Edward Banfield has suggested that much of the crisis atmosphere characterizing discussions of urban problems is a result of a rise in standards and expectations rather than an absolute deterioration of conditions. See his *The Unheavenly City* (Boston: Little Brown, 1971).

30. *Gideon* v. *Wainwright* 372 U.S. 335 (1963) and *Argersinger* v. *Hamlin* 407 U.S. 25 (1972) are the two most significant cases in this development.

31. Peter F. Drucker, "Managing the Public Service Institution," *The Public Interest* 33 (1973): 43–60.

32. The grand jury is extinct in some jurisdictions, and even where it has survived it is invariably controlled by the prosecution. Rarely if ever does it function as an instrument of the community as it once did, and as theory still has it.

33. Professionals with a monopoly of information and technical expertise are also in a position to manipulate those who are dependent upon them, and as the discussion in chapter six indicated, officials are not immune from this temptation.

34. Indeed, as discussed in chapter four, there is a strong incentive for defendants not even to bother to show up for their scheduled court appearances. While many frustrated defense attorneys attribute this to the "irrationality" or "slowness" of their clients, given the court's lack of interest in penalizing FTAs and the generally lenient sentences, it may be perfectly reasonable. Occasionally defendants who have been informed that their cases will be nolled do not appear to accept the nolle.

Chapter 9

1. Malcolm M. Feeley, "Two Models of the Criminal Justice System," *Law and Society Review* 7 (1973): 407–425, 421.

2. For an insightful discussion of the tensions among various conceptions of law, see Philippe Nonet and Philip Selznick, *Law and Society in Transition: Toward Responsive Law* (New York: Harper & Row, 1978).

3. See David Matza, *Delinquency and Drift* (New York: John Wiley, 1964), especially chapter four, "The Sense of Injustice."

4. Lon Fuller, "Collective Bargaining and Arbitration," *Wisconsin Law Review* (1963): 3–46, 18.

5. Joseph Goldstein, "Police Discretion Not to Invoke the Criminal Process: Low Visibility Decisions in the Administration of Justice," *Yale Law Journal* 69 (1960): 543–589, 588.

6. Herbert Packer, *The Limits of the Criminal Sanctions* (Stanford: Stanford University Press, 1968): 290.

7. Fuller, "Collective Bargaining and Arbitration," p. 43.

8. For a polemic against the ideal of *perfectibility* which underlies much modern judicial thinking, see Macklin Fleming, *The Price of Perfect Justice* (New York: Basic Books, 1974).

9. For a review of this literature with implications for the American setting, see Richard Abel, "A Comparative Theory of Dispute Institutions in Society," *Law and Society Review* 8 (1974): 217–343; William Felstiner, "Influences of Social Organization on Dispute Processing," *Law and Society Review* 9 (1974): 63–94. See also the several articles on dispute processing published in the symposium "Litigation and Dispute Processing," *Law and Society Review* Nos. 1 and 2, 9 (1974, 1975). More recently the Department of Justice has committed millions of dollars to promote neighborhood justice centers, although there is little if any systematic research which points to the benefits they might afford within the American urban setting.

10. I recognize that one person's analogy can be another's distortion. The technology used to identify speeders and those operating under the influence of alcohol is on the whole more precise than a police officer's determination of a "breach of peace" or "disorderly conduct," and these differences cannot be ignored.

11. Prior to 1975 the penal order in Germany could be used to impose jail sentences up to three months. Since then no cases providing for a jail sentence of any length can be disposed of by a penal order. Yet even excluding many motor vehicle cases in 1976 there were more penal orders than judicial proceedings in German courts, 436,000 to 423,000. See Abraham S. Goldstein and Martin Marcus, "The Myth of Judicial Supervision in Three 'Inquisitorial' Systems: France, Italy and Germany," *Yale Law Journal* 87 (1977): 240–283, 267. See also John H. Langbein, "Controlling Prosecutorial Discretion in Germany," *University of Chicago Law Review* 41 (1974): 439–505; and William L. F. Felstiner, "Plea Contracts in West Germany," *Law and Society Review* 13 (in press). I am indebted to William Felstiner and to Klas Lithner, State's Attorney in Karlskrona, Sweden, for discussing the implications of the bond forfeiture in light of the functioning of the penal order with me.

12. Since at least biblical times due process has been a "variable" concept. The Sanhedran imposed such high standards of proof in capital crimes that despite the large numbers of capital offenses, execution was a rare event. Similarly Charles Black argues that capital punishment should be permitted only if *all* chance of caprice and mistake is eliminated. He readily acknowledges that this is an impossibly high standard, and as a consequence concludes that capital punishment should be held unconstitutional not on cruel and unusual punishment grounds, but on due process grounds. See Charles L. Black, *Capital Punishment: The Inevitability of Caprice and Mistake* (New York: W. W. Norton, 1974). At the other extreme, while the Supreme Court has continued to insist upon higher standards for lower criminal courts, it has permitted less than full-fledged adversarial proceedings for other public institutions dispensing sanctions and benefits. See, for example, *Goldberg* v. *Kelly*, 397 U.S. 254 (1970); *Bell* v. *Burson*, 402 U.S. 535 (1971); and *Goss* v. *Lopez*, 419 U.S. 565 (1975). More generally, see Kenneth C. Davis, *Discretionary Justice: A Preliminary Inquiry* (Urbana: University of Illinois Press, 1971); and Jerry Mashaw, "The Management Side of Due Process: Some Theoretical and Litigation Notes on the Assurance of Accuracy, Fairness, and Timeliness in the Adjudication of Social Welfare Claims," *Cornell Law Review* 59 (1974), 772–824. The problem is, of course, one of

fitting the procedure to the punishment, a problem that is a concern in a society which increasingly relies on government to dispense sanctions and benefits. Despite the special constitutional status of the rights of the criminally accused, it is also one that links theoretically criminal with administrative law. This connection is most obvious when confronting the problems of coping with the high volume of low-stakes cases in the lower criminal courts. See, e.g., Justice Rehnquist's dissent in *Argersinger* v. *Hamlin* 407 *US* 25 (1972).

INDEX

"accelerated rehabilitation," 176–
177
actor, focus on, 23
adjudication: process of, 123ff.,
154ff.; alternatives in, 127–130;
ambiguity in, 167–177; and arbitration, 289; and bargaining,
156–158; case worth determination, 158–167; determinants of,
130–136; and negotiation process, 192–195; and plea bargaining, 185–192
adjudicative ideal, 280ff., 297; and
criminal court system, 280–283;
and pretrial costs, 290–292; and
substantive justice, 283–290
adversary process: decline in, 13,
266–270; and felony time, 266;
nature of, 8, 250–254; self-regu-
lation in, 18; social control in,
17–18; training in, 245
adversary process model, 17
age: and crime statistics, 42–43;
and sentences, 147
aggravated assaults, rates of, 38
aides: appointment of, 50; of public defenders, 120
alcoholism: and crime, 4; problems from, 152; programs for,
113
aldermen, and police, 45
appeal: lack of, and due process,
33; right to, 15
arbitration, and mediation, 288–
289
Argersinger v. Hamlin, 7, 60, 82
armed robbery, xv, 5, 9
arraignments: and jurisdiction, 47;
police at, 116; and prosecutors,
75–76, 178
arrests: court responses to, 162; as
ends in themselves, 46; and police character, 158, 161, 165–
166, 168; procedures in, and narcotics possession, 273–274; prosecutor attitudes on, 47; rates of,
comparative, 39
assaults, 9; classes of, 190; preven-
tion of, 161–162

"assembly line," metaphor for
lower courts, 12–13
attorneys, general: and fees, 30,
217–219; pretrial payment of,
238–239; procurement of, 216–
222; and public defenders, 135–
136; and sentencing, 144–145;
see also defense attorneys

bail: in court, 146, 258; and PTA,
173; and rearrest, 150; and sanction, 15, 100–107; schedule on,
10, 67, 160, 210; setting process,
211–213; see also bail commissioners
bail commissioners, 94, 161, 107–
111, 206–207; and pretrial release, 202–203, 209; role of,
211–212
Bailey, John, 71
bailiffs: advice of, 184; and personnel, 20; and fines, 156; and information, 119; responsibilities
of, 120–122
Bail Reform Act of 1967, 108, 109,
229
ballistic tests, 275
Banfield, Edward, 312, 319
bar associations, and judicial candidates, 59
bargaining/competition: and caseloads, 253; and nolles, 156
"Baxter Street bar," New York, 78
Beeley, Arthur, 305
Bethany, Conn., 51
black box, 152
Black Panther case (1970), 79
Blacks: and crime statistics, 42, 43;
as defendants, 4; and defense attorneys, 79, 80; discrimination
against, 122, 147, 249; FTA of,
231–232; as judges, 63; sentencing of, 143; in urban population,
36; see also race, and judicial
behavior
blood tests, 275
Blumberg, Abraham, 12–15, 250,
299, 300, 301, 304, 307, 310,
314, 316